Explore the World

NELLES GUIDE

SOUTH PACIFIC ISLANDS

Author:
Michael Brillat

*An Up-to-date travel guide with 144 color photos
and 21 maps*

First Edition
1999

W9-AYY-966

Dear Reader,

Being up-to-date is the main goal of the Nelles series. To achieve it, we have a network of far-flung correspondents who keep us abreast of the latest developments in the travel scene, and our cartographers always make sure that maps and texts are adjusted to each other.

Each travel chapter ends with its own list of useful tips, accommodations, restaurants, tourist offices, sights. At the end of the book you will find practical information from A to Z. But the travel world is fast moving, and we cannot guarantee that all the contents are always valid. Should you come across a discrepancy, please write us at: Nelles Verlag GmbH, Schleissheimer Str. 371 b, D-80935 München, Germany, Tel: (089) 3571940, Fax: (089) 35719430.

LEGEND

★ Place of Interest	🚏 Bus Station	**Otemanu** 727 Mountain (Alt. in Meters)
▣ Public or Significant Building	☀ Beach	▬ National Border
■ ⌂ Hotel	Pago Pago Place Mentioned in Text	═ Highway
● Restaurant, Casino	♣ National Park	═ Provincial Road
Golf Course	✈ International Airport	─ Secondary Road
○ ▣ Market, Shopping Center	✈ National Airport	━ Railway
✝ Church		

SOUTH PACIFIC ISLANDS
© Nelles Verlag GmbH, D-80935 Munich
 All rights reserved

First Edition 1999
ISBN 3-88618-104-9
Printed in Slovenia

Publisher:	Günter Nelles	**Translation:**	Judit Szász,
Editor-in-Chief:	Berthold Schwarz		Marianna Henning-Schroeder,
Project Editor:	Michael Brillat		Paul Lorenger, Marton Radkai
Editors:	Susanne Braun,	**Cartography:**	Nelles Verlag GmbH,
	Elke Eberhardt		Munich
Photo Editor:	K. Bärmann-Thümmel	**Lithos:**	Priegnitz, Munich
English Editor:	Marton Radkai	**Druck:**	Gorenjski Tisk

- X01 -

TABLE OF CONTENTS

FEATURES

TRAVEL INFORMATION

LIST OF MAPS

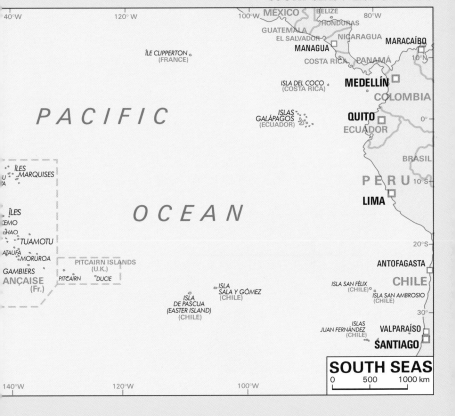

SOUTH SEAS

0   500   1000 km

LIST OF MAPS

THE ISLANDS AND THEIR PEOPLE

THE NATURE OF THE SOUTH PACIFIC ISLANDS

The Pacific ("still") Ocean was named by the Portuguese seafarer and explorer Magellan after he and his ships experienced more than one lull in the otherwise active winds.

The dimensions of this ocean are very impressive indeed: it is over 9000 miles (15,000 km) long from north to south and about 11,000 miles (18,000 km) from east to west. All land masses on Earth could easily find space in its inner section, which is about 64 million square miles (166 million sq km). Its deepest spot, along the Mariana Trench, which extends from near Guam to the Mariana Islands, is 36,198 feet deep (11,200 m). The Pacific's average depth is 13,440 feet (4200 m), and it contains enough water to fill 3.5 trillion bathtubs!

The exact number of islands in the Pacific Ocean remains uncounted to this day and for very good reason: that number is constantly changing. Nevertheless, exact figures are frequently given for certain island groups or states, but what is often overlooked is the accounting method.

Can, for example, a large rock poking out of the water be considered an island, or must it be of a certain size in order to be considered an island? Must an island be inhabited, or is it enough that it be used for agricultural purposes? Is distance to other islands a decisive factor,

Preceding pages: Moorea (French Polynesia) – just one of many dream islands in the South Seas. Corals are the distinctive mark of the South Pacific's underwater world. Left: Welcome!

and is that perhaps the reason why Sala y Gomez, an uninhabited rock about 260 x 650 feet (80 x 200 m), lying 210 miles (346 km) northeast of Easter Island, has been drawn on virtually every map, while many islands, some forming an atoll and often much larger, are given the name of a single island?

The number of islands in the South Seas is subject to speculation, though the figure lies between 5000 and 100,000. The figures in this book are taken from official bulletins.

Islands and Islands!

The actual landscape of the South Pacific islands is a lot more diverse than the small scale of most general maps seems to suggest. The geological and geomorphologic events on the one hand, and animal and plant life on the other are very varied in the gigantic natural space dominated by the great ocean. Earth-bound flora and fauna in particular had to cross huge expanses of water. But even for many of the sea's denizens, the great distances, the different currents, the various depths and temperatures were also significant distribution factors.

The geological genesis of the islands can be reduced to a few simple principles. With the exception of New Caledonia and some of the Solomon Islands in the western Pacific area, which were once upon a time part of a continent, all the islands were born out of the sea, and many are former volcanoes. The difference in their appearance today has to do with age, rock type, position within certain climatic zones and erosion by the ocean.

Geologically speaking, we can distinguish two main types of islands. The islands of the first type (Tonga and Fiji, for example) stand on the border between the oceanic and continental plates, which press against each other. The weaker oceanic plate is forced under the con-

tinental plate (a process known as subduction). The cracks which then appear in the plates form a perfect upward conduit for the molten stone below, which is under great pressure. The ocean floor is marked by numerous deep trenches (the Tonga Trench, for example, is over 30,000 feet/10,000 meters deep) where the two plates meet. Earthquakes are frequent here.

Other islands, those of French Polynesia, for instance, evolved over so-called hot spots; a stationary hot area below the solid crust of the earth. Magma rises here during periods of high activity; a submarine volcano appears.

If these periods continue long enough, the mountain will ultimately break through the surface of the water and ultimately become an island. A chain of islands appears when the tectonic plate

Above and right: Volcanic activity (here the Yasur volcano on Tanna, Vanuatu) and reef-building corals were the main natural forces that built the geography of the islands in the South Pacific.

slowly moves across a hot spot over a period of millions of years.

Atolls and Other Coral Islands

Types of coral that form reefs have given rise to those famous South Sea "paradises." Charles Darwin, who undertook an exploratory journey in the Pacific between 1831 and 1836, was the first to find a scientific explanation for the genesis of atolls. The following postulates of his theory are still valid:

1) Corals grow in the shallow coastal zone of a volcanic island that has risen out of the sea: a seam reef develops.

2) The island gradually sinks back into the sea, because as the rock masses rose to the surface, they left an empty chamber below, which cannot carry the weight of the island. The rate of sinking can be anywhere from a few millimeters up to 10 cm (four inches) per century.

3) The coral shelves adhering to the volcanic rock base are also affected by the sinking. But because they grow verti-

cally, they are able to adapt to the downward movement. This gives rise to a barrier reef, and thus the lagoon between the reef and the shore expands.

4) Weather and other erosion processes add rock and earth to the lagoon. A sediment made up of rubble, gravel and sand settles on the rock and the coral shelves.

5) Bits of sand and shell also settle on the coral reef where the waves break, turning the coral base into coral rock.

6) If the sinking motion is slow enough, the stabilized coral reef begins to expand sideways.

7) Further deposits ultimately lead to a flat island emerging up to 6 feet (2 m) above sea level at high tide. A wreath of small islands has thus risen on the barrier reef around a high volcanic island. Bora Bora is a famous and excellent example of this particular stage of island growth.

8) The wreath of islands remains even after the main island has sunk back into the sea. A high, mountainous island thus becomes a low-lying atoll.

Another type of coral island arises when blocks of coral or coral rock formations are later heaved upward by movements in the earth's crust. A typical example of this is Tonga's main island Tongatapu.

Underwater Fascination

All islands of the South Seas have one thing in common: submarine life is by far richer than terrestrial fauna. All the average visitor needs to inspect this spectacular, colorful and diverse underwater world is a diving mask, a snorkel and flippers. But do be very careful of the coral reefs, which can leave nasty cuts that only heal slowly in the tropical climate.

No amount of written words can properly describe the unbelievable variety of exotic fish, the corals in all shapes and colors, the sea cucumbers, sea stars, urchins, shells, snails and anemones. Let us here at least explain the origin of coral, which is such an important aspect of the region's nature.

Coral can be found above all in tropical seas, and to a lesser extent in subtropical waters. The corals that form reefs are of quintessential importance to the genesis and shaping of islands in the South Pacific. The coral animals are polyps with a bone or limestone skeleton. Coral shelves come into being when the young animals settle on the skeletons of the earlier, defunct generations.

Water temperature, its salt and oxygen content and the amount of light are all vital growth factors in the life of corals. The polyps are very sensitive creatures, who react quickly to any pollution or temperature variations in the water. They are unmistakable indicators of any ecological damage. The seam and barrier reefs fulfill a vital protective function against violent swell from the sea and tidal waves.

Above: A red fire fish looks for food in the coral seascape. Right: The flying fox is the only type of mammal to have reached Polynesia under its own "steam."

What Lurks in the South Seas

Such a wealth of submarine life naturally must have its share of poisonous or aggressive animals. There are the sea snakes, with light and dark stripes, the highly poisonous, colored cone shells (*conidae*), stonefish and crown-of-thorns, moray eels, sharks and poisonous corals and anemones, to name but a few. Snorkelers who do not venture too far out will seldom encounter these dangerous underwater species. At any rate, while they are often described in dramatic terms, they usually only attack if frightened.

Certain simple rules should be followed when swimming, snorkeling or diving to avoid difficulties, for example: always wear shoes when walking along rocky shorelines; always use flippers when snorkeling; do not touch anything you are not 100 percent familiar with; inform yourself of local dangers and currents; and, when in doubt, go swimming in a shallow, protected lagoon.

A Modest Animal Kingdom

In comparison to the fauna of the continents, animal life in the South Pacific is quite poor when it comes to number of species. Those animal species that spread without the help of humans diminish notably in number as one goes from west to east in the Pacific. The longer the sea route and the smaller the tract of land lying in the midst of this vast ocean, the more difficult – or coincidental – the ability of species to reach other islands.

Reptiles are a good example, crocodiles are native to the Solomon Islands, but they are only found in isolated cases on Vanuatu, where they are occasionally swept away by hurricanes. However, they have never been able to actually settle the island.

One type of iguana did succeed in reaching the Fiji Islands and one of the Tonga Islands. There are two types of land snakes living on the Fiji Islands, only one on Samoa and not a single one in French Polynesia. Skinks and geckos

follow the same diminishing pattern, although some of these species have made it into the eastern Pacific. Of all land mammals, only the flying fox has been able to get as far as Polynesia.

Accidentally, no doubt, the seafaring of the first islanders did help many species, such as insects, Polynesian rats, mice and maybe even some birds to reach other islands. They also brought domestic animals, mostly chickens, pigs and dogs.

The Europeans introduced hitherto unknown domestic animals such as cattle, horses, goats, sheep and cats. They also brought a crowd of less desirable creatures. The arrival of mosquitoes and Norwegian rats can be precisely dated on some islands (thanks to reports on the arrival of ships from certain countries). Some of these animals were able to spread like wildfire thanks to an absence of natural enemies. They sometimes did irreparable damage to the environment. The sugar-cane toad (*Bufo marinus*) and the mongoose (*Herpestes auropunctatus*)

species, the result is that in many places only one type of plant arrived in many thousands of years. The large and tall islands, with their overall fertile volcanic soil and greater precipitation, provided a good basis for the further spread of plant life. Extensive tropical forests arose here, and in some more leeward places there are even grassy fields. On the other hand, the vegetation in the low-lying coral atolls is extremely poor in terms of species, but not necessarily lacking in body.

The first settlers brought about 20 to 30 plants on their journeys to the islands, and seeds were sown. Missionaries and white settlers introduced further species. Some time toward the beginning of the 20th century, a fad for decorative plants swept through many of the islands, botanical gardens were established, and many of the newly-introduced flowers and flowering plants quickly spread. Today they have become a symbol of the South Sea islands. Tourist brochures like to advertise with great bouquets and especially with girls from the islands all covered with flowers.

Flowers have also become an important aspect of everyday life and have nothing to do at all with tourism. The inhabitants of the South Seas islands simply love plants – especially what they call "exotic" ones, meaning those not from the region. In spite of very strict regulations concerning the import of plants, and the repeated outbreaks of foreign diseases, large numbers of foreign species are still smuggled to the islands.

on Fiji, or the mynah bird, which is very common in the South Seas, are just three examples.

The ecosystems of the islands are extremely sensitive, and the very strict import regulations are more than justified, even if they seem exaggerated and annoying to the tourist.

Dense Rain Forests and Floral Splendor

As with the animal kingdom, the diversity of vegetation diminishes from west to east in the Pacific. By far the bulk of flora can be found in the Malayan area. Marine currents, winds and birds gradually spread the vegetation throughout the islands. If you examine the relationship between the geological age of the islands and the number of "immigrant"

Summer Forever

Almost all islands of the South Pacific lie within the tropical bandwidth, only a handful are subtropical. For much of the year they are caressed by the eastern trade winds. The gentle sea breezes that often waft over the waters temper the tropical climate. The basic fact is that the

Above: Frangipani flowers are a favorite in the ubiquitous garlands. Right: Thor Heyerdahl's Kon-Tiki – an exciting adventure in the name of knowledge.

amount of precipitation in the South Pacific increases the further east one goes. On the higher islands, the amount and frequency of rain can vary from one place to another, even over small distances. The damp season is between November and March or April. This is also the season for hurricanes, which also increase in frequency the further west the latitude.

The rainier season is also somewhat warmer. Daytime highs are between 79 and 90° F (26 and 32° C), nighttime lows lie between 68 and 77° F (20 and 25° C). During the dry months (from June to September), daytime highs reach 71 to 82° F (22 to 28° C), while at night temperatures can sink to 50 to 64° C (10 to 18° C).

THE CULTURE OF THE SOUTH PACIFIC ISLANDS

The Divided Ocean

Oceania is usually divided up into three broad regions. The islands lying to the north, the northern Marianas, Palau, Guam, Yap, Truk and Pohnpei, belong to what is called Micronesia. Melanesia (the "black island world") consists of Papua New Guinea, the Solomon Islands, New Caledonia and Vanuatu (New Hebrides). Polynesia, the "world of many islands," includes islands in the triangle formed by Hawaii, New Zealand and Easter Island.

A rough ethnographic and geographic classification was already made in the 19th century. Many small islands simply don't fit any specific category, and borders, too, are changing and not perfectly defined. Over the centuries, the South Seas inhabitants were always ready to travel, either with friendly or bellicose intention, resulting in an intense mix of the various ethnicities. Scholars have long puzzled over the exact origin of the peoples of the Pacific.

Discovering the Pacific

In 1947, the Norwegian Thor Heyerdahl proved with his Kon-Tiki expedition that it was possible to sail from Peru to the Tuamotu Islands in French Polynesia using South American reed rafts. However, he could not prove conclusively that the Pacific islands had indeed been settled from South America.

After Heyerdahl went public with his hypothesis, hundreds of researchers assiduously set about their work trying to answer unanswered questions about the South Pacific and its population shifts. Today they are almost unanimous in their belief that the South American continent was not the origin of the South Seas peoples.

The generally accepted theory is that Asian ethnic groups, perhaps even from inland regions, over a period of thousands of years gradually became more adapted to a seafaring way of life. Australia was settled between 40,000 and 50,000 years ago, which was fairly easy back then, as the sea level worldwide was about 300 ft (100 m) lower, and the Torres Strait separating New Guinea and Australia was almost dry. The Aborigines are in fact only distantly related to the Melanesian people, if at all.

Much later, about 12,000 to 15,000 years ago, the islands close to the New Guinea coast in the north were settled. And a few millennia later, some ethnic groups went on an extended island hopping jaunt in an easterly direction.

The Fiji islands were reached around 1500 B.C. Archeological finds show that Samoa and Tonga have been inhabited for at least 3000 years. The settling of these islands is thought to have been the result of renewed migration wave, which may have begun in southern China, and ended up in Polynesia via the Micronesian islands. Finally, the three corners of the Hawaii-Easter Islands-New Zealand

triangle of Polynesia were established from the Marquesas Islands, which, it is assumed, were themselves settled no later than 200 B.C.

There is no doubt that the inhabitants of the South Seas also sailed back and forth between distant archipelagos. They might indeed have reached the South American continent on one of these journeys and brought back people, supplies (fruit and vegetables) and new knowledge to their islands.

At any rate, Thor Heyerdahl has earned the highest respect for his scientific and human integrity. Polynesians love and honor him – his work played a vital role in drawing attention to them worldwide and encouraging research into their traditional culture. His book *Kon-Tiki* was translated into about 60 languages.

World Champion Navigators

The seafarers from the Pacific knew how to sail great distances from west to east over the tropics, against currents, against the dominant easterly trade winds (which the Europeans only succeeded in doing much later).

For all intents and purposes, they had excellent knowledge of the stars and their progress throughout the year. We can assume that they used certain constellations to stay on course during longer trips. A star appearing on the horizon remains a reliable point of reference for two hours at the outside, then it slips off course or moves too high. But in the meantime, a new star has appeared on the horizon to provide guidance. The sun was used as a reference point during the day.

Knowledge of the currents, about the salt content of the water, the behavior of birds and fish, of the play of light in the sky and cloud movement once made the inhabitants of the Pacific the world's finest navigators. The long trips were made using double-hulled canoes about 110

Right: Building an outrigger canoe on the Cook Islands – a job with a tradition going back ages.

feet long (35 m) powered by large sails shaped like lobster claws. They could carry about 40 to 60 passengers including supplies and animals, for shorter trips even up to 200 people.

When the Europeans took control of the islands, the natives ceased their long journeys. They may even have been prohibited from doing so.

Unfortunately, over time, the details of their navigational art and the various aspects of their ship-building technique were by and large forgotten. Since Heyerdahl's expedition, several long sea journeys have been undertaken without the benefit of modern technology. These adventurous and often spectacular ventures have proven that the trips were possible, but they have revealed little about the art of navigation of the South Pacific peoples.

Organized Communities

In large sections of Polynesia and the neighboring Fiji Islands, society is strictly structured to this day. The extended family is ruled by a chief, who is ruled in turn by a higher chief and an even higher, differentiated nobility. Specialists in the art of handicrafts such as tattooers, boat builders and priests, enjoyed a special reputation in ancient Polynesia. The authority of the aristocracy rested on the divine origins of its ancestors, and is therefore seen as hereditary, absolute and unimpeachable.

As a rule, the titles go to the first born. Exceptions are possible, since several family members have the same divine origin. In addition, women can occupy all the same political positions as men, which guarantees a certain flexibility and maintains the social structures.

In the lowest strata a chief is elected every now and then. At any rate, they do have special social responsibilities toward their community. These include granting land rights or material and financial help. If a chief fails to fulfill these responsibilities, he – or she – can be stripped of the title.

The situation in Melanesia is different from that in Polynesia. The traditional structures here are marked by strong cultural divisions. This can be seen in the great linguistic diversity of the region, and the structuring of society in small, non-centrally organized clans and family units whose origins go back to a common ancestor. Men often belong to secret societies or religious associations with hierarchical structures that in turn control community life.

Basically speaking, Melanesia's social structures have survived better than those of Polynesia, which have become completely meaningless, especially on those islands under foreign dominion, such as Hawaii, French Polynesia and Easter Island.

Above: The giant statues on Easter Island, thought by some to represent ancestors who direct their mana onto people. Right: The figurehead of a war canoe representing the helpful spirit of an ancestor (Solomon Islands).

But even on islands where the ancient system has remained intact, such as Fiji, Tonga and Samoa, because of increasing material needs and the growing desire to achieve higher educational levels, the process of dissolution as begun.

Of Gods and Taboos

All Polynesian societies had a more or less uniform polytheistic religion, at least where basic structure and myths were concerned. They worshipped hundreds of gods, demigods and spirits, who were all connected through a system of hierarchical dependencies.

Every aspect of day-to-day life was determined by divinities; their spirits were seen in trees, stones, fish and turtles. They were honored and pacified in rituals, ceremonies, sacrifices and obeisance to certain taboos.

A *tabu* (also called *tapu* or *kapu*) always had a counterpart in *mana*, a special power that could live in not only gods but also people, animals, objects and places. One theory holds that the great statues of Easter Island represent ancestors directing *mana* toward the inhabitants of the island.

Tabu (taboo in English) meant that a creature or object filled with *mana* – permanently or temporarily – was not supposed to be touched or injured, in order to avoid trouble or the wrath of the gods. The speaking of certain names and words, walking in a certain place or touching certain special animals, plants or symbols, could also be *tabu*.

Mana, however, can also be inherited – for instance, as the power of a chieftain – or earned by certain achievements or abilities. Extraordinary performance by a warrior or a particular weapon is usually attributed to *mana* in man or object. Naturally, what is gained, can also be lost again.

A *tabu* was rooted in religion, magic or ritual, and was accepted by society at large. Breaking a *tabu* had dire consequences, and was punished by the gods or the very powers that had proclaimed the *tabu*. It was the "civilized" Western world that generalized the word *tabu* and imbued it with negative moral connotations and values.

On many islands in the more remote regions, some taboos are still taken quite seriously. Foreigners to these parts would do well to inform themselves of the taboos that have been declared over certain places or actions.

Ancestor worship has always been cultivated in Melanesia. Certain rituals and ceremonies are designed to show gratitude and respect to these ancestors, whose spirits are thought to be present in everyday life. Achieving this guarantees continuity of life's order.

Cannibalism

At some time, all islands in the South Seas experienced cannibalism. Just when and for what extent of time differs quite

drastically from island to island, even within island groups. Eating human flesh took place for two important reasons: On the one hand, consuming another person's flesh was one way of acquiring his particular power or *mana*; on the other hand, being eaten could be seen as a sign of the highest disrespect and indignity for the deceased.

Cannibalism, for what it's worth, was reserved mostly for certain people and was performed along with special rituals. Eating another human for purely gastronomical reasons was seldom the case, though apparently hands and feet were coveted for their especially tender and lean meat...

The Babylon of the Pacific

The Tahitians say *Mauruuru no te ha'amaramara'* or "Thanks for the information" (using an image meaning to bring light into a matter). This is just one example of the multifaceted qualities of Polynesian languages.

23

In all, about 1200 languages and dialects are spoken in the South Pacific, in other words, about 25 percent of all languages in the world. The languages of Polynesia are by and large quite closely related to one another, though the islanders from different nations do not understand each other.

The western Pacific, on the other hand, is very clearly divided along linguistic lines. 110 different languages are spoken on Vanuatu, 90 on the Solomon Islands, and 720 in New Guinea. Needless to say, this incredible diversity makes for extremely difficult communication in the centrally-governed islands, and has been the main reason for the development of a pidgin in the nations mentioned above, a hodgepodge of English, Melanesian and other languages that has become the *lingua franca* in that region. Many of the languages and dialects are currently threatened with extinction, and when they disappear, it means that small ethnic groups will lose a significant part of their cultural identity.

Polynesian languages, including Tongan, Samoan, the languages of French Polynesia and of the Maori in New Zealand, Hawaiian, and Rapa Nui of Easter Island, is written using only 12 to 14 letters. Thanks to the missionaries, many of these tongues were put down in writing; many might otherwise have become lost.

The pronunciation and emphasis of the vowels are extremely differentiated for Western ears, and one word frequently has several definitions. The context of the sentence usually suggests its meaning. The language of the colonial owners of the islands, Spanish, French or English, has often established itself as the second language of the respective islands. Children grow up with two or three languages as a rule.

Right: Dances were one way to tell stories and pass on history without writing – here on Fiji.

None of the old Pacific cultures ever developed a written language (the runes of Easter Island will be treated in the chapter dealing specifically with that island).

Whatever has come down from the past has done so orally, often in legends and songs, or in dances and ceremonies. Consequently, the stories told over many generations were gradually modified or embellished, interpreted and changed. This is especially obvious in the case of the myths and tales, which appear in many different versions sometimes even on a single island.

You Can't Live in the Sea...

Land in the huge watery expanse of the South Seas has acquired a special meaning simply by virtue of it's being rare. Land ownership in the Western sense is unknown in the South Seas and, luckily, buying and possessing land is carefully regulated on most of the islands in the region even today.

Even in the past a system was in place to deal with the issue: There were administrators of the land, namely the aristocracy and the chieftains, and there were those who actually made good use of the land. However, even if a family had cultivated a plot for generations and generations, it still belonged to the extended family in the end. This is still the case on many of the islands, although economic interests are gradually making inroads into the old system.

Even the natives on Easter Island are not allowed to deal in property among themselves. The law can be circumvented, however: one party gives another a present of US $20,000, and the second party donates his land officially to the first. And many a European, having thus purchased or leased a plot in the South Seas, wakes up one morning to find that the seller never had any rights over the piece of land in the first place.

Mine? Yours? Ours!

Ownership is relative in the South Seas. Piling up property does not necessarily lead to higher status as it might do in our Western world, at least not out in the rural areas. Respect is earned by social behavior that is becoming to the community at large. In other words: a well-to-do person is welcome, but the South Seas people expect that family members, friends and close acquaintances also see some of that wealth. This kind of communal thinking is deeply anchored in society even in modern cities: it is not unusual for neighbors to make small gifts of food to each other daily.

This idyllic system can only function if everyone in the community has the same attitude and principles and material differences are not too stark. Just as in Western countries, when a present has been accepted, the giver expects a return on the investment at a given time. This principle has placed many a visitor in an embarrassing position. He will admire a beautiful shell in a private home, for example, and receive it as a gift on the spot; the next day, the former host makes admiring remarks about the visitor's golden wristwatch. So what can you do? The most important thing is to communicate to your interlocutor that you have understood the system (see "South Seas Etiquette" in the *Guidelines* section).

Stealing does not occur frequently on most islands, but the incidents of it are on the rise especially in the larger cities and where western influence is more acutely felt. Whenever it does happen, it is usually a case of easy opportunity: one person owns something that another one needs, so the coveted object is simply "borrowed." Ownership, as mentioned at the start of the section, is relative.

Free Love?

All European voyagers were fascinated by the physique, the facial traits, the light brown skin, the grace and gentle character of the Polynesian, especially

the women. The early seafarers were already thrilled by the islanders' total lack of sexual inhibition; women offered their bodies generously, men offered their wives and daughters as a sign of hospitality. But even some tough sailors lost their courage and appetite when encouraged to perform sexual acts in front of a curious and expectant crowd. Many anecdotes have survived from that period of Polynesian history, and the experiences of yore survive in the clichés that were soon to be applied to the entire South Seas.

Missionary work in the South Seas gradually transformed the moral expectations of the people, many women now live according to more austere Christian precepts. Nevertheless, they love to laugh and dance, their warmth is proverbial, and sexuality is by no means a taboo

Above: The beauty and openness of Polynesian women fascinated painter Paul Gauguin. Right: Ferdinand Magellan, the great seafarer who sought the "Sea of the South."

issue. Women traditionally take care of the home and the hearth, and in Melanesia also work in the fields. This old-fashioned division of roles is slowly falling apart now that young women are receiving an education, engaging in family planning, studying, taking on paid jobs and even supporting their entire family.

The American anthropologist Margaret Mead, who lived many years in the South Seas, did a great deal of research on family ties, sexuality and the life of women in Samoa and New Guinea. Her book *Coming of Age in Samoa*, published in 1928, contrasted the ease with which South Seas girls grew into womanhood with the difficulties experienced by American girls. It became a best seller instantly.

THE EUROPEAN ERA

European Explorers and Scientists

The European era in the South Seas dawned with the first journey around the world by the Portuguese captain Fernão de Magalhães (better known as Ferdinand Magellan), who was in the service of Spain. In 1513, Vasco Nuñez de Balboa, a Spanish explorer, had come across an unknown "ocean" on the yonder coast of Panama and called it *Mar del Sur* (Sea of the South). In 1519, Magellan set out with five ships. He was convinced that this sea measured about 1000 nautical miles from west to east, and that, therefore, the wealthy Moluccas (Spice Islands), which were in Portuguese hands, were in fact in the officially-decreed Spanish sphere.

Magellan was by no means acting in the spirit of exploration alone. Besides the post of viceroy, he had been promised a twentieth of all revenue generated from newly-discovered territories. An undiscovered continent, known as *terra australis incognita*, which geographers suspected existed in the Pacific as a counterweight to the land masses on the northern hemisphere, had not yet been found. The incentive was great, as everyone expected to find extraordinary wealth there.

The journey was eventful indeed, plagued by illness, death and mutiniy. In October 1520, Magellan discovered the long-sought 350-mile (563 km) strait between the mainland of South America and the Tierra del Fuego archipelago, henceforth named after him.

The journey across the "Sea of the South" began on November 28 with three ships only and the crew virtually on a starvation diet. Magellan ultimately called the sea "Pacific," after his ships got stuck in yet another long lull. These hardy seafarers failed to make landfall at any of the main islands in the South Seas, but they did stop on some smaller ones, notably Guam.

Finally, on April 27, 1521, Magellan was killed during a battle with natives in the Philippines. Of the fleet that started out, only a single ship with 18 men on board actually managed to circumnavigate the globe

At first, the Spanish instigated a number of voyages of discovery throughout the Pacific. The main thrust of these trips was to increase their territorial holdings and to proselytize for the Catholic Church. In the process, however, they discovered the northern west wind zone, which allowed them to travel the ocean from west to east.

No complete roster exists of the individual islands they discovered while shuttling back and forth between their Central and South American and Philippine trading posts. lvaro de Medaña discovered the Solomon Islands in 1568 and the Marquesas in 1595.

Toward the end of the 16th century, English privateers, the most famous of whom was Sir Francis Drake, increasingly began encroaching on Spanish turf.

FERDINAND MAGELLANUS.

The discovery of Vanuatu (New Hebrides) by Fernandez de Quiros in 1606 finally put a cap on the Spanish era in the South Seas.

The Dutch were the next European power to arrive. They in fact discovered the hitherto unknown Australian continent, but the arid, inhospitable western coast did not fulfill the common expectation of the long-sought wealthy part of the globe. The voyages of Roggeven, Tasman, Schouten, LeMaire and others, were financed by trading companies. Yet in spite of the discovery of many islands, for example, the Fiji and Tonga groups, economic results were not up to the sponsors' expectations, so the Dutch voyages of discovery were ultimately canceled.

Expeditions during the 18th century were usually financed by consortiums of mercantile companies, governments and research societies. The captains had longer and longer lists of commissions, and the general public also awaited reports from the expeditions with great curiosity. Count Louis-Antoine de Bou-

gainville was the first Frenchman to sail around the world (1767-1769). His gushing narration became a best seller. The world had finally found the "noble savage" living on a "happy isle," and ever so slowly the cliché of the paradisical South Seas that still survives to this day was born.

In 1768, Captain James Cook embarked on the first of three Pacific expeditions. Cook, who was an excellent mathematician and astronomer, discovered hundreds of islands and explored them with the help of his team of scientists. They studied the lifestyle of the islanders, described flora and fauna, and drew the first exact maps.

Cook was killed in Hawaii in 1779. The name of this brilliant navigator, however, has been immortalized throughout the Pacific.

Above: A copperplate engraving by J. T. de Bry depicting the Dutch arriving on a South Seas island. Right: Protestant church service in Avarua, Cook Islands.

Christian Missions

The first missionaries (from the *London Missionary Society*) landed on Tahiti in 1797. They had a great deal of trouble getting the message across at first, many were chased away, some were even eaten. The inimical attitude of the islanders was no surprise, as the missionaries declared their age-old, natural way of life to be bad. In addition, the prudish Europeans brought new and devastating diseases along with them.

Nevertheless, the Reformed Church of Thomas Haweis, and John Wesley's Methodist Church, were able to get a toe hold on the islands by the early 19th century and gradually spread their influence throughout all of Polynesia and parts of Melanesia. Protestant and Anglican creeds also succeeded in planting themselves on Vanuatu and the Solomon Islands. The Catholic missionaries arrived too late, it seems: the inhabitants of most of the larger islands had already converted to Protestant Christianity. The

Catholics did find receptive ears on the more remote islands, and later particularly on those under French protectorate. The missionaries introduced constricting clothing and equally constricting and bigoted moral codes, but by and large they were unable to eradicate the sheer sense of joy, the dancing, the sensuality of the islanders.

Colonization of the South Seas

Whalers and seal hunters also started turning their attention to the Pacific Ocean around 1800. The crews of the ships consisted of coarse fellows generally, whose shore leaves were often quite tumultuous.

More and more Europeans sailed to the Pacific as well to settle the islands. Some had deserted the harsh life on whaling ships or had escaped from convict transports, others had "merely" been shipwrecked. Their knowledge of firearms, unknown to the islanders, certainly gave them an advantage. They exacerbated the existing rivalries between tribal chiefs, who became increasingly anxious to have a white man or a group of them on their side. The latter were taken care of accordingly and often lead a genuinely paradisical life.

The economic exploitation of the islands started at about the same time. Of value were sandalwood, pearls, tortoise shell and sea cucumbers (*bêche-de-mer*), which fetched a pretty penny in China. The first trading posts opened their doors at first to supply ships. They were followed by settlers, who purchased land more or less legally and established the first plantations.

Labor was needed everywhere. From 1840 onward, the trade in human beings became a valuable source of cash. The price of a ship could be made with two or three holds full of human workers. The *blackbirders*, as they were called, were no shrinking violets when it came to the business of recruiting. The future labor force was brought on board by force, partly kidnapped using cunning, partly thanks to false promises. The Solomon Islanders and the Ni-Vanuatu were carted off to plantations on the Fijis and in Australia, and to harsh labor in the French-run nickel mines of New Caledonia. Cook and Easter Islanders ended up on Tahiti. In the 1860s, Peru brought over 3000 islanders to the guano islands to work.

Contact with the Europeans confronted the South Sea inhabitants with diseases their immune systems could not handle, such as measles, tuberculosis, smallpox, typhoid, whooping cough, intestinal infections, common influenza and other sicknesses, which took on epidemic proportions. The population of some of the islands was reduced to 5 to 10 percent of its original figure (notably Easter Island), so it's partially a miracle that some islands are still inhabited. Other European "giveaways" were venereal disease, alcohol and firearms.

The Great Powers gradually recognized the strategic significance of the South Sea islands, and the second half of the 19th century was marked by busy competition for protectorates and colonies mainly between England, France, the USA and Germany.

By mid-century, New Caledonia and parts of Polynesia including Tahiti became French colonies. And other portions of the "Pacific cake" were also taken by greedy powers, with agricultural products (copra, sugar, spices and cocoa) and natural resources such as nickel promising high profits. By the dawn of the 20th century, all islands in the South Seas had been colonized with few exceptions: the kingdom of Tonga, for instance, had assured itself its autonomy under British protection.

Right: Keeping the peace, Western style – for 40 years, the USA, Great Britain and France tested their atom bombs in the South Pacific (here Bikini Atoll, 1946).

The Road to Independence

At the beginning of the First World War, Germany's possessions in the Pacific (including northeastern New Guinea, West Samoa and Micronesia) were taken over by Japan and Great Britain. Thereafter, they became a mandate of the League of Nations.

After the Second World War, which saw major action especially in the waters around the Solomon Islands (Guadalcanal, for example), Japan's former trust territories were taken over by the USA and the mandates of the League of Nations were turned over to the new United Nations.

The actual move toward independence, or at least autonomy, began around 1950. Samoa was the first state in the South Seas to actually achieve independence, followed a few years later by Nauru (1968), the Fiji Islands (1970), Niue (1974), the Solomon Islands (1978) and Vanuatu (1980). France, having handily lost Viet Nam and Algeria in the 1950s, kept its grip on its colonies of French Polynesia and New Caledonia, as well as Wallis and Futuna, in spite of some resistance in recent years. Pitcairn remained British, and Easter Island is still in Chilean hands.

The desire for self-determination was – and for all intents and purposes still is – certainly understandable, but the reality today inevitably means collaboration with one or more larger nations. Because of the high cost of transportation and lack of financial backing to actually turn a profit from natural resources and the sea, the new states have remained economically dependent on help from abroad. Good fishing grounds, in particular huge tuna reserves, attract fishing boats from Japan, Korea, the USA and the former Soviet Union, whose large trawling nets also catch dolphins and sea turtles. Manganese lumps containing copper, cobalt and nickel were discovered on the ocean

floor. The moment the ownership issue is cleared, exploitation will begin. The French colony of New Caledonia is the world's third-largest producer of nickel.

For the past 40 years, the USA, Great Britain and France have also used the South Pacific area for over 250 atomic tests above ground and underground, and islanders have in part been used as guinea pigs. The Americans and British stopped testing in 1963, but the French continued until 1992. In September 1995, Jacques Chirac, France's new conservative president, resumed testing on Moruroa. Massive international protest, which included boycotting French products, forced the French government to put an end to the test series by the beginning of 1996.

For a while now, international investors have been entertaining plans to create an atomic "world final disposal repository" on the uninhabited Palmyra atoll in the north of Kiribati. In spite of hefty resistance by several South Sea states, western industrial nations have definitely been toying with the idea.

The collision with European culture has often brought the "happy isles" little more than questionable Western needs and degradation, or – much worse still – the total loss of a cultural identity and life itself.

When traveling the region with open eyes, the visitor will quickly become aware of the conflicts and problem areas; from the influence of modern life in the era of air travel, Coca-Cola and TV, to pollution, to fenced-off and over-priced luxury hotels. And yet, signals of a gentler form of eco-tourism are beginning to be heard.

Go beyond the beaten paths in the South Sea islands, and you are liable to rediscover the legendary free and easy paradise in which you will experience a child-like sense of wonder. It might be a landscape that caresses the senses or indigenous people welcoming you as a friend. It is indeed that same magic that drew in artists of the stamp of Paul Gauguin or more recently the poet and singer Jacques Brel.

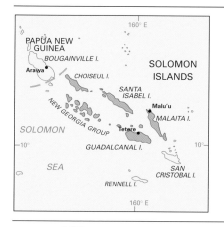

SOLOMON ISLANDS

GUADALCANAL

MALAITA

OTHER SOLOMON

ISLANDS

Of Nature and War

Beyond its surprising cultural variety – about 90 languages are spoken on the Solomon Islands – the special charm of this archipelago lies in the many untouched areas visitors will encounter. Thick rain forests, imposing mountains, roaring waterfalls and lonely beaches are a Mecca for all those who love nature. Snorkelers and divers may experience the highlights of their careers here when studying the fauna and flora of the ocean. The relics of the battles that raged between Americans and Japanese during the Second World War attract many tourists – mainly from the two countries involved. But generally the tourist trade of the Solomon Islands is still in its infancy.

Almost a Thousand Islands

The almost 1000 islands that range in size from big to tiny, stretch from the northwest to the southeast over a distance of about 900 miles (1500 km). Dry land adds up to about 10,800 square miles (27,000 sq km), while the area covered

Preceding pages: Gone fishing in Malaita, Solomons. Left: Necklaces of shell money offered for sale at Langa Langa Lagoon (Malaita).

by the maritime economic zone is more than 520,000 square miles (1,300,000 sq km). The six big islands – Choiseul, New Georgia, Santa Isabel, Guadalcanal, Malaita and San Cristobal (Makira) – are mountainous and the interiors are quite difficult to penetrate. The capital, Honiara, is on Guadalcanal, the biggest island of the country.

Among the smaller islands in the group there are a number of raised coral islands and atolls. The country is situated in the area of the contact and subduction zone of the Pacific and Australo-Asian continental plates. This accounts for the frequent earthquakes, and in various places visitors can witness active volcanoes and geothermal phenomena. Some of the bigger islands exhibit a significant amount of crystalline rock, some of which contains valuable minerals. This rock was originally part of an older continental plate that broke off and drifted away.

Orchids and Crocodiles

The relative closeness to Asia and also to the archipelago of Papua New Guinea allowed many plants to settle here naturally. It is said that there are 4500 kinds of plant on the islands, among them almost 250 various orchids. Inland, the bigger islands are covered as a rule by a

thick cloak of rain forest. Only where growth conditions were unsuitable or where the primal forest was destroyed was it possible for shrub and bush vegetation to get established. Plantations were set up almost exclusively along the coast. At the mouths of the rivers thick mangrove forests have taken over.

The fauna of the Solomon Islands is considerably richer than on other South Pacific islands. As far as mammals are concerned, only various rodents (including opossums), mice and fruit bats have reached the islands. As for reptiles, you will find skink lizards, one species of iguana and seven species of land snake, of which four are poisonous. One of the two kinds of crocodile is dangerous and lives in salt water. Among the numerous insects are 150 species of butterflies (about one quarter of them particular to these islands). Birds also exhibit remarkable variety. Of the over 300 species and

Right: There are 250 types of orchids on the Solomon Islands!

sub-species (parrots, pigeons, kingfishers, herons, eagles, hawks, frigate birds, finches, etc.), more than 40 are found exclusively on the Solomon Islands.

Heat and Humidity

All the islands are situated in the hot and humid tropical region. The average temperature is between 79° F and 81° F (26° C and 27° C), with minor variations between the cooler months of June to August and the warmer period of December to February. The amount of rain can vary considerably on the higher islands, even over small distances.

In Honiara, which lies in the shadow of the southeasterly trade-winds that carry rain, 84 inches (2150 mm) of rain fall per year. This is one of the lower levels in the country: in many areas, 117 to 160 inches (3000 to 4000 mm) of rain a year is not unusual and on exposed mountains levels can reach twice that or even more. For the most part, the cooler periods are also the drier ones.

The People

The total population of the Solomon Islands is about 400,000, nearly half of whom are younger than 15. More than 95 percent are Melanesians and 4 percent Polynesians. Micronesians, Chinese and Europeans together account for the remaining 1 percent. Melanesians living here are partly very dark skinned and partly light. Some individuals also reveal a striking combination of pysical features, namely dark skin and blond, often almost white curly hair. This is particularly noted on Malaita, and it is by no means due to any kind of "touristic influence."

The distribution of people within the country varies greatly. More than 55 percent of the population live on the two islands of Guadalcanal and Malaita, with more than 40,000 people concentrated in and around Honiara.

The inhabitants of the Solomon Islands excel in arts and crafts: they make wood carvings, often inlaid with mother of pearl, and beautiful necklaces out of shells. Visitors can buy other traditional jewelry and textiles. If you venture outside the main settlements, be careful to find out which locations – and also what activities – are considered taboo.

Settlers, Missionaries, Slavers

Very little archeological research has been conducted here, but existing work certainly seems to offer a safe basis for speculating on when the islands were first settled. Finds on the island of Tikopia, in the east, where the inhabitants are of Polynesian origin, have been identified as part of the Lapita culture and are dated at more than 3500 years old. Australian scientists discovered that the Poha cave on Guadalcanal was inhabited as early as 6000 years ago and the first human settlers probably reached the islands a few thousand years before that.

Inca legend speaks of two islands in the west, rich in gold and silver and inhabited by dark-skinned people. In search of these "Islands of King Solomon," the Spaniard Álvaro de Mendaña was the first European to arrive – in 1568 – on the island today called Santa Isabel. He soon found other islands in the archipelago, though no precious metals. Despite this, Mendaña sailed again for the islands in 1595 with four ships and 450 followers ready to leave their country and establish a new settlement on the unknown islands. Their attempt to found a colony eventually failed.

The Dutchmen Schouten and Le Maire (1616) and Tasman (1643) sighted the atoll of Ontong Java north of the Solomon Islands. British and French sailors (Carteret, Bougainville, Surville, Shortland and others) mapped most of the Solomons in the 18th century.

From the middle of the 19th century, sandalwood traders anchored here to load supplies and to acquire goods that they could use in exchange for the much desired wood they found on other islands. Whalers would also drop anchor. Colonists and other traders settled slowly over the years. In 1845, Catholic missionaries tried to establish a station on San Cristobal, but left the island disappointed three years later.

The subsequent Melanesian Mission also proved initially unsuccessful, and only after new missionary stations were founded in 1875 did Christianity begin to spread. The intensive contact with Europeans led here, as elsewhere, to a fall in population due to newly introduced diseases.

In addition, between 1870 and 1911, almost 30,000 inhabitants were deported voluntarily or involuntarily by slave traders to work on the sugar cane plantations in Australia and the Fiji Islands.

Colonial Times and Independence

The increasing trade interests of the European powers, conflicts between white settlers and locals, tribal wars, reports of cannibalism and the brutal behavior of slave traders led in 1886 to a contract dividing the territory into German and British spheres of influence. In 1893 Britain declared the southern islands to be a protectorate. Germany took over the northern islands but resigned its claim on the islands of Ontong Java, Shortland, Choiseul and Santa Isabel in exchange for West Samoa. At the beginning of the 20th century, Western companies started to establish coconut plantations, but otherwise the islands remained a backwater.

The Second World War rudely awoke the sleepy Solomons. The Japanese invaded beginning in April 1942 with the capture of Shortland Island in the northwest and the then capital Tulagi situated

Right: Honiara became the capital of the Solomon Islands after serving as a US base during World War Two.

on a little island north of Guadalcanal. On Guadalcanal the Japanese started to build an airfield, but this was captured in August by the Americans. The subsequent sea battle near the island of Savo numbers amongst the bloodiest in the Pacific war, and ended in victory for the Japanese. Despite this reverse, and with great loss of life on both sides, US troops managed by 1943 to liberate almost all the Solomon islands. Japanese troops did remain on Choiseul and Shortland until 1945.

After the war, Honiara on the island of Guadalcanal was designated the new capital. Anti-colonial and other radical movements sprang into being at this time. The Maasina (or Marching) Rule, similar to the cargo cults of Vanuatu (see pages 56 and 57), was officially suppressed at the end of the 1940s. At the beginning of the 1960s other nationalist and anti-European movements gained influence. Meanwhile, the country was being led step-by-step to self-rule, and in 1978 it obtained its independence as a member of the Commonwealth.

Fish, Palm Oil and Copra

About 80 percent of the population can provide for themselves in the subsistence economy. The country exports fish, palm oil, copra, wood and cocoa. In recent years, both exports and imports have increased. Although the trade balance is negative, it is still better than that of almost all the other South Pacific nations. The most important trade partner is Japan, followed by Britain. With about 12,000 visitors a year, tourism is still just beginning. The unique diving facilities and the relics of the Second World War are attractive mainly to Australians, New Zealanders, Americans and Japanese. The government sees a chance to encourage ecological tourism and hopes to attract more visitors with carefully targeted promotion.

GUADALCANAL

Guadalcanal covers more than 2000 square miles (5300 sq km) and is the biggest island. It is covered by thick, impenetrable forest. **Mount Makarakomburu** and **Mount Popomanaseu** stand at 8075 and 7695 feet (2447 and 2332 meters) respectively, the highest mountains in the country. The north lies in a dry belt; the southern beaches, which are exposed to the southeasterly trade winds, get far more rain, hence the name *Weather Coast*. In the central part of the northern coastal region is a large (184 square miles/460 sq km) inundation plain used for intensive agriculture. A 42-mile (72 km) road leads out of Honiara to the west all the way to Lambi Bay. To the east is another road that takes you to Aola 45 miles (75 km) away.

The Capital Honiara

The Americans established their most important bases in the north of Guadalca-nal. They built an airfield and various other facilities. When the old capital of Tulagi was destroyed in the fighting of World War Two, it was obvious that the infrastructure set up by the US troops could be recycled. Honiara became the new capital. It quickly developed into a modern industrial center and also the center of Guadalcanal's tourist industry. It now numbers 40,000 inhabitants.

Although Honiara has no impressive historical sights, the modern town, with its concrete buildings and greenery, is lively and friendly. Palm trees and blossoming hibiscus, frangipani and flame trees give shade. Bright colors and sweet smells bewitch the senses.

The most important street is **Mendaña Avenue**, which runs near the coast. Here, you will find shops and banks. The parallel street inland is called **Hibiscus Avenue** where there are public buildings like the **Parliament** and the missions of Australia and of the United States, as well as the King Solomon Hotel. At the **Central Market**, about 200 meters (200 yards) from the Town Hall, one can buy mainly fruits and vegetables. The market is worth visiting, especially in the morning or on a Saturday: the fresh goods and the busy crowds offer a colorful picture.

Next to the Town Hall stands the **Holy Cross Cathedral**. Mendaña Avenue branches off shortly afterwards to the right. The **City Library** is located here. The street crosses the Mataniko River and leads to picturesque **Chinatown**, where a totally different world opens up. The wooden houses have pretty verandahs, Chinese shops and restaurants offer their goods and services.

It is said that a Spanish sailor, Alvaro de Mendaña, erected a wooden cross in 1568 on the spit of land called **Point Cruz** and declared that the islands he had discovered were the property of the Spanish Crown. On the east side of the little peninsula a **harbor** was built. A nearby fuel storage depot is to be moved to a new location outside town following a recent fire there. Further west along Mendaña Avenue the **tourist office** will offer information and help. The **Point Cruz Yacht Club**, to be found right behind it on the shore, is a popular meeting place not only for yachting people. Travelers consider the **Solomon Kitano Mendaña Hotel** the best and biggest in the country.

Opposite the hotel is the **National Museum and Cultural Center**, where curators have shown great commitment in assembling a collection dedicated to the culture and history of the country. On show are typical houses from the various regions of the Solomon Islands, canoes, woodwork, shells and cult objects. The museum sells books and artifacts. The nearby **Central Bank** has a permanent exhibition showing traditional money made out of feathers and shells, with an occasional temporary exhibition of woodcarving and paintings.

Right: The Vilu War Museum exhibits relics from World War Two.

The **Botanical Gardens**, open permanently, lie a little outside the town to the west. They charm their visitors with typical plants of the country, a lake covered in lilies and a herbarium with thousands of dried plants. There are paths leading into the surrounding rain forest for those who want to venture on longer walks. **Watapamu Village**, not far away, is an idyllic Solomon village with houses on stilts and roofs made from palm leaves. It is an absolute must for anyone visiting the island.

From Honiara to Lambi Bay

The many crashed planes and sunken warships, testimonies to the dramatic battles between the Japanese and Americans in the Second World War, give the area the name of **Iron Bottom Sound**. The wrecks, overgrown with algae and coral and surrounded by shoals of brightly colored tropical fish, are an attraction for divers. The wrecks are often so close to the surface of the water that even snorkelers can explore them easily. Water sports agencies and the tourist office provide information about these underwater sights.

About 5 miles (8 km) from Honiara, near **Poha**, you'll find the **Vatuluma Posori Cave**. Decorated with rock carvings, it represents the oldest archeological find on the islands to date. It is accessible to tourists only with a special permit issued by the museum and the villagers.

As is common practice in the South Pacific, an entrance fee must be paid for the beaches near **Bonegi** (8 miles/13 km) and **Ndoma** 14 miles/23 km). Further to the west, a bit away from the main road, is the village of **Vilu**. The small **Vilu War Museum** shows relics from World War Two.

After another 6 miles (10 km), one reaches **Cape Espérance**, where at the beginning of 1943 the Japanese began the secret evacuation of their troops from

Guadalcanal following their defeat. The **Tambea Village Resort** (27 miles/45 km), with its Melanesian-style bungalows, is one of the few tourist developments to be found outside the capital. It is conveniently located for a break during the trip on this road. The road ends 15 miles (25 km) further at **Lambi Bay**.

From Honiara to Aola

Mount Austin road branches off in **Kukum**, the eastern district of the capital. **Mount Austin** (1353 feet/410 m) was one of the strategically critical positions of Japanese troops in the fight for Henderson Airfield. A road leads to the top. Halfway up the hill the **Solomon Peace Memorial Park** honors the fallen Japanese. The hill offers marvelous views of Honiara and the north coast.

Henderson, now the international airport, lies 6 miles (10 km) outside Honiara. Names like **Bloody Ridge**, **Hell's Point** and **Red Beach** are testimony to the bitter fighting that once took place in this area.

The road continues across the **Guadalcanal Plains**, the largest flatlands on the island. **Tetere** (20 miles/34 km from Honiara) lies at the center of the oil palm plantations established at the end of the 1970s.

Two miles (3 km) off the main road is **Tetere Beach**, which has a cross in memory of four Austrian explorers who were killed in 1896 by locals. In the vicinity lies the sad wreckage of some landing craft from the Second World War.

If arrangements are made in advance, you can cross from **Komuninggita** (39 miles/65 km) to the island of **Vulelua**. There are day trips on offer from Honiara. The road ends at **Aola** (45 miles/75 km).

MALAITA AND OTHER SOLOMON ISLANDS

Malaita, the second biggest island of the Solomons, has 80,000 inhabitants and the highest population density. A ferry shuttles from Honiara to the main town **Auki**. You will find a relaxed atmosphere

here, hotels, banks, a market, shops and restaurants. In the shallow waters of the **Langa Langa Lagoon** the inhabitants of the lagoon made artificial islands out of blocks of coral and sand, initially as a defense against enemy mountain tribes. Many families still live here, although they have to go to the mainland to work on their fields. "Shark callers" perform rituals and make offerings to pacify the sharks, which, according to tradition, are hosts to the souls of the villagers' ancestors.

In the south of the lagoon is the little island of **Laulasi** with its big "spirit houses" (tours via Auki Lodge). The thickly forested island has several roads (often in bad condition!) on which you can travel in converted passenger trucks. There are good facilities for bathing, diving and snorkeling, for example near the friendly village of **Malu'u** in the north or

Above: The watering hole of the village, a place to meet for a little gossip while washing up (here on Malaita).

near **Atori** in the east (popular with surfers). From Atori one can cross to the idyllic island of **Kwai**. The inhabitants are friendly and the Rest House, built out of coral blocks, offers comfortable accommodation for the night. There are dozens of little inhabited islands in the **Lau Lagoon** to the northeast.

The **Nggela (Florida) Islands** north of Guadalcanal are made up of two main islands, Nggela Sule and Nggela Pile, which have beautiful and quiet beaches. Below the Nggelas, there is the little island of **Tulagi** with the former capital, also of that name.

The island of **Savo** in Iron Bottom Sound has an active volcano with two craters and various geothermal phenomena, such as fumaroles, mudholes and geysers. The megapode, an indigenous bird (*Megapodius prichardis*), buries its eggs in the warm sand.

A number of hotels, restaurants and diving facilities are located in the Western Province on **Uepi Island**, **New Georgia Island** and **Gizo Island**.

SOLOMON ISLANDS
There is no area code. The country code is 677.

Arrival / Departure / Vaccinations
Most nationals receive a three-month visa on entering the country. For information check with a British consulate or embassy. Airport tax on departing is SI$ 40. Anti-malarial drugs and vaccinations against smallpox, yellow fever and cholera are recommended. Water should be boiled before drinking.

Air Travel
International flights: **Solomon Airlines** (Tel: 20031, Fax: 23992), **Air Pacific** (Tel: 23791), **Air Niugini** (Tel: 22895, Fax: 24025) and **Air Nauru** (Tel: 22587, Fax: 23887) to Australia (Brisbane, Melbourne, Sydney), Fiji (Nadi, Suva), Nauru, New Zealand, Papua New Guinea and Vanuatu. **Solomon Airlines** (Tel/Fax see above) and **Western Pacific Air Services** (Tel: 30533) fly to over 25 airports in the country.

Accommodation
A selection of lodgings with varying standards and in various price categories can only be found in Honiara on Guadalcanal. More remote parts of the country have simple guest houses as a rule. The tourist office has a list.
GUADALCANAL: *LUXURY (from SI$ 150 per double):* **Honiara Hotel**, near Chinatown, Honiara, Tel: 21737, Fax: 20376, air-conditioned rooms, balcony, restaurant, bar, pool, also some simple, inexpensive rooms. **Iron Bottom Sound Village**, west of the center, Mendaña Ave., Tel: 30407, Fax: 30460, 42 air-conditioned rooms, Chinese restaurant, bar. **Kitano Mendaña Hotel**, Honiara, Tel: 20071, Fax: 23942, on a small beach offering no swimming, 96 air-conditioned rooms, restaurant, bar, pool, diving shop. **King Solomon Hotel**, Hibiscus Ave., Tel: 21205, Fax: 21771, 58 air-conditioned rooms, restaurant, bar, nightclub, pool. *MODERATE: (from SI$ 70 per double)* **Testimony Guest House**, Tel: 21530, Fax: 21341, Lenggakiki Ridge southwest of the center, idyllic location, cooking opportunities, friendly and quiet.
OUTSIDE HONIARA: *LUXURY:* **Lelei Resort**, 2.5 miles (4 km) west, Tel: 20720, Fax: 22970, 6 air-conditioned rooms, restaurant, pool. **Tambea Hotel Beach Resort**, 28 miles (45 km) west, Tel: 21737, Fax: 20376, bungalows, ventilator, restaurant, pool, water sports. **Vulelua Island Resort**, Tel/Fax: 29684, 9 Melanesian bungalows on a small island 40 miles (65 km) southeast , restaurant, water sports.
MALAITA: *BUDGET:* **Auki Lodge**, Auki, Tel: 40131, Fax: 40220, restaurant, bar, tours. **Malu'u Lodge**, Malu'u (no Tel), tours.
WESTERN PROVINCE: *MODERATE (from SI$ 100 per double):* **Uepi Island Resort**, Uepi Island, New Georgia Islands, (Roco Ltd., Honiara, Tel:

26074, Fax: 26076), 6 bungalows, 2 rooms, restaurant (full board oblig.), tours, water sports, diving. **Agnes Lodge**, Manda / New Georgia Island, Tel: 61133, Fax: 61225, rooms of varying prices and standards, restaurant, bar, tours, diving. **Gizo Hotel**, Gizo, Tel: 60199, Fax: 60137, air-conditioned or ventilated rooms, restaurant, pool, dive-shop.

Restaurants
HONIARA: La Pérouse Restaurant, Tel: 23720, located near the Guadalcanal Club on Mendaña Avenue, excellent French cuisine, seafood (lunch and dinner), cozy. The **Kitano Mendaña** Hotel and the **Honiara** have good restaurants, Japanese and Chinese respectively.

Museums
HONIARA: National Museum and Cultural Center, Tel: 22309, weekdays 9:00 a.m.-noon and 1:00 p.m.-4:00 p.m., donation appreciated.

Nightlife / Entertainment / Clubs
HONIARA: Dancing and disco are offered in some clubs on specific days. Inquire when there. **Honiara Casino**, Tel: 25222, Fax: 25369, gambling machines, roulette, blackjack, poker, baccarat, opens at 11 a.m. Gambling, too, in the **Super Club** and **Club 88**. **Point Cruz Yacht Club**, Tel: 22500, and **G Club** (Guadalcanal Club, Mendaña Ave.) Tel: 22212, offer temporary membership for tourists.

Excursions
HONIARA: Organized tours on Guadalcanal and other islands: **Guadalcanal Travel Service**, Tel: 22587, Fax: 26184; **Tour Solomons**, Tel: 21630.

Diving
Explore the terrific underwater world including World-War-Two wrecks: **GUADALCANAL: Dive Solomons**, Tel: 20520, Fax: 23110. **Dive Tambea**, at the Tambea Hotel Beach Resort 28 miles/45 km west of Honiara, Tel: 21737, Fax: 20376. **Island Dive Services**, Tel: 22103, Fax: 21493. **GIZO: Adventure Sports**, Tel: 60253, Fax: 60297.

Rental Cars / Charters
GUADALCANAL: **Avis**, Tel: 24180, Fax: 24181. **Budget Rent-A-Car**, Tel: 23205. **MV Solomon Sea**, Tel: 24936, Fax: 25300, 80-ft (25 m) yacht, 5 double cabins. **Bilikiki Cruises Ltd.**, Tel: 20412, Fax: 23897.

Currency / Sales Tax
1 US$ is ca SI$ 2,20. Sales tax is 10 percent.

Business Hours / Electricity
BUSINESS HOURS: Mon-Fri 8 a.m.-5 p.m., Sat 8 a.m.-noon. *ELECTRICITY:* 240 V AC.

Tourist Information
Solomon Islands Tourism Assoc., PO Box 321, Honiara, Tel: 22442, Fax: 23986. **Western Province Tourism Assoc.**, PO Box 71, Gizo, Tel: 60251.

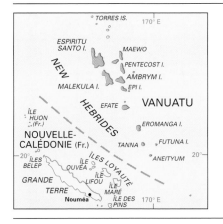

VANUATU
(New Hebrides)

EFATE

TANNA

ESPIRITU SANTO

PENTECOST

MALEKULA

AMBRYM

Vanuatu is a Pacific travel destination that is highly recommended by insiders. You will find here the romantic atmosphere of the South Seas for which you might have looked in vain on other islands: emerald green rain forests, dreamlike white beaches, lonely coves fringed by coconut palms, gorgeous lagoons, reefs and waterfalls. But Vanuatu offers still more: highly active volcanoes with all their breathtaking effects, plus an ancient culture of great variety. The locals, who call themselves Ni-Vanuatu, are warm-hearted and friendly. Life is quiet and easy.

Smoking Volcanoes and Tropical Forests

The Republic of Vanuatu (previously New Hebrides) consists of at least 68 inhabited tropical islands and many more uninhabited ones. They lie between the lines of 166 and 171 eastern longitude and 13 and 21 southern latitude. The group stretches over about 780 miles (1300 km) from the Torres Islands in the northwest to the little islands of Hunter

Preceding pages: Champagne Beach on Espiritu Santo. Left: Traditional tower jumping on Pentecost, the original version of bungee jumping.

and Matthew in the southeast. Officially, the country covers 4876 square miles (12,190 sq km). The main island, Efate, is the third biggest of the group.

Geologically speaking, the islands straddle the meeting point of the Pacific and Australo-Asian continental plates. This explains the phenomena of rising and sinking ground levels and the active volcanoes. On Ambrym and Tanna islands, the craters permanently bubble away, and smoke columns rise majestically over the mountaintops. Mount Yasur on Tanna is considered the most accessible of the earth's active volcanoes.

Most of the high-rising volcanic islands are overgrown with thick tropical vegetation. Subsistence farming, plantation clearances and wood felling – and also the occasional severe tornado – have radically reduced the once widely spread tropical rain forests. In many places, lower secondary forests have grown over the empty ground, but even here the big old banyan trees (*ficus benghalensis*) frequently stand out, with their huge trunks and roots and broad crowns. The Ni-Vanuatu call this majestic shade-providing tree "king of the forest." In areas where original forests survive, the richness of plant species is remarkable. It is said that there are more than 1500 different types, among them 160 kinds of orchid, a quar-

ter of which are particular to these islands. Along the coast, one will often find *casuarina equisetifolia*, Barringtonia (the fruit of which is used as a poison in hunting fish, though this practice has been outlawed) and *hibiscus tiliaceus*. Mangroves grow in many muddy, shallow bays.

Reptiles, Insects and Birds

Eight kinds of bat – in particular four kinds of fruit bat, one of them now only found here – appear to be the only land mammals to have reached the islands on their own. All other mammals on the islands, including the partly wild ones, were imported by humans. 13 kinds of reptile, including five kinds of gecko, are at home here, in addition to the striped iguana imported from the Fiji Islands and two types of non-poisonous snake. One of them, the Pacific boa, can reach a

Above: The smoking crater of Mt. Yasur on Tanna, a still-active volcano. Right: A brightly-colored coconut crab.

length of up to 8 feet (2.5 meters). It is often noted that on Banks Island in the north one will occasionally meet crocodiles, but they are probably from the Solomon Islands, and lost their way in the ocean.

There is considerably greater variety among invertebrates and birds. More than 70 species of snails and slugs, 60 kinds of butterflies and 120 kinds of insect populate the islands, among them, unfortunately, malaria-carrying mosquitoes. There are almost 90 species of land birds (seven of them particular to the islands) and 30 species of sea birds.

Climate

The average temperature in the capital, Port Vila, is 76 °F (24 °C), and the average rainfall is chalked up at 84 inches (2160 mm), although with marked seasonal variations. The warmest time is between December and March, when most of the rain falls. The cooler and drier season is between June and September,

when temperatures are a few degrees cooler than in the warm season. The dominant winds are southeasterlies (trade winds) and so the eastern sides of the easterly islands get most rain. Two or three times a year a cyclone will hit Vanuatu and storm damage is frequent. But a cyclone causing severe damage in the region is only reckoned to happen every 20 years or so.

Cultural Diversity

The number of inhabitants has doubled over the past 15 years to 170,000. Almost 98 percent of the population are the Melanesian locals (Ni-Vanuatu). They are ethnically quite homogeneous. Marked decentralization was the tradition on the islands and remains typical. This isolated way of life, with about 60 percent of the people living in villages of fewer than 50, has often led to cultural divergence over even small distances.

This is most clearly shown in the 115-plus languages spoken on the islands.

Linguists have discovered so-called "language chains," whereby an islander can understand the language spoken in immediately neighboring villages but understands increasingly less in more distant settlements.

With the first regular contact with Europeans at the beginning of the 19th century, a generally understood dialect evolved from pidgin English called *Bislama* (French: *Bichlamar*). This made it possible to cross the language barrier with Europeans but also barriers between the locals themselves.

Today, *Bislama* is the official language of Vanuatu. English and French are also official languages, especially in education. In addition to their local dialect, many people speak Bislama and one or both of the European languages.

Kava and Copra in the Tax Shelter

"Try some kava," says the headline in a tourist brochure. Port Vila alone is reputed to boast more than 100 *namakal*

49

(kava bars). Kava is a relaxing drink made from the root of the kava plant. It is more than just a national drink: it has also become an export item for Vanuatu. In 1995, 52 tons of the dried plant were exported and demand is growing (see Fiji Islands, page 96). The biggest export however is copra (dried coconut meat), followed by beef and wood. Cocoa and shellfish are also exported. The main customers are countries of the European Union, Japan, Australia and Bangladesh. Trade is far from balanced, however; imports are four times greater than exports.

The number of visitors in 1995 surpassed 100,000 for the first time, although 57 percent stayed only one day, being cruise ship passengers. More than 50 percent of visitors come from Australia and a quarter from New Zealand or New Caledonia. Tourism is a growing industry.

Above: Wood is one of the commodities that keep Vanuatu's economy going.

At the beginning of the 1970s the legal conditions were established to transform the New Hebrides into an attractive international financial center. The independent Vanuatu has continued this initiative with big tax breaks and liberal banking laws. Many banks and international management companies today have a branch in Port Vila.

Seafarers, Settlers, Sandalwood and Slaves

It is believed that the first settlers reached Vanuatu 5000 years ago via Papua New Guinea and the Solomon Islands. The oldest finds to date are believed to be about 3400 years old. The first European to reach the islands was the Spaniard Fernandez de Quiros in 1606. He gave the name to the island, Espiritu Santo, and was convinced that he had found the big unknown southern continent, Terra Australis Incognita. His attempts to establish a permanent settlement failed, however. In 1768, Louis

Antoine de Bougainville landed on Ambae and Malo. It was eventually Captain James Cook who, on his second journey in 1774, sailed around the islands and mapped them. In honor of the Scottish isles, he called them the New Hebrides.

In 1825, an Australian trader discovered rich sandalwood forests on Erromango. News of the find spread quickly. More forests of the valuable wood were discovered and by 1865 this resource was totally exhausted. At the same time, a new and lucrative business started: slavery. Plantations in Australia and Fiji and the mines of New Caledonia needed labor. Hiring agents had no scruples. Many inhabitants were kidnapped, while volunteers often did not know on what terms they would be working. Only at the start of the 20th century did the trade in humans stop, following pressure from the Church.

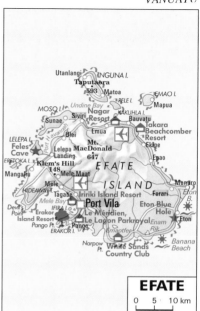

EFATE

0 5 10 km

Missionary Troubles

In 1839 the English missionaries James Harris and John Williams arrived in the New Hebrides. They visited Tanna and Futuna, and came full of hope of increasing the Christian flock, but on Erromango the islanders beat them to death and ate them. This unfortunate incident forced a change in strategy; the British Missionary Society subsequently sent Polynesian missionaries, hoping that they would prove more acceptable. But language problems, malaria and repeated acts of aggression by the islanders made their work extremely difficult and unrewarding.

In 1848, Presbyterians founded the first missionary station on the island of Aneityium. The Anglican-Melanesian mission meanwhile took locals to schools in New Zealand to prepare them for missionary work back on their islands. In 1887, the first Catholic missionary station was established on Malekula. Today 90 percent of the population are Chris-

tians; about half of them Presbyterian with the rest roughly divided between Anglicans and Catholics.

Contact with Europeans in the early days brought lethal epidemics: cholera, measles, smallpox, whooping cough and flu were only a few of the imported diseases. Experts believe that the population of Vanuatu in 1800 was about one million. At the end of the 19th century there were only 100,000 people left, and by 1935 numbers had been further reduced to 45,000.

British and French Settlers

In 1853, France annexed the New Hebrides in order to continue its support for French traders and settlers in the Pacific. Beginning in 1854, British farmers from New Zealand and Australia also settled on the islands. During the American Civil War, they considered cotton to be particularly lucrative. But cyclones, malaria, falling world prices and lack of support from the British government all contributed to the ruin of many farmers by the beginning of the 1880s.

John Higginson, an Irish-born French land speculator, founded the Compagnie Calédonienne des Nouvelles-Hébrides (CCNH) in 1882. In that year, the company bought about 222,000 acres (90,000 hectares) of land from locals and impoverished British farmers. By 1905 it possessed 55 percent of the arable land on the islands. At the same time the immigration of French farmers was encouraged.

Australian businessmen tried to protect British interests with their Australian New Hebrides Company (ANHC). Conflicts between British and French settlers grew worse and worse until eventually, in 1906, a solution was attempted with the establishment of a British-French condominium on the New Hebrides. Almost all offices and public organizations soon had parallel French and British structures. The cost of this system of joint government was huge, but the results – for want of cooperation – meager.

From the Second World War to Independence

After Japanese troops landed on the Solomon Islands in 1942, the Americans immediately sent troops to Vanuatu. The establishment of a US base on Efate was followed by another on Espiritu Santo, where soon more than 100,000 troops were bivouacked. This made a deep impact on the quiet, traditional life of the locals. Thousands of the inhabitants of Vanuatu found unusually well-paid jobs with the Americans and everybody was fascinated by what – for them – were the enormous treasures that were unloaded, practically overnight. But after 1945, as swiftly as they had arrived, the Americans disappeared.

Right: A panoramic view of Vanuatu's capital Port Vila and of the island of Iririki.

In the 1960s and 1970s, independence movements and the first indigenous political parties began to be established. Shortly before the last step to independence there were serious disturbances, mainly on the northern islands. In many places people were afraid that a central government in Port Vila with a strong English orientation would not represent local interests sufficiently. On July 30, 1980, however, the independent Republic of Vanuatu (*Our Country*) was declared.

EFATE

The Capital Port Vila

Port Vila, the small capital of Vanuatu (about 30,000 inhabitants) on the island of Efate, is considered among the most beautiful spots in the South Pacific because of its marvelous location – a broad bay, with views to the forest-covered mountains of the southern peninsula and the two tiny islands of Iririki and Ifira. A mixture of Melanesian, British and French flair gives the town an unusual charm.

The main street, the **Kumul Highway**, runs parallel to the bay. The bigger shops, many restaurants, boutiques and cafés, offices of the airline companies and travel agents are situated along this somewhat commercial strip.

The **Main Post Office** is remarkable for its expressive ornamental reliefs by Aloi Pilioko. Pilioko has become one of the most well-known contemporary artists of the South Pacific. He originally came from the island of Wallis but has lived for decades on Vanuatu.

Many of his richly colored tapestries have found their way into public buildings. Pilioko is also known for his collaboration with another brilliant local artist, Nicolai Michoutouchkine. A way northward from the Post Office, in Lolam House, is the **tourist office**, where staff

are always ready to help with advice and information.

Walking up Rue Emile Mercet, you pass the pink **Pilioko House**, its façade decorated with reliefs by Aloi Pilioko. Nikolai Michoutouchkine designs and sells unique fabrics in this house. About 200 yards (200 meters) further down this street is the **Mairie**, the Town Hall, where in condominium times the French Tricolor and the British Union Jack fluttered side by side. Opposite the **Reserve Bank of Vanuatu** stands a memorial to the soldiers who died in the First World War. From here a marvelous panoramic view stretches over town. A few hundred yards/meters up the hill is the beautiful old wooden building of the **Supreme Court**. In colonial times it was the home of the *Joint Court*, the common French and British courts of the New Hebrides that used to regulate conflicts between settlers and locals and between the settlers themselves.

Parallel to the Kumul Highway runs the broad **Shore Promenade** with lawns on either side. At its southern end the market hall invites visitors with its colorful displays of agricultural goods. Some stalls sell shells, simple handicrafts and colored fabrics.

From the quay south of the market hall there is a free 24-hour shuttle service to the nearby **Iririki Island Resort**, which opened in 1986. The villa perched on the hill of the island used to be the seat of the British Commissary. The main building of the resort offers a beautiful view back to Port Vila. The island is well wooded and one can walk around it comfortably in 30 minutes. It offers marvelous possibilities for swimming and snorkeling, especially at **Snorkeler's Cove**. From the quay in Port Vila boats also go to **Ifira Island** (get a permit first).

Two important sights are located to the the south of the town on Avenue Edmond Colardeau, the **National Museum** and the **Vanuatu Cultural Center**, with the library and archives. This modern building stands a block away from the Windsor Hotel. The permanent exhibition

53

shows objects illustrating the history of Vanuatu, its art and historical photographs from various islands as well as ceremonial objects.

The **Parliament Building** opposite the museum was built with Chinese help in 1992. The bronze sculpture by the entrance figures a Ni-Vanuatu family.

About 3 miles (5 km) to the south on the road to the village of Pango, is the **Michoutouchkine and Pilioko Foundation Art Gallery**. The two artists have gathered here a collection of South Pacific art worth visiting. One can also inspect and buy the works of these two internationally-recognized figures.

On the coast between **Pango** and **Pango Point** are marvelous beaches, attractive also for surfers. The beach of Pango Point has an entry fee. The island of **Erakor** lies in front of **Erakor La-**

Above: Colorful batik cloth being sold at Port Vila's harbor, an ideal souvenir. Right: Bronze sculpture of a Ni-Vanuatu family.

goon, and from the quay near **Le Lagon Parkroyal Resort**, a ferry shuttles 24 hours a day. The island is ideal for a daytrip. You can relax amid rich vegetation on a dream of a beach, while accommodation and fine food are offered by the **Erakor Island Resort**.

Around Efate

The approximately 84-mile-long (140 km) main road (mostly unpaved) follows the coast for long stretches at a time. Because of the rather steep gradients encountered in the west, it is advisable to drive around the island counter-clockwise, as described below.

The southeast of Efate consists of acres of abandoned coconut palm plantations transformed into pastures for cattle and also pumpkin fields (for export to Japan). After 5.5 miles (9 km), the road passes the biggest river on the island, the Teouma, and soon afterwards appears the **White Sands Country Club** with its golf course. **Banana Beach** and **Dry Creek** are beautiful public beaches. It is worthwhile, however, driving on a further 3.5 miles (6 km) to the wonderful **Eton Beach** (directly behind the village of that name). Shortly before entering the village, on the right side, you will find the **Eton Blue Hole** surrounded by rich vegetation. A rich variety of colorful fish swim about this saltwater hole located right by the roadside.

In **Forari**, 6 miles (10 km) further, intensive surface mining of manganese was conducted between 1961 and 1978. The rusty, overgrown buildings are a grim feature of the landscape here. As the volcanic ground around Forari is good for the production of cement, new investors have shown interest.

The journey continues to the north partly along the coast and also through small settlements and rich vegetation. In the **Takara Beachcomber Resort** (50 miles/82 km) you can inspect some rusty old relics of World War Two. The resort, with restaurant and a waterside bar and views of **Emao Island**, offers a pleasant opportunity for a break in the journey or even for a night's stay.

Quoin Hill airfield, not far away, was built by the Americans during the Second World War. Near Bauvatu are the wrecks of two fighter planes lying in shallow waters offshore. There are also wrecks in the forest to the west of the landing strip, but you will need a local guide to find them.

From the simple but beautifully situated **Nagar Resort**, also with restaurant and bar, you can see three islands. The nearest is the uninhabited little **Kakula Island**, on lease and awaiting construction of a luxury resort hotel. **Pele Island** is inhabited, just like the big island of **Nguna**.

The impressive picture book volcano, **Taputaora**, standing almost 2000 feet (600 meters) high, is a defining feature of the tableau that presents itself from over the water to the north. **Siviri** (59 miles/98

km), on the western edge of **Undine Bay**, is reached by a side road. For a small fee you can visit the little **Valeafau Cave** and hear its story.

Shortly before the village of **Ulei**, the main road hits the coast at **Port Havannah**, which offers a first class protected anchorage formed by the islands of **Moso** and **Lelepa**. In 1942, American troops landed here and set up base, and for a few years life returned to this little harbor.

In a few places one can see relics of these times: a quay, a water reservoir, the remains of a sunken seaplane and the ruins of the officers' mess. Here, roadside vendors offer fruits and mussels, and also finds from the American times like field canteens and cutlery and old bottles (mainly Coca Cola).

After **Samoa Point** (70 miles/116 km) you will reach **Lelepa Landing**. Lelepa Island has some beautiful, lonely beaches, caves (**Feles Cave** with rock paintings more than 1000 years old) and again relics from the Second World War: a crashed Corsair and an anti-aircraft gun. Day trips are on offer from Port Vila to Lelepa.

About 2 miles (3 km) from Lelepa Landing (and only to be found with the help of a local guide) is the former **Manga'asi**, a settlement founded about 1500 years ago. It developed during the reign of Chief Roymata in the 13th century and was once upon a time the most important place on the island.

Roymata was reputed to have been buried on the uninhabited island of **Eretoka** (also called **Hat Island** because of its shape), in the company of 18 of his chieftains and 22 wives, all of them alive at the time. Excavations led by the French archeologist José Granger at the end of the 1960s indeed brought to light what was obviously a chieftain's grave with 41 skeletons.

The road starts rising and then falls steeply in several sections until finally reaching **Klem's Hill** (76 miles/127 km). From the parking lot on the left, directly behind the hill, there is a marvelous view of Port Vila and **Mele Bay**. The road descends steeply to **Mele Maat**, where the great sight is the **cascades**. Before the road cuts away to Mele, continue to the right for another 7 miles (12 km) to **Devil's Point**.

In front of **Mele Village** lies diminutive **Mele Island** (also called **Hideaway Island**), a popular place for swimming and snorkeling. Past the **Port Vila Golf Club**, the road returns to the capital. 2 miles (3 km) before the town center a side road to the right takes you to the wealthiest district, called **Malapoa**.

TANNA

Tanna, 226 square miles (565 sq km) in size, numbers amongst the most frequently visited islands of Vanuatu.

Right: A suckling pig is the prize for these proud hunters (Tanna).

James Cook was the first European to reach the island, in 1774. He anchored in **Port Resolution Bay** and gave the island its name. A good quarter of today's population are followers of so-called "kastom" religions, i.e., religions or ways of life based on traditional customs. The most popular is the **Jon Frum Movement**, a "cargo cult," which came about in the 1930s but only received its impetus as a consequence of the flood of goods arriving on the island with the advent of American troops during World War Two. The followers of this creed believe that Jon Frum, undoubtedly an American, will return one day and again bring prosperity and health. John Frum villages and other such *kastom* villages can be visited with a local guide.

At irregular intervals, mostly between August and the end of the year, the three- to five-day *Nekowiar* festival takes place. The wild toka-dance, with the participation of the men from the villages, celebrates the circumcision of the young boys.

For its comparatively small size, Tanna offers a quite a varied landscape, including two mountains, **Mt. Tukosmera** and **Mt. Mareun**, which reach altitudes of more than 3000 feet (1000 meters) respectively.

But the main attraction is the modest 1200-foot (361 meters) and easily approachable active volcano, **Mount Yasur**, on the east of the island. The last great eruption took place there in 1878 when the southeastern part of Tanna was raised by about 65 feet (20 meters). Smoke columns, earth movements and explosions occur regularly, and flying rocks are quite common. The view into the crater at night is most impressive (sensible shoes and a flashlight recommended).

Agencies in Port Vila offer day-long tours to Tanna. They are frequently designed to coincide with the popular Nekowiar festival.

ESPIRITU SANTO

This is Vanuatu's biggest island, with a surface area of more than 1600 square miles (4000 sq km) and approximately 30,000 inhabitants. It's usually simply called Santo. A mountain range more than 3000 feet (1000 meters) high, covered in thick forest, stretches from north to south. **Mount Tabwemasan**, at 6260 feet (1897 meters), is the highest peak of Vanuatu. The east of Santo is mostly flat, so the majority of the people, plantations and pastures are there. The biggest settlement, **Luganville**, is in the south-east of the island and has 10,000 inhabitants.

Santo was discovered in 1606 by the Spanish captain Quiros and later visited by de Bougainville and Captain Cook. The first resistance movements in Vanuatu against the European merchants and plantation owners who settled after the 1850s began on Santo in the 1920s. The arrival of 100,000 American soldiers in 1942 brought about radical change.

Dwellings, roads, docks and airfields were swiftly built. About 10,000 Ni-Vanuatu from other islands found work on Santo.

Santo also gave birth after the war to fresh "cargo cults" and, in 1963, under the leadership of Chief Buluk and Jimmy Stevens, the *Nagriamel* movement came into being. In 1971, *Nagriamel* lodged a petition with the United Nations demanding independence for Vanuatu. Beginning in 1975, the pro-French movement fought for an independent Santo. A few weeks before the declaration of independence the so-called Coconut Rebellion broke out, which was eventually stifled. Its leaders, including Jimmy Stevens, were punished.

Santo is a paradise for divers, especially wreck-divers. The wreck of the 664 foot-long (202 meters), 22,000-ton luxury cruiser *SS President Coolidge* – sunk by its own mines during a military mission in 1942 – lies 3.5 miles (6 km) east of Luganville at a depth of between 65 and 230 feet (20 and 70 meters) of

ESPIRITU SANTO

0   20   40 km

water. At **Million Dollar Point** (5.5 miles/9 km) the Americans sank a vast amount of war materials and other goods at the end of World War Two, after neither the colonial administration of the island nor the European settlers could make up their minds to buy them despite the bargain basement prices being offered. This protected area is a popular spot for snorkelers, divers and souvenir hunters.

In **Saraoutou** you can visit the **IRHO Coconut Research Center**. In **Matevulu** (12.5 miles/21 km), the island's biggest Blue Hole – a deep pool fed by a spring – promises a refreshing bath.

Thirty-four miles (55 km) north of Luganville, near the pleasant English-speaking settlement of **Hog Harbour**, is the most spectacular beach of Vanuatu, **Champagne Beach**. The romantic name is by no means an exaggeration: a crystal

Right: Waiting anxiously for the great jump, land diving on Pentecost.

clear lagoon lined by cream-colored sand fine as powdered sugar. Coconut palms sway in the breeze, behind them rises a mellifluous line of shining green hills. The cruiser *Fristar* anchors here regularly, releasing a flood of passengers. The white beach of **Port Olry** and the dark beach in **Big Bay** are ideal for swimming, dreaming and being lazy.

The *kastom* village **Tanafo** (also known as Fanafo or Vanafo, and lying 14 miles/23 km from Luganville) is the former home of Jimmy Stevens and the center of the *Nagriamel* movement. It can be visited only on an organized tour with a local guide.

PENTECOST

This 200-square-mile (500 sq km) island with its 13,000 inhabitants has become internationally known for its spectacular land diving (*naghol*). This traditional test of bravery ultimately gave birth to modern bungee jumping. Every April and May a 30-meter (100-feet) tower is built around a tree trunk using flexible branches. Men prepared to jump tie strands of liana creepers around their ankles, fix them to the top of the platform and dive head first into the abyss. This ceremony at the beginning of the yam harvest marks the renewal of fertility and is also an initiation ritual.

Visitors now attend the land diving ceremony and tour companies have included it in their programs, leading those locals conscious of their culture to fear that the ritual may turn into a shabby tourist show.

MALEKULA

Malekula, with its surface area of 828 square miles (2070 sq km) and 21,000 inhabitants, is the second biggest and one of the most densely populated islands of Vanuatu. Settlements are concentrated on the coast.

The island is culturally diverse, as demonstrated by the fact that about 30 languages are spoken on it. At the same time, despite earlier European settlement, old traditions have succeeded in surviving more or less intact to this day – especially in the isolated mountainous regions. The name for the two groups of natives – Big Nambas and Small Nambas – refers to the different size of the penis sheaths (*nambas*) which the men wear suspended from a belt.

Visitors land at the airstrip in Norsup. A few simple rest houses and restaurants have opened 3 miles (5 km) to the south in **Lakatoro**. The **Cultural Center** there gives information about the island and the availability of tours. In **Aop Bay** a marvelous white beach beckons – but beware of the sharks in the waters around Malekula. The **Wala Island Resort** on Wala Island is an ideal place for Robinson holidays. Another possibility is spending the night on nearby Ranoi island.

There are many places in Malekula that are considered taboo, so visitors should get exact information before they set out on a trip about where they may go.

AMBRYM

This 280-square-mile (700 sq km) island is dominated by three volcanoes: **Mt. Marum** (4190 feet/1270 m), **Mt. Benbow** (3825 feet/1159 m) and **Mt. Vetlam** (3877 feet/1175 m). After eruptions in 1950, several hundred inhabitants were forced to move to Efate. Today, almost 8000 people live on Ambrym. They are regarded as exceptionally good wood carvers. Their huge slit drums (*tam tam*), and their sculptures made from fern tree wood, tufa and pumice stone, are famous all over Vanuatu.

The **Milee Resthouse** in **Sanesup** (south Ambrym) hires out guides for a tour into the volcanic area surrounding Mounts Benbow and Marum. In the north one can climb up to Mount Vetlam via **Linbul** and **Ranon**. The friendly **Solomon Douglas Rest House** in Ranon is a good base for further treks.

VANUATU

No local area codes, the country code is 678.

Arrival / Departure

Most nationals have to get a one-month visa on arrival, extensions up to four months are possible. Airport tax on departure is VT 2000.

Air Travel

There are international flights to Auckland, Sydney and Brisbane, Nouméa (New Caledonia), Nadi (Fiji Islands) and Honiara (Solomon Islands). They are flown by **Air Calédonie**, Tel: 228950; **Air Pacific**, Tel: 22836; AOM, Tel: 241212, Fax: 241213; **Solomon Airlines** and **Air Vanuatu**, both Tel: 23848, Fax: 23910. A host of other international airlines have offices in Port Vila. The local company, **Vanair**, flies regularly to about 30 destinations, Tel: 22643.

Currency

The national currency is the vatu (1 US$ = ca 110 VT). US dollars are often accepted.

Business Hours

Shops: Mon-Fri 8-11:30 a.m. and 1:30-5:30 p.m. Sat 8 a.m.-noon. **Offices**: Mon-Fri 7:30-11:30 a.m. and 1:30-5 p.m. **Post office**: Mon-Fri 7:30 a.m.-4:30 p.m.

EFATE ISLAND

(Unless otherwise indicated, the establishment is near Port Vila).

Accommodation

LUXURY (over US$ 100): **Iriri Island Resort**, on the private island of Iriri off the coast of Port Vila, Tel: 22388, Fax: 23880, 24-hour free shuttle service, 72 air-conditioned bungalows, restaurant, bar, pool, beach, water, events. **Le Lagon Parkroyal**, 1.5 miles/3 km south of Port Vila on Erakor Lagoon, Tel: 22313, Fax: 23817, 141 air-conditioned rooms, bungalows, 2 restaurants, conference room, nightclub, 2 pools, own beach, golf, tennis, water sports. **Le Méridien Port Vila Resort & Casino**, over a mile west of the center on Erakor Lagoon, Tel: 22040, Fax: 23340, 165 air-conditioned rooms, 2 restaurants, bar, pool, beach, casino, water sports, tennis, golf, conference room, disco on weekends. *MODERATE (over US$ 50)*: **Coral Motel**, north of Vila Bay, Tel/Fax: 23569, 10 studios with kitchenette, ventilator, bistro and bar. **Erakor Island Resort**, ca 3 miles/5 km south of Port Vila on Erakor Lagoon, 5 min by ferry (24-hour service), Tel: 26983, Fax: 22983, 18 bungalows with ventilator, beautiful white sand beach, restaurant, bar, water sports. **Kaiviti Village Motel**, south of the Parliament, Tel: 24684, Fax: 24685, 28 studios, 9 apartments, snack bar (dining in the adjacent Windsor Hotel can be put on the bill), pool. **Hideaway Island Resort & Marine Sanctuary**, on the small island of Mele 5 miles (9 km) northwest of Port Vila, Tel: 22963, Fax: 23867, bungalows with telephone and kitchenette, rooms, dormitory, restaurant, bar, water sports, diving, often overcrowded. **Iriri Centre Ville Hotel**, on the private island of Iriri Tel: 22464, Fax: 22953, 21 air-conditioned rooms, studios and suites, all amenities of the Iriri Island Resort are available. **Pacific Lagoon Apt's**, 1.5 miles/3 km east of Port Vila on Erakor Lagoon, Tel: 23860, Fax: 24377, 12 three-room apartments, ventilator, sea and garden view, patrons are welcome to the amenities of nearby Le Lagon Parkroyal. **Vila Chaumières**, 2.5 miles/4 km east of Port Vila on the road to Forari, Tel: 22866, Fax: 24238, 4 air-conditioned bungalows with kitchenette, restaurant, bar with terrace over water, canoes, paddle boats, no children. **White Sands Country Club**, 11 miles/16 km southeast of Port Vila, Tel/Fax: 22090, close to the beach, 11 bungalows with ventilator, restaurant, bar, pool, golf, tennis. **Windsor Hotel International**, south of the Parliament, Tel: 22150, Fax: 22678, 53 rooms, most air-conditioned, TV, Tel: 30 studios and apartments with kitchenette, 2 restaurants, bar, gambling hall, pool, tennis. *BUDGET (under US$ 50)*: **Beachcomber Takara Springs**, Takara Beach 2 miles (3 km) east of Nagar, north coast, Tel: 23576, Fax: 26458, has 8 rooms with ventilator, restaurant, bar, thermal pool, water sports, yacht charter. **Nagar Beach Bungalows**, north coast, near Paonangisu, Tel: 23221, Fax: 27289 (Tour Vanuatu), 6 simple bungalows with ventilator, community toilets and showers, restaurant, camping. **Talimoru Hotel**, Cornwall St., Port Vila, Tel: 23740, Fax: 25369, has 42 rooms with ventilator, some with balcony, restaurant, kava bar, clean and friendly establishment.

Restaurants

Among the best establishments in Port Vila is: **Le Rendez-Vous Restaurant**, Tel: 23045, south of the center, near the Windsor Hotel, fine French cuisine, closed Sundays. **Pisces Restaurant**, on the Kumul Highway in the north of the city, Tel: 24940, Italian cuisine, seafood. **L'Houstalet**, on the main road south of the city, Tel: 22303, has some unusual fare such as flying foxes, fruit pigeons.... **Chez Gilles et Brigitte**, Tel: 26000, 3 miles (5 km) south of the road to Pago, on the beach near the Michoutouchkine & Piliko Foundation, French cooking, seafood. **Le Rossi**, near the tourist office, on the water, Tel: 22528, seafood, meat, pretty terrace, closed Sun and Mon. The hotel **Vila Chaumières** (see above), Tel: 22866, has an excellent, atmospheric restaurant with a terrace and a romantic view of the lagoon; serves delicious seafood. **Waterfront Bar & Grill**, Kumul Highway south of the city, Tel: 23490, fish, meat, salads, cakes, closed Sun.

Casino / Nightlife

The Palms, casino in the Le Méridien hotel, Tel: 24308, Fax 22394, with one-arm bandits, black jack, roulette, daily from 11:30 a.m. The disco **L'Houstalet**, in the restaurant by the same name is a favorite, especially with locals, opens at 9 p.m. **Le Flamingo**, Tel: 25788, near the post office is the city's best disco, opens at 8 p.m. The larger hotels arrange for **Melanesian Nights** with dance performances.

Museums

National Museum, Cultural Center and **National Library and Archives**, Avenue Edmond Colardeau, Tel: 22129, Mon-Fri 9 a.m.-5 p.m., Sat 9 a.m.-noon.

Excursions / Charter Boats

Island ferries and tours: **Surata Tamaso Tours**, Tel: 25600, Fax: 24275. **Tour Vanuatu**, Tel: 22733, Fax: 23442. **Tropical Adventure Tours**, Tel: 22743, Fax: 24452. *Excursions and charters:* **Coongoola Day Cruise**, Tel: 25020, Fax: 229 79, 74-ft/23-m ketch up to 50 passengers, diving. **La Violante Charters**, Tel: 83143, Fax: 26331, deep-sea fishing, diving, 112-ft/35-m luxury sailboat (1922) for six people. **Nautilus Scuba**, Tel: 22398, Fax: 25255, 3 boats, diving school. **Sailaway Cruises**, Tel: 22743, Fax: 24452, diving too.

Tours / Rental Cars

Aéro Club de Vila, Tel/Fax: 22514, Tours, charter, tandem parachuting. **Helicopters Vanuatu**, Tel: 24424, Fax: 24693, tours, various programs, charter.
Avis, Tel: 24816. **Budget Rent-a-Car**, Tel 23 170, Fax: 24693. **Discount Car Rentals**, Tel: 23242, Fax: 23898, packages with overnight stays, **Hertz**, Tel: 25700, Fax: 25511.

Sports

GOLF: **Port Vila Golf & Country Club**, Tel: 22564, 18 holes, Mele Bay, open 7:30 a.m., reservations on weekends. **White Sands Country Club**, 11 miles/16 km southeast of Port Vila, Tel: 22090, Fax: 22899, 18 holes.
DEEP-SEA FISHING: **Club Marine**, Tel: 26660. **Tuku Tuku Ranch Vanuatu**, Tel: 23096, Fax: 27215, two 34- and 21-foot boats (11 and 6.5 m), lodgings for fishermen on 6000-acre ranch.
RIDING: **Club Hippique**, Ranch de Colle, Tel: 23347. *DIVING:* **Nautilus Scuba**, Tel: 22398, Fax: 25255. **Tranquillity Island Dive Center**, Tel: 25020, Fax: 22979. *TENNIS:* **Port Vila Tennis Club**, Tel: 22437.

Tourist Information

National Tourism Office Vanuatu, Kumul Hwy, Lolam House, PO Box 209, Port Vila, Tel: 22515, Fax: 23889, e-mail: tourism@vanuatu.com.vu. Gives information on other Vanuatu islands.

TANNA ISLAND
Accommodation

Port Resolution Yacht Club, Tel/Fax: 68653, 6 simple bungalows without electricity, breakfast, dinner. great location, beaches nearby. **White Grass Bungalows**, Tel: 68660, Fax: 68688, northern west coast, very isolated. 11 bungalows, restaurant, bar. **Paradise Bay Guest House**, Tel: 68695, Fax: 68625, in Lenakel (west coast), colonial-style house, 6 rooms, communal kitchen, TV, beautiful gardens, comfortable, friendly. Snorkeling, tours. Nearby supermarket and bank.

ESPIRITU SANTO ISLAND
Accommodation

LUGANVILLE: *BUDGET:* **Hotel Santo**, in the center, Tel: 36250, Fax: 36749, 30 rooms (22 with air-conditioning), restaurant, bar, pool, tours. *BUDGET:* **Jaranmoli Bungalows**, over a mile (2 km) eastward toward the airport, Tel: 36857, Fax: 36396, 9 bungalows, ventilator, communal kitchen. **Natapoa Motel**, behind the Hotel Santo, Tel: 36643, rooms with bath. **New Look Motel**, in the center, Tel: 36440, Fax: 36095, 9 rooms with bath, communal kitchen. **Unity Park Motel**, in the center, Tel: 36052, Fax: 36025, 13 rooms, communal kitchen. **NEARBY:** **Aore Resort & Plantation**, Tel: 36705, Fax: 36703, on Aore Island opposite Luganville, shuttle 10 min., well-planned for children on a white sand beach, 10 bungalows with bathroom/WC, ventilator, restaurant, bar, pool, credit cards accepted. Diving (through Aquamarine Santo), tours. Coffee, copra and cocoa are grown on the plantation. **Bokissa Island Resort**, Tel/Fax: 36855, on a coral island between Aore and Tutuba, 6 miles/10 km from Luganville, great diving grounds, 12 bungalows on the beach, restaurant, bar, pool, water sports. **Bougainville Resort**, 3 miles (5 km) west of Luganville on a pretty beach, Tel: 36257, Fax: 36647, 8 bungalows, restaurant, bar, pool. **Lonnoc Beach Bungalows**, west of Champagne Beach, Tel: 36141, simple bungalows without electricity, community showers and toilet, restaurant, bar. Romantic, friendly lodgings, wonderful diving and snorkeling grounds. **Oyster Island Bungalows**, Tel: 36390, Fax: 36753, located 9 miles/15 km north of Pekoa airport on a smaller island, 6 bungalows, restaurant, bar, yacht tours, scuba diving.

Excursions / Diving

TOURS: **Butterfly Tours**, Tel: 362570, Fax: 36647. **Espiritu Santo Travel & Tours**, Tel: 36391. **Hibiscus Tours**, Tel: 36675, Fax: 36085. *DIVING:* **Aquamarine Santo**, Tel/Fax: 36196. **Bokissa Island Dive**, Tel/Fax: 36855. **Santo Dive Tours**, Tel: 36822. **Troppo Dive Espiritu Santo**, Tel: 36638, Fax: 36101, also arranges lodgings.

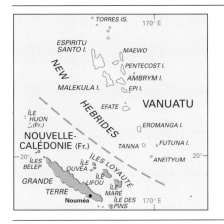

NEW CALEDONIA
(Nouvelle-Calédonie)

GRANDE TERRE

ÎLE DES PINS

LOYALTY ISLANDS

The first impression of New Caledonia's diverse natural scenery is on the airborne approach to the international airport of Tontouta, a breathtaking flight by small islands and the *Massif du Humboldt*. A closer look reveals large-scale cattle farms established by Europeans on the west coast of Grande Terre. On the east coast, however, the traditional lifestyle of the Melanesians has by and large been kept intact. Mountains streaked with deep valleys and great splashing waterfalls flow into sylvan hills and dense rain forest, to end at turquoise lagoons rimmed with shell-covered beaches offering paradisical peace.

A contrasting program, i.e., big city atmosphere, is also available in the capital Nouméa, the "Paris of the South Seas," which seduces its visitors with a broad variety of wares, with exquisite restaurants and French *savoir vivre.*

New Caledonia, a land mass of 7367 square miles (almost 20,000 sq km), comprises the main island of Grande Terre (popularly known as *le caillou*, the pebble), the Loyalty Islands to the east, the Bélep Islands to the northwest, Île des

Pins and a peppering of other islets. Grande Terre, which measures 248 miles long and about 31 miles at its widest point (about 397 by 50 km), is the largest of the South Pacific islands after Papua New Guinea and New Zealand.

Wind and Weather

New Caledonia lies on the edge of the tropics in the path of the southeastern trade winds. The average yearly temperature in Nouméa is about 73° F (23° C), with a variance of 43° F (6° C) during the course of the year. From June to September, nighttime lows can drop to about 53° F (12° C), while the lows during the warm months from November to April seldom go below 68° F (20° C), and the highs hover around 86° F (30° C). Thanks to the mountain chain running the length of Grande Terre, precipitation is very unevenly distributed. The western section of the country receives far less rainfall per year (39 to 58.5 inches/1000 to 1500 mm) than the eastern section (over 117 inches/3000 mm).

Fauna and Flora

Flying foxes are the only mammals that were able to reach the islands without help. Some of the domestic animals

Preceding pages: The northwestern region of New Caledonia is known for its cattle raising. Left: Dancers in Nouméa clad in their colorfully-painted tapa cloths.

NEW CALEDONIA

0 20 40 60 80 km

introduced by humans, such as cats, dogs and pigs, became wild after a while. Cattle was introduced for livestock, and a vast number of rats also arrived on European ships.

The ornithological kingdom is far more diverse, boasting about 70 species. The national bird is the kagu (*Rhynochetus jubatus*), a gray, flightless and endangered bird of the crane family, which moves very slowly and broods a single egg per year. As for reptiles, there are skinks, geckos and three types of land snake. Water snakes, which are found quite frequently, are extremely poisonous, but not aggressive.

Over 3000 higher species of plants flourish on the islands, three quarters of them are part of the natural vegetation. Thanks to the country's impassable terrain and thinly-settled population, many endemic plant types have survived in the more remote regions. The eastern half of Grande Terre has large stretches of dense, tropically humid vegetation, whereas the western side consists more of a grassy savanna dotted by small forests. Common here is the native eucalyptus-like niaouli tree (*Melaleuca quinquenervia*), whose white bark is used to make a medicinal oil. The tall Norfolk pines (*Araucaria*) are quite impressive. Some of the 14 species are endemic to the island.

New Caledonia's barrier reef is one of the largest and most splendid in the world, a veritable paradise for deep-sea divers and snorkelers, who can admire a wonderful world of coral gardens, colorful reef fish and shells here.

Nickel, Coffee and Tourism

New Caledonia, a split of section of the old continent of Gondwanaland, has a great deal of natural resources. It is the world's third largest producer of nickel, which accounts for 90 percent of the country's export revenues. Its chrome,

iron, manganese and cobalt ore deposits have not yet been properly exploited. Most of the mined ore is processed in Nouméa and exported as a partial product. Tourism started becoming a significant economic factor during the 1980s. The number of visitors per year has now crossed the 100,000 mark. Coconut oil and coffee are among the main agricultural products exported, albeit in small quantities. The trade deficit is growing.

Kanaka, Caldoches, Foreign Workers

New Caledonia only numbers about 170,000 inhabitants, but they are a variegated bunch indeed. The indigenous Melanesians proudly call themselves *Kanaka* (humans), a word that in some European languages is used disparagingly to describe certain foreigners, especially those of color.

Until after World War Two, the Kanaka population was diminishing. Nowadays they constitute about 45 percent of the population. These original inhabitants, who are struggling hard to maintain their culture and traditions in the face of strong French influence, generally live in the east of Grande Terre and on the surrounding islands. Islanders who trace their origins to the early European settlers are called *caldoches*. Thirty-four percent of the population are Europeans, 21 percent were born on Wallis, Futuna, Tahiti, or in Indonesia, Vietnam, or other countries, and came to New Caledonia in the wake of increased mining activity. The official language is French, but the native people speak about 30 different Melanesian languages.

James Cook Again

Just when New Caledonia was settled is a matter of contention. Dating of Lapita ceramic did prove, however, that Melanesians had already arrived on the islands several millennia ago, possibly

via the Solomon Islands and Vanuatu. When the Europeans arrived, at least 50,000 people were living there.

Captain James Cook was the first European to arrive in the area, landing near **Balade** in the northeastern part of Grande Terre. He called what he saw as a stark and craggy landscape *Caledonia*, borrowing the old Roman term for northern Scotland.

Around the beginning of the 19th century, French seamen explored and mapped Grande Terre and the Loyalty Islands, and soon the usual South Seas scenario was being enacted, with European influence-taking and exploitation. Whale hunters, sandalwood and sea-cucumber dealers, slave traders, escaped convicts and deserters moved to the islands. The first Protestant missionaries,

Above: The flightless kagu, considered the symbolic bird of New Caledonia. Right: Ninety percent of the country's earnings come from the mining of nickel.

from the London Missionary Society, came to Grande Terre in 1840, the first Catholics, from the Marian Order, three years later.

Flying the French Flag

Emperor Napoleon III found sufficient reasons to annex New Caledonia officially: its good strategic location in the South Pacific, the need to create some more penal colonies and continued attacks on French missions. In 1853, Admiral Auguste Febvrier-Despointe hoisted the French *tricolore* over Grande Terre and Île des Pins. In 1864, the first deported prisoners arrived. They were to be followed by thousands more, including many political prisoners, especially after the Commune in 1871.

The French engineer Jules Garnier discovered nickel ore in 1863. A short while later gold was found in the north of Grande Terre. Mining in a big way began in 1876, and in 1878 the Kanaka made a desperate attempt at rebellion on the west

coast. Their protest against the merciless land-grabbing practices of white settlers was in vain. As a result, the dispossessions became even more brutal, and Kanaka were partly forced to live on reservations.

The mining industry benefited at first from cheap or free labor performed by the convicts, but abolition of the transports led to a lack of workers. The Kanaka and other peoples from Asia and the islands were invited to take up the slack under the worst conditions.

In 1942, 40,000 US soldiers arrived on Grande Terre to defend it against the Japanese, just in case. They built four landing strips, and – as happened on many of the South Sea islands during the war – suddenly the Kanaka had well-paid work. For many it was also a revelation to see white and black Americans working together as equals, and to be treated with human respect. In 1946, the colony of New Caledonia was declared a French overseas territory, and the Kanaka were given French citizenship.

On the Way to Freedom

The first independence movements began taking shape at the beginning of the 1950s, but it was only in the 1970s that well-organized political parties emerged, including some whose platform was full separation from France. The tension between settlers of European origin and Kanaka, as well as between the various political parties, reached a climax in 1984. The FNLKS (*Front National de Libération Kanaka Socialiste*) boycotted the territorial elections. A short while later, a heavily-armed band of French settlers brutally murdered a group of Kanaka.

The violence escalated. Kanaka took revenge by resorting to desperate acts of terrorism such as blowing up French-owned nickel mines. New Caledonia seemed at the brink of a civil war. In 1985, then president Mitterand ordered new elections, and the situation quieted down a bit. However, under Jacques Chirac, who became Prime Minister in

1986, the French government once again took a hard line. In 1988, the murderers of the ten Kanaka were acquitted in a transparent and ridiculous political farce. 40 Kanaka promptly occupied a police station on Uvéa, killing four police officers and taking hostages. 300 elite French troops stormed the cave where the Kanaka were hiding out, causing a bloodbath with 21 dead. In the same year, right- and left-wing parties finally came to terms with France in the *Matignon Accords*. These stipulated, among other things, that New Caledonia was to be divided up into three provinces: North, South and the Loyalty Islands.

In 1998, a referendum will decide the issue of independence. Many Kanaka are longing for the day they will be free of French rule, while pro-French islanders, most of whom are of French ancestry, would rather not have to do without the economic support of the motherland. It is

Above: Nouméa's yacht marinas, a draw for sailors from around the world.

also doubtful whether the French government will want to forego its strategic bastion in the South Pacific with its wealth of natural resources.

GRANDE TERRE

Nouméa, a Metropolis in the Pacific

Nouméa (pop. 70,000), the capital of New Caledonia, lies on a hilly peninsula framed in wonderful sandy bays and with a fine view of small offshore islands. This most modern of all South Sea cities has a cosmopolitan flair, thanks to its large yacht harbor, its variegated crowd of Melanesians, Polynesians, Europeans mixed with tourists, its French restaurants, boutiques, well-supplied supermarkets and – last but not least – very high prices.

A day begins with *café au lait* and *croissants* or a *baguette*, before attacking the grid of streets that makes up the inner city. Right a the center of town is the elongated **Place des Cocotiers**, with

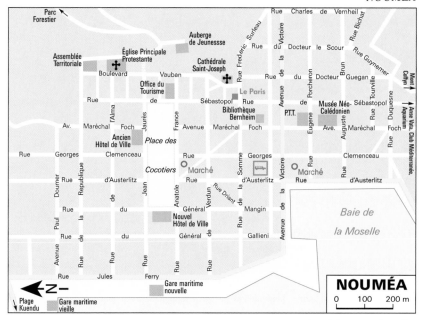

its stand of generous royal poinciana (*Delonix regia*), whose ostentatious scarlet and orange flowers can only be seen in winter, unfortunately.

The 25-foot (8 m) fountain in the middle of the plaza was created by Malhoux in 1893. The gazebo hails back to the days when a French military band used to play here regularly. The **Town Hall** stands on the western edge, behind the **statue** of Vice-Admiral Olry, who served as governor from 1878 to 1880. The old **Town Hall** is a beautiful colonial building dating to 1875 and located on Rue Jean Jaurès. At the southern end of Place des Cocotiers, on Rue du Gouverneur Sautot, is the **Office du Tourisme**, which provides good travel tips.

Elegant shops offering Parisian fashions, perfumes, wine and other French specialties, have established their supremacy over the streets around the plaza, in particular Rue de l'Alma. The latter runs into Blvd. Vauban, site of the simple **Protestant Church**, built in 1893, and its neighbor the **Assemblée**

Territoriale, the local house of parliament.

The Catholics were less modest. To the south of Blvd. Vauban (named after an architect whose grand opus includes an infamous penitentiary on the Île de Ré in France) is the majestic Cathédrale St. Joseph, built by convicts and inaugurated in 1894. It is the most visible hallmark of Nouméa. Especially noteworthy are the stained-glass windows and its 604-pipe organ, the only one to be found in a church in the South Seas.

The **Bibliothèque Bernheim** on Avenue Maréchal Foch has a very complete collection of books and articles published on New Caledonia. Two blocks southward, the **Musée Néo-Caledonien** documents the country's history and the culture of the Kanaka, using various finds (e.g., petroglyphs and Lapita ceramics), masks, wood carvings, houses, canoes and an ethno-botanical garden. The itinerary can now continue either up **Mont Coffyn** to the southeast for a great view, or to the Baie de la Moselle in the west,

71

where peddlers sell fruit, vegetables and fish (daily from 5 a.m. to 10 a.m., best to visit weekends in the early hours).

The southern part of the Nouméa peninsula is consists of fairly expensive neighborhoods and fine beaches to go along with them. Good hotels also provide tourists with accommodation. It's a fine place to relax, swim or surf, but not quite the spot to discover the solitude and romance of the South Seas. The quarter is served by a public bus. If coming by car, you must take Rue de Sébastopol southwards and turn right onto Route Jules Garnier at the attractive La Louisiane restaurant on **Baie de l'Orphelinat**. You soon arrive at **Baie du Pêcheur**, with a yacht harbor, luxury apartments and an elegant shopping center. The real tourist quarter of Nouméa begins in **Baie des Citrons**, which has a beautiful white sand beach. The spit of land known as **Roche à la Voile** (with lookout) is where Baie des Citrons becomes the beach-lined cove of **Anse Vata**.

The **Nouméa Aquarium** is the special highlight here. Over 250,000 gallons (ca 1 million liters) of sea water are pumped into the basin daily. The aquarium offers a unique look into the rich underwater world of New Caledonia, including brightly-colored reef fish, octopi, sea snakes, nautilus snails and phosphorescent corals.

A plethora of hotels, restaurants, snack bars, souvenir shops and tour organizers make Anse Vata the veritable tourist center of Nouméa. In the east of the cove stands the headquarters of the **Commission du Pacifique Sud**, an association of Pacific states founded for the promotion of trade and culture, where local handicrafts are often exhibited. The **Club Méditerranée** is just a few steps away.

Right: Anse Vata has become a major center of tourism, especially for sunbathing, swimming and surfing.

The coastal road winds its way along the foot of **Ouen Toro**. This 410-ft (128 m) hill can be climbed in 15 minutes for a most rewarding view.

In the north, Nouméa shows its industrial face. On the **Pointe Doniambo** sprawls the gigantic nickel smelter of the *Société Le Nickel*.

The zoo and botanical gardens, the **Parc Forestier**, lies 3.5 miles (5 km) northeast of the center of town at the foot of Mt. Montravel (534 ft/167 m). This nature park is the last parcel of land in the greater Nouméa area where the island's natural vegetation has more or less survived. It includes two lakes and enclosures inhabited by native animals, above all birds such as the kagu and the rare Ouvéa parakeet.

To the west of town is the **Île Nou** and the town of **Nouville**. This erstwhile penal island was attached to the main island by a causeway in 1972. Some of the buildings of the old penitentiary have remained intact.

Kuendu Beach, with the Kuendu Beach Resort, is a very popular place for excursions. **Fort Tereka**, perched atop 402-foot (126 m) Mt. Tereka, provides a terrific view of the island and the surrounding sea.

Travel agents offer excursions to the offshore islands (regular ferry service), among others **Îlot Maître** (hotel resort), **Îlot Signal** (ruins of a fort), **Îlot La Reignière** (beautiful reef).

The attraction on little **Amédée** (15 miles/23 km south of Nouméa) is the metal **Lighthouse**, which was assembled in Paris in 1862, taken apart and then shipped to New Caledonia. It is one of the world's tallest, standing a proud 179 feet (56 m). However, the lighthouse is no longer in operation, so you cannot enjoy a vigorous climb up 231 steps to the top. The island also has good swimming, snorkeling and diving.

16 miles (25 km) west of Nouméa, the **Seahorse Pontoon** was anchored to the

reef (also called **Coral Garden**). The glass walls of the pontoon, and snorkeling as well, provide a view of the delightful underwater world here (half-day tours on weekdays, all day on weekends).

The Lonely South

A 60-mile (ca. 100 km) road begins at the eastern side of Nouméa and accesses a small part of Grande Terre's southern regions. The way there is through arid plains, by the sparsely-grown slopes of red earth mountains and bouquets of niaouli trees.

The villages of **La Concéption** and **Saint Louis** lie in the greater Nouméa region. The former has a well-frequented church of pilgrimage (completed in 1874), the latter was founded as a mission town in 1856. Its church, built in 1860 and named for Louis Napoleon III, Emperor of France (1852-1870), is the oldest of the island group. Shortly beyond Saint Louis, a road leads off to the left up **Mont Doré** (2470 ft/772 m, can

be climbed for superb view) and to the beach of **Plum**.

The 22,000-acre (9000 ha) nature reserve **Parc Provincial de la Rivière Bleue** stretches along the western tip of the reservoir lake **Lac de Yaté**. The park is very popular with the residents of Nouméa for excursions and hiking tours thanks to its interesting stands of kaori and araucaria trees, waterfalls, beautiful views, rich bird-life, and recreational activities from camping to bicycle and canoe tours.

The road to Yaté hugs the shoreline until **Creek Pernod** at kilometer stone 67.5. A little road forks off here to the south and the lacustrine plain **Plaine des Lacs**. In good weather, you can go as far as the **Chutes de la Madeleine** waterfall in a normal vehicle, but from then on you will need a four-wheel-drive.

To the left when driving on toward Yaté is the **Barrage de Yaté**, a dam about 1.5 miles (2 km) from the road. This imposing construction was built between 1956 and 1958. It is 736 feet (230

m) long and 192 feet (60 m) high. Walking along its crest is not allowed. An old and bumpy road follows the Yaté River for about 4.5 miles (7 km), passing by a dramatic waterfall.

Finally, there is **Yaté**, a little town dwarfed by a huge water power plant, which supplies more than just Nouméa and its suburbs with electricity. The roads to **Mamié** in the north and **Goro** in the south lead through settlements, where you still find traditional houses (*cases*), and by mountains, bays and beautiful beaches. Local tour operators have trips to the Plaine des Lacs and **Île Ouen** on their schedules.

The Wild West

Route 1, which unravels northwestwards from Nouméa, is the island's most

Above: The Parc Provincial de la Rivière Bleue is a very popular area to hike and enjoy nature at close range. Right: A carnivorous plant.

important road. The Voie E 2 highway runs parallel to it for the first 10.5 miles (17 km). Right behind **Païta** (the first settlement of the French colonists), at Col de la Pirogue, a small road climbs up to the nature reserve of **Mont Mou** (3901 ft/1219 m). The international airport is in **Tontouta**, 28 miles (45 km) from Nouméa. Shortly after crossing the eponymous river, a path forks off to the right into the valley to the deserted **Galliéni** mine (difficult walking). Hikes up New Caledonia's second largest mountain, **Mt. Humboldt** (5177 ft/1618 m), begin here, with refuges at 3136 feet (980 m) and 4416 feet (1380 m), but count on three to four days depending on the weather. Route 4 toward the east coast and Thio begins in the little town of **Bouloupari**. If you keep heading to the northwest, then make a detour at km 100 (60 miles), you come to the beach of the **Ouano Peninsula** (6 miles/10 km from the main road, camping).

La Foa is a ponderous town boasting a supermarket and hotels. A Kanaka rebellion began in La Foa on June 25, 1878, with the storming of the local police station. Cultivation of sugar cane and a rum distillery later kindled an economic upswing. On the way to the center of town, the road crosses a bridge spanning the La Foa River. On the right is the old **Passerelle Marguerite** bridge, which was built in France and assembled here. It weighs only four tons.

At km 129 (80 miles), a little over a mile from the road, are the ruins of **Fort Teremba**, which served as a penitentiary until 1898. The village of **Moindou** was founded by immigrants from Alsace in 1874. An **Arab cemetery** was set up right before Bourail to accommodate the Algerian rebels of 1871 who had been deported to, and died in, New Caledonia. A little further on is a **cemetery for New Zealanders**, for the members of the Commonwealth who died during the Second World War.

Bourail had a military garrison from 1868 on, and shortly after opened a penal camp. The **Bourail Museum**, located in some buildings of the former camp, shows exhibits from the history and culture of the region. The town's **church** was completed in 1877. Though it's the second largest community in New Caledonia after Nouméa, Bourail is not nearly as lively and multifaceted.

The beach of Poé is on a covered road leading in southwesterly direction left off the main route just short of Bourail. A few miles on is the grandiose **Roche Percée** rock formation. The high cliff was eroded by the powerful swell over millennia, leaving a single rock behemoth, called *Le Bonhomme* by the locals, stuck in the sea. A tunnel-like gate was hammered out of the rock which can be traversed at low tide. Less than a mile further, the **Belvédère** lookout on top of a cliff is the place to enjoy a 360-degree panoramic view.

To the right, a road snakes down to the **Baie des Tortues** (Turtle Bay), thus

named because turtles sometimes brood here from November to March. Finally, you come to the **Plage de Poé,** an 11-mile (18 km) white sand beach covered in sea shells, considered to be one of the most beautiful on the island. It boasts a moderately-priced beach resort (with a restaurant, tennis, golf and riding) and camping sites.

The main road *RT1* continues on to **Poya**. About 1.5 miles (2.5 km) beyond the village, a turn-off leads 9 miles (15 km) to the **Grottes d'Adio** caves. The last 2500 feet (800 m) have to be negotiated on foot. In order to investigate the caves, you will need a flashlight and preferably a guide.

The town of **Népoui** was founded in 1969 by the *Société Le Nickel*. The local area is severely scarred by the great, deep gashes left by strip-mining. The somewhat monotonous **Plaine des Gaïacs** separates Népoui from **Pouembout**, where a street leads to a horse racetrack. Just beyond is another road that leads off to the east for about 16 miles (25 km) to

the **Cascade de Ouendé**, which plunges down 320 ft (100 m). It is accessed from the road by a 20-minute walk along a path. The tribal community (*tribu*) of **Forêt-Plate** is also nearby.

Just before Koné, the new road connecting to the eastern side of Grande Terre breaks away from *RT 1*. **Koné**, founded in 1887 as the administrative center in the northern province, is surrounded by pastures and cattle farms. The Australians introduced ranching here, and cowboys on horseback call themselves *stockmen*, just like in Australia, and drive the cattle. A rodeo festival in December attracts huge crowds, and of course tourists are invited to explore the region in the saddle on tours that can go on for days. *Air Calédonie* has regular flights to Koné.

About 4 miles (6 km) south of town is **Foué** beach (camping available). In 1917, the Frenchman Piroutet discovered ancient ceramicware, which was subsequently named **Lapita** after the place it was found in the Foué plain.

Over 5 miles (9 km) beyond the town of Voh, a small road leads off to the northeast to the clan community of Témala. The **Momies de Faténaoué** (mummies) in the holy tomb in the cave of Pafoua can no longer be visited.

The main road continues through flat pasturelands to **Koumac**, the northernmost "business city" of the island. The interior of the **Église Sainte Jeanne d'Arc** (which was completed in 1950) was done by a local sculptor named Charles Weiss. From this point, about 4 miles (7 km) inland are the **Grottes de Koumac**, a series of caves that go about 2 miles (3 km) into the mountain. They haven't been prepared for the public, so spelunkers go about their hobby at their own risk!

North of Koumac, RPN 7 crosses the interior of the island and becomes RPN 3 to accompany the eastern coastline all the way to Houaïlou.

Above: The view from the Belvédère over the Baie des Tortues. Right: Mission church in Arama on the northern coast.

The Untrodden North

On its way to the northern tip of Grande Terre, *RT1* passes by the abandoned mining town of **Tiébaghi**, which is visible from far and wide as it stands atop a mountain. Chrome and copper ore were mined here from 1902 to 1964. 16 miles (25 km) further on, the **Hotel Malabou Beach** on the **Baie de Néhoué** offers fine accommodation for the night. *RT1* then ends in **Poum**, a little town with not a great lot to offer its visitors. Nearby, however, nature has provided beautiful, remote beaches, some with camping sites. The northern extremity of the island is another 19 miles (30 km) away. A Catholic mission was established in **Arama** on the northern coast of the peninsula, and its church completed three years later.

The Verdant East

The east coast is without a doubt the more attractive side of Grande Terre. The vegetation is far denser, the picture is completed with clear rivers alive with fish, lonely sand beaches, forest-covered mountainsides and traditional Kanaka villages, especially in the northeast. Five roads cross the island, connecting the east and west coasts.

Shortly after Bouloupari on *RT1* (leaving from Nouméa) comes the intersection with *RT4*, which rolls along for 30 miles (48 km) before reaching the drab mining town of **Thio** on the east coast. The French started digging for nickel here at the end of the 1880s. Thio at times produced 3 percent of the world's nickel. An old colonial building of the *Société Le Nickel* has been turned into the **Musée de la Mine** (a mining museum).

The perilously winding road from Thio to Canala (23 miles/37 km) traverses a wonderful mountain landscape. There's a lookout platform at the **Col de Petchécara** (pass) at 1400 ft/435 m. The road is

single lane for 8 miles (13 km). It opens for traffic to Thio on every even hour, and to Canala at the top of every odd hour. At night the road is particularly dangerous, as it is open in both directions. Whatever you do, inquire about its state before embarking on a journey.

Canala, a European settlement founded in 1859, grew up quickly to be the hub of an important mining region. Economically speaking, it has no significance any longer, but it has become a major center of the Kanaka independence movement. Just before town, a little road connects the 2.5 miles (4 km) to the **Cascades de Ciu** waterfalls. 9 miles (14 km) to the west of town are the sulfur springs of **La Crouen**. A dip in the hot thermal pool (109 °F/43 °C) is good against rheumatism and arthritis (avoid if you have heart problems). Camping is possible here. A few miles further, *RPN 21* heads north to the mining town of **Kouaoua**.

A road runs from La Foa, mentioned above, on the west coast through the interior of the island to the east coast. It

crosses a mountainous land in heady green striated with waterfalls and rivers. The little communities of **Farino** (population about 250, beautiful view of the coastal plain) and **Sarraméa** (population 500 and one hotel) are a few miles off the main road. The old meeting house in **Petit Couli** and the auracaria alley leading to it are worth the trouble (ask permission!). The road then crosses the **Col d'Amieu**, a 1360-foot-high (425 m) pass, to reach the eastern slopes of the mountains before going to Canala or Kouaoua.

Another east coast-west coast connection is *RPN 6*, some 4 miles (7 km) north of Bourail. The road crosses a dry savanna, twists and turns up to the **Col des Roussettes** (pass at 1187 ft/371 m, nice view), and then descends into the tropical vegetation of the east coast. 40 miles (65 km) later, you arrive at the coastal community of **Houaïlou** (under a mile/1 km

Above: Nickel mining in Thio. Right: Diahoue near Pouébo is home to the sculptor François Toibat.

off the road). To the northwest of town near the landing strip is a solitary beach.

After Houaïlou, it's *RPN 3* that follows the east coast. Stopping in **Bâ**, 9 miles (15 km) northwestwards, is advisable. A 1-mile (1.5 km) footpath leads from the road to a remarkable waterfall.

Ponérihouen, founded in 1879, is a pleasant little town. One local product is coffee. Several clan communities straddle the river **Nimbaye** (or Nabai). Driving to them requires a four-wheel drive.

Poindimié, the administrative center of the northeast coast, was born after World War Two. Visitors will find lodgings here, as well as restaurants, banks and a supermarket. Operators offer tours on horseback and boat rides, even diving expeditions. The public **swimming pool** has a great jewel of art history to show, namely a beautiful 1961 mosaic by the Hungarian-born French creator of op-art, Victor Vasarely. The town's most beautiful beach is the **Plage de Tiéti**, which lies to the northwest and has two hotels and a public camping site.

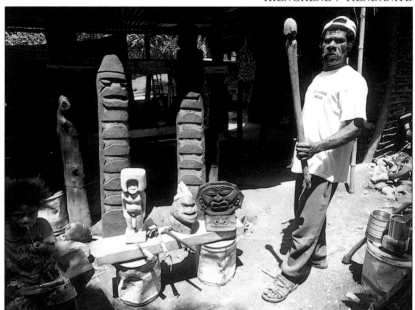

A road to the left will take you through an idyllic valley to **Napoémien** (camping and guest house); continuing for 3 miles (5 km) along the coast leads to a detour through the valley of the **Amoa River** and to the **Pic d'Amoa** mountain (1952 ft/610 m). To the north of the Amoa estuary lies the **Tié Mission**, whose church dates to 1866. Soon after, you reach a left-hand turn into the **Tiwaka Valley** and onto the new road to Koné (42 miles/68 km away) on the west coast.

Beach after beautiful beach line the way to **Touho**, a pretty fishing town that sprang up in 1884. Fruit and coffee are cultivated in the area. The small, nicely situated church was completed in 1889.

The countryside between Touho and Hienghène is the most attractive on Grande Terre. The view takes in the turquoise sea and the occasional islet, white beaches and black rocks, and luxuriant tropical vegetation interspersed with tall araucaria trees.

The valley of the **Tipindjé River** is well worth a brief upstream excursion be-fore continuing along the coast to Hienghène. Another stop should be made at the mighty limestone formations known as the **Roches de Lindéralique**. The **Club Mediterranée Koulnoué Village** was built just under 4 miles (6 km) outside Hienghène. Look out for the path (2 miles/3 km from the village) leading to the **Grotte de Lindéralique**. Besides the wonderful cave, you'll also find a small beach and a camping site here. Another sight is the **Col de Hienghène**, a 960-ft (300 m) pass accessible on a side road, with a superb view of the region. There are two remarkable formations in the bay of Hienghène, one called the **Sphinx** (480 ft/150 m high), the other is the comical **Brooding Hen** (192 ft/60 m high).

As for Hienghène itself, it is not terribly attractive in spite of the promising countryside around it, though the **Centre Culturel Mélanésien** does keep one room as a museum to exhibit ceramics and other works by local artists. The valley of the Hienghène River was one of

the early hatching spots of Kanaka resistance against the French colonial bosses, in particular the village of **Tiendanite**, birthplace of the Kanaka leader Jean-Marie Tjibaou. Many of the villagers were killed or deported by the French authorities, especially between 1914 and 1917, and the village was burned down. It was here in 1984 that a gang of French settlers brutally murdered ten Kanaka, who were members of the liberation movement FNLKS, almost sparking a civil war. A memorial monument was set up about 4 miles (6 km) up the valley from the **Ganem** settlement. The ten graves are in Tiendanite, 7.5 miles (12 km) beyond the river.

Northwest of Hienghène, a car ferry shuttles across the **Ouaïème River**. The coastal road now runs by **Mont Panié**, at 5314 feet (1660 m) the highest mountain in New Caledonia. Hikers will find refuges along its paths. A few miles further, the waterfall of **Tao** tumbles down the slope to the left of the road. In 1847, Catholic missionaries tried to set up shop in **Pouébo**, but were chased away by the natives. A second attempt five years later was successful, and in 1863, a police station was opened to protect the Europeans. The historic **Balade** is 6 miles (10 km) to the north of the 1875 mission church of Pouébo. It is here that Captain James Cook made landfall, the first European to come to Grande Terre. The first Catholic missionaries also touched down nearby, on the beautiful beach of **Maamaat** (a memorial cross was erected). Two monuments on the road recall the French annexation of New Caledonia on September 24, 1853.

In the meantime, however, the landscape has changed. The overwhelming mountains and rich valleys have given way to a flatter, drier countryside. **Col d'Amos** (1177 ft/368 m) offers one last, grand view of resplendent nature, and then the road makes a sharp bend to the

Above: Carved totem poles at Baie de Saint-Maurice, Île des Pins. Right: The crystal waters of Baie de Kanuméra, Île des Pins.

southwest and joins Koumac on the west coast. On the way is **Ouégoa**, a community founded in 1879 in the midst of a region rich in zinc, lead, copper, manganese and gold ore, which were all mined at one time.

ÎLE DES PINS

58-square-mile (152 sq km) **Île des Pins** lying to the southeast of Grande Terre is rightly called the "Jewel of the South Seas." James Cook discovered it in 1774, and gave it the name "Pine Island" because of its proliferation of araucaria trees, many of which have grown near to the 200 foot (60 m) mark. Île des Pins, known to the Kanaka as *Kunié*, is breathtakingly beautiful, with heavenly beaches covered in fine, white sand, jagged, rocky coastline and picture-perfect lagoons. The reef area is full of superb diving grounds, and stalagtitic caves are a joy to explore for spelunkers.

About 1500 people live on the island, and they welcome visitors with great friendliness. The largest village and the administrative center is **Vao** in the south. The **Town Hall** and the so-called *Chefferie* (the house of the chief) are both on the main street. A path begins behind the **Mission Church** (built in 1860) and leads up to the chapel **Notre-Dame-de-la-Salette**. The view from here is worth the little climb. Queen Hortense was buried in the **cemetery**. After the death of her father Great Chief Vandegou II in 1855, Hortense acceded the throne, ruling until 1883. She was skilled in cutting deals with the Catholic missionaries, who had started arriving from France in 1848. About a hundred yards from the village, on the **Baie de Saint-Maurice**, stands a memorial to these missionaries. The monument is surrounded by totem poles.

The **Baie St. Joseph**, about 1.5 miles (2 km) from Vao, has a beautiful beach. It is also called **Baie des Pirogues**, because of the many canoes (*pirogues*) that ply its waters, with their sails puffed up in the wind. Glass-bottom boat tours are available around the splendid **Baie d'Upi**. A

45-minute walk takes you from the bay to the **Oro Peninsula**, where the **Baie d'Oro** invites its visitors for a swim. It can also be reached by car on two roads that fork off of *RM 3*.

A 30-minute march on a path leading off the main road east of the airport leads to the **Grotte de Wemwanyi** (also known as **Grotte de d'Oumagne**). Even people without any experience need not fear this light cave with large stalactites. An unmarked path leads about 2 miles (3 km) southeastwards to the **Grotte de Waacia** (also: **Grotte d'Ouatcha**), but you should hire a guide to see it. Queen Hortense allegedly hid in this cave for months during the political unrest that shook the isle from 1855 to 1856.

Following the main road further in a northwesterly direction toward Kaaji (Gadji), you should stop in **Wapwanga** (Wapan) for a shopping spree at the **Grande Case**, where shells, handicrafts and jewelry are on sale. At he beginning of the century, **Kaaji** was the capital of the island and the residence of the big chiefs. *RM 1* leaves starts here to follow the western flank of the island, crossing a plateau before descending to the south. Penal camps once lined the road, which, after 1872, received numerous political prisoners sentenced in the wake of the Paris Commune.

Just before the left-hand turnoff toward the airport, there is a right fork to the **Grotte du Paradis** (also called **Grotte de la Troisième**, after the third penal camp. The entrance of this freshwater cave is easily accessible, and the pools before it are nice for a dip. Only experienced divers should attempt to explore the mostly flooded cave with its forest of stalactites. Two miles to the south (3 km), a track leads to the beach of the **Baie d'Ouro**; and shortly thereafter, to the left, a path takes you to the **Cime-**tière des Déportés**, a cemetery where 250 political deportees are buried. In the community of **Ouro** a little way southward, you can see the ruins of old prison buildings that once belonged to the penal colony. The village of **Kuto** is on the **Baie de Kuto**, and the **Baie de Kanuméra** has clear, calm waters. Both bays are lined with white sand beaches fringed with tropical vegetation. The highest point on the island, **Pic Nga** (838 ft/262 m), can be climbed in just about an hour.

THE LOYALTY ISLANDS

The four raised coral islands, Maré, Tiga, Lifou and Uvéa, which lie about 60 miles (100 km) to the east of Grande Terre, constitute the New Caledonian province **Îles Loyauté**. Together, these isles have a land surface of nearly 775 square miles (2000 sq km), and a population of about 19,000 Melanesians with at times Polynesian influence. The islands are relatively flat, have no rivers and lower precipitation than Grande Terre, so vegetation is accordingly scarce.

The Loyalties were first chartered by captain Dumont d'Urville. But the European influence was always weaker than on Grande Terre, so traditional social structures survived better. Visitors should respect this at all times. The inhabitants are relaxed and friendly. The beaches are some of the best in the entire South Seas.

Maré, 251 square miles (650 sq km), is a raised atoll, whose interior is lower-lying than its coast. The cliffs on the southern coast to the south of **Medu** reach the 377 foot mark (118 m), which is the highest point in the Loyalties. The fertile basin in the middle of the island is ideal for agriculture; fruit and vegetables are even exported to Nouméa. The airport was built near the old Catholic mission of **La Roche** on the north coast, the main town and port **Tadine** lies in the west. Five miles (8 km) to the south of Tadine is a wonderful beach called **Ceigeïté**.

Right: A vanilla farmer checks the ripeness of the coveted beans (Loyalty Islands).

Lifou, the largest of the Loyalty Islands (463 sq miles/1200 sq km), is also a raised atoll. Many caves were carved into the coral limestone. Great cliffs and fine sand beaches mark the contours of the island. The highest elevations are in the south (max. 345 ft/108 m). The main town and administrative center is **We**, situated on a dream beach on the eastern coast. To the west of the airport **Wanaham**, in **Hnathalo**, are two imposing buildings. The first is the **mission church** built in 1883 and still boasting its original interior furnishings; the second is the *case* of the big chief of Hnathalo surrounded by palisades. The delicate little chapel of **Notre-Dame-de-Lourdes** (1898) quaintly stands on a spit of land overlooking the **Baie du Santal** on the east coast and offers a terrific view of the island. We is connected by a good road to nice beaches near **Luengoni**, **Mou** and **Xodé** in the southeast.

Uvéa (surface: 51 square miles/132 sq km) is only raised in its eastern section. The lagoon, protected by a barrier reef and a chain of islets, consists of nearly 16 miles (25 km) of breathtaking sand beaches along a turquoise sea. The narrow, crescent-shaped main island is connected to the island of **Mouly** in the south by a bridge. Another fabulous beach lines the Baie de Mouly. The east coast is harsher, the ocean roars in to break upon cliffs that reach a height of 130 feet (40 m). The main town is **Fayaoué** (or Fajawe), 3.5 miles (5 km) from the airport.

Polynesian seafarers reached Ouvéa in the 18th century and settled in the northern part of the island. The ethnic tensions between Melanesians and Polynesians were exacerbated in the 19th century by conflicts between Protestants and Catholics. In 1988, Uvéa became the symbol of the Kanaka's struggle for freedom: it was here that a small group of Kanaka were surrounded by hundreds of elite French soldiers and massacred.

Tiga, another raised atoll with a surface area of almost 5 square miles (12 sq km) and a population nearing 350, is the smallest of the Loyalty Islands.

NEW CALEDONIA
No area code, country code is 687.

Arrival / Departure
ARRIVAL: A passport and a return ticket suffice for nationals of: EU states, Switzerland, the USA, Canada, Japan, Australia, New Zealand. Visa and information is available at French consulates or embassies. *DEPARTURE:* No departure tax.

Air Travel
The international airport is in Tontouta 28 miles/45 km northwest of Nouméa. Taxis are expensive and rare. Buses go into town. Book your transfer ahead of time. Flights to Wallis & Futuna and Fiji with connecting flights to Tahiti, Port Vila (Vanuatu), Sydney, Paris, Tokyo (Japan) and Auckland. International airlines: AOM, Corsair, Air France, Air Calédonie International, Air Vanuatu, Qantas and Air New Zealand. National flights from Magenta airport, a few miles outside Nouméa. Air Calédonie, Tel: 286564, Fax: 281340, flies to Koné, Koumac, Poum and Touho on Grande Terre, the Bélep islands, Île Art, the Loyalty Islands Uvéa, Lifou, Maré, Tiga and the Île des Pins, and sells overnight packages.

Currency / Banks / Post Office
Pacific francs (CFP): US$ 1 = ca CFP 105. Fixed exchange rate with the French franc: FF 1 = CFP 18,18. US$ accepted almost everywhere. Banks and post offices open as a rule Mon-Fri 7:45 a.m.-3:45 p.m.

GRANDE TERRE
NOUMÉA AREA
Accommodation
LUXURY (from US$ 100): **Isle de France**, 20, rue Boulari, Anse Vata, Tel: 262422, Fax: 261720, near the beach, 102 air-conditioned apts., restaurant, bar. **Kuendu Beach Resort**, Kuendu beach, western tip of Île Nou, Tel: 278989, Fax: 276033, beach, 20 air-conditioned bungalows on the beach or in the garden, Melanesian style, restaurant, pool, water sports. **L'Escapade Resort**, private island Îlot Maître, southwest of Nouméa, Tel/Fax: 285320, 30 min by boat, 44 rooms with ventilator, restaurant, bar, pool, beaches, water sports. **Le Lagon**, 143, rue de l'Anse Vata, Anse Vata, Tel: 251255, Fax: 261244, 59 air-conditioned apartments with ventilator, restaurant, bar, water sports. **Le Méridien**, southern tip of Anse Vata, Tel: 265000, Fax: 265100, 253 air-conditioned rooms/suites, restaurant, bar, casino, fitness, pool, water sports, tennis. **Le Stanley**, Baie de Ste. Marie, Quémo, Tel: 263277, Fax: 252656, sea view, 2 suites, 56 air-conditioned studios, restaurant, bar, pool. **Nouvata Parkroyal Nouméa**, 123 Prom. Roger Laroque, Anse Vata, Tel: 262200, Fax: 261677, beach, 101 air-conditioned rooms, restaurant, bar, pool. **Novotel Nouméa**, 55, promenade Roger Laroque, Anse Vata, Tel: 286688, Fax: 285223, 235 air-conditioned rooms/suites, restau-

rant, bar, casino, sauna, pool. tennis and water sports nearby. *MODERATE (under US$ 100):* **Hôtel Ibis**, 9, promenade Roger Laroque, Baie des Citrons, Tel: 262055, Fax: 262044, has 60 air-conditioned rooms, 2 restaurants, bar, boutique, pool, water sports. **Hôtel Le Paris**, 45, rue de Sébastopol, Nouméa, Tel: 281700, Fax: 276080, 48 air-conditioned rooms, restaurant, nightclub. **Lantana Beach Hôtel**, 113 promenade Roger Laroque, Anse Vata, Tel: 262212, Fax: 261612, 37 air-conditioned rooms, bar, shops, bank. **Marina Beach Hôtel**, 4, rue Auguste Page, Baie des Citrons, Tel: 287633, Fax: 262881, near the beach and the yacht harbor, 20 air-conditioned studios. *BUDGET (under US$ 60):* **Hôtel Mocambo**, 49, rue Jules Garnier, Baie de l'Orphelinat, Tel: 262701, Fax: 263877, 40 air-conditioned rooms. **Motel Anse Vata**, 19, rue Gabriel Laroque, Anse Vata, Tel: 262612, Fax: 259060, 22 air-conditioned apartments. **Motel Le Bambou**, 44, rue Spahr, Anse Vata, Tel: 261290, Fax: 263058, 16 studios with ventilator.

Restaurants / Nightlife
French cuisine if not otherwise indicated. Hotels not included. **Bilboquet-Plage**, 127 Promenade Laroque, Tel: 262811. **Café de Paris**, 47 rue Sébastopol, Tel: 282000. **Dolce Vita**, Route de l'Anse-Vata, Tel: 262441, Italian. **El Cordobes**, 1 rue Bichat, Tel: 274768. **Jade-Palace**, Baie des Citrons, Tel: 264215, Chinese. **La Coupole**, 57 Promenade Laroque, Tel: 262811. **Le Petit Train**, 22 Baie des Citrons, Tel: 262811, also Chinese. **Monsieur Buf**, 5 rue Jules Garnier, Tel: 262572, steakhouse. **Saint-Hubert**, rue Sébastopol / rue A.-France, Tel: 272142.

Nouméa does not have a wild nightlife. The tourist areas (Anse Vata, Baie des Citrons) are busier evenings. Some piano bars serve drinks in a pleasant atmosphere. Dancing in *Nouméa:* **Eden**, rue Sébastopol/rue A.-France. **Étoile 81**, 47 rue Sébastopol. **Guingette**, Anse Vata. **Joker**, 41 rue Sébastopol. **Privilège**, 20 rue Boulari, Polynesian dances as well. Dancing in *Anse Vata:* **Kaluha** and **Startruck**. The **Novotel** and **Le Méridien** hotels have casinos.

Museums / Parks
Aquarium de Nouméa, Tel: 262731, Fax: 261793. **Musée Néo-Calédonien**, Tel: 272342. **Parc Forestier**, Tel: 272674.

Excursions
Alpha International, Tel: 261313, Fax: 264786. **Apouéma Pacific Tours**, Tel: 287864, Fax: 289375. **Pacific Paradise Tours**, Tel: 241924, Fax: 252566. **Entreprise Viratelle** to Îlot Maître, Tel: 274849. **Mary D Cruises** to the Amédée lighthouse among others, Tel: 263131, Fax: 263979. **Lagon Loisir**, to Îlot Maitre, Tel: 262440. **Le Caretta**, to Île Quen, Tel: 285362. **Club Med II**, to Île des Pins, Hienghène, Tel: 274339, Fax: 263387.

Air Tours / Air and Boat Charters / Rental Cars

AIRPLANE: **Aviazur**, Tel: 253709, Fax: 254662. *HELICOPTER:* **Heliocean**, Tel: 253949, Fax: 276517. **Air-Mer-Loisir**, Tel: 282197, Fax: 259477. **M. Filippi**, Tel: 275410. *BOATS:* **Air-Mer-Loisir**, Tel: 282197, Fax: 259477. **Alize Voiles**, Tel/Fax: 275043. **Gin Fizz Croisière**, Île des Pins, Tel: 461000. **Nouméa Rent a Boat**, Tel: 262528. **Nouméa Yacht Charter**, Tel: 286666, Fax: 287482. **Rehutaï IV**, Tel/Fax: 435408. **Pacific Charter**, Tel: 261055, Fax: 285755. **Vagabond Charter**, Tel/Fax: 261493. *CARS:* **Budget**, Tel: 275733, Fax: 275272. **Discount Location**, Tel: 241042, Fax: 269998. **Hertz**, Tel: 261822, Fax: 261219. **Pacific Charter**, Tel: 261055, Fax: 285755, RVs. **Tour des Îles**, Tel: 264142, Fax: 262928.

Sports

DEEP-SEA FISHING: **M. Delorme**, Tel: 284400. **M. Jeantet**, Tel: 282325. **Pacific Charter**, Tel: 261055, Fax: 285755. *PARASAILING:* **Loisirs Bord de Mer**, Tel: 271150. *SAILING:* **M. Frei**, Tel: 262685, HobbieCat. *SQUASH:* **Squash-Club**, Tel: 262212. *DIVING:* **Amédée Diving Club**, Tel: 264029. **Marine Sports Services**, Tel: 261167. **Nautac Alizé**, Tel: 262585. **Nouméa Diving**, Tel: 251688. **Sub Austral Plongée**, Tel/Fax: 241258. *WATER-SKIING:* **Water-Ski Center**, Tel: 284494. *WINDSURFING:* **M. Cali**, Tel: 272384.

Tourist Information

Nouvelle Calédonie Tourisme, BP 688, Nouméa, Tel: 272632, Fax: 274623. **La Maison des Îles Loyauté**, 113 Av. R. Laroque, Anse Vata, Tel: 289360, Fax: 289121. **Bureau du Tourisme en Province Nord**, 39 rue de Verdun, Nouméa, Tel: 277805, Fax: 274887. **Office de Tourisme de Nouméa et de la Province Sud**, 24 rue A. France, Nouméa, Tel: 287580, Fax: 287585.

OUTSIDE NOUMÉA
Accommodation

Many guest houses and *gîtes*, usually simple and inexpensive bungalows. *LUXURY:* **Novotel Malabou Beach**, 9 miles/15 km south of Poum, Tel: 356060, Fax: 356070. **Club Mediterranée Koulnoué Village**, 6 miles/9 km south of Hienghène, Tel: 428166, Fax: 428175. *MODERATE:* **Auberge du Mont Koghi**, 12.5 miles/20 km northeast of Nouméa, Tel: 412929. **Tontoutel Hôtel**, Tontouta, Tel: 351111, Fax: 351348. **Les Paillotes de la Ouenghi**, 4.5 miles/7 km south Bouloupari, Tel: 351735. **Poé Beach Resort**, 9 miles/16 km southw.of Bourail, Tel: 441850, Fax: 441070. **Le Bougainville**, Pouembout, Tel: 355255, Fax: 355060. **Koniambo**, Koné, Tel: 355186, Fax: 355303. **Monitel Koné**, Koné, Tel: 355261, Fax: 355535. **Le Grand Cerf**, Koumac, Tel: 356131, Fax: 356016. **Monitel Koumac**, Kou-

mac, Tel: 356666, Fax: 356285. **Monitel Tiéti**, Poindimié, Tel: 427273, Fax: 427224. **Le Nukuhiva**, near Plum, Tel: 434141. *BUDGET:* **Hôtel Banu**, La Foa, Tel: 443119. **Evasion 130**, Sarramea, 12.5 miles/20 km from La Foa in the mountains, Tel: 443235. **Hôtel El Kantara**, 5 miles/8 km from Bourail, Tel: 441322, Fax: 442033. **Hôtel La Néra**, Bourail, Tel: 441644, Fax: 441831. **La Maison de Passage**, Népoui, Tel: 471228. **Gîte Le Tamaon**, near Pouembout, Tel: 355726. **L'Escale de Koné**, Koné, Tel: 355109. **Relais Madiana**, Koné, Tel: 355009. **Gîte d'Ateou**, 10.5 miles/17 km from Koné in the mountains, Tel: 355613. **Le Passiflore**, Koumac, Tel: 356210. **Gîte de Poingam**, near Boat Pass, Tel: 356340. **Le Normandon**, Ouegoa, Tel: 356828. **Gîte de Galarino**, 22 miles/35 km north of Hienghène, Tel: 428812. **Gîte de Weouth**, 5 miles/8 km north of Hienghène, Tel: 428142. **Gîte Mangalia**, 8 miles/13 km north of Touho, Tel: 428760. **Relais Alison**, Touho, Tel: 428812. **Gîte Napoémien**, near Poindimié, Tel: 427477. **Hôtel de la Plage**, Poindimié, Tel: 427128, Fax: 427044. **Hôtel Tapoandari**, Poindimié, Tel: 427111. **L'Oasis**, Kouaoua, Tel: 42 4485. **Gîte Ouroue**, 2.5 miles/4 km from Thio, Tel: 445163. **Chez Minette**, Thio, Tel: 445196. **La Nouvelle Siesta**, near Plum, Tel: 433910, Fax: 434404. **Gîte IYA**, 2.5 miles/4 km south of Waho, Tel: 464232. **Gîte Saint-Gabriel**, 5.5 miles/9 km south of Waho, Tel: 464277. **Relais de Wadiana**, just south of Goro, Tel: 464190.

Sports

GOLF: **Dumbea Golf Club**, Tel: 368181. **Bouloupari Club**, Tel: 351735. *RIDING:* **Koné Rodeo**, Koné, Tel: 355151, horseback tours, 3-7 days. **Randonnée Equestre**, Koné, Tel: 355368. *DIVING:* **Kuni Scuba Centre**, Île des Pins, Tel/Fax: 461122, 461227, Heli-diving.

OTHER ISLANDS
Accommodations

ÎLE DES PINS: Gîte Nataiwatch, Tel: 461113, Fax: 461229, Kanuméra Bay. **Hôtel Kou-Bugny**, Tel/Fax: 461123, Kuto Bay. **Kuberka Res.**, Tel: 461118, Fax: 461158, Kuto Bay. **Ouré Resort**, Tel: 461120, east Kanuméra Bay. **Relais de Kodjeue**, Tel: 461142, Ouaméo Bay. **ÎLE OUEN: Auberge Wokoue**, Tel: 285767. **Turtle Club**, Tel: 285362. **ÎLOT CASY: Îlot Casy**, 10 min from Prony, Tel: 264777. **LIFOU: Drehu Village**, We, Tel: 450270, Fax: 450271, thatched huts, best around. **Relais des Cocotiers**, We, Tel: 451136. **Fare Falaise**, Jokin, Tel: 451648. **Gîte Hnaxulu**, Wedrumel, Tel: 451642. **Gîte Neibash**, Luengoni, Tel: 451568. **Hôtel Lifou Plaisance**, Jozip, Tel: 451444, Fax: 451333. **MARÉ: Gîte Si Hmed**, Wabao, Tel: 454151. **Hnala**, Tadine, Tel: 454396. **OUVÉA: Gîte Beaupré**, Tel. 457132. **Gîte Fleury**, Tel: 457136. **Gîte Hwattau**, Tel: 457125, all three near Fayaoué.

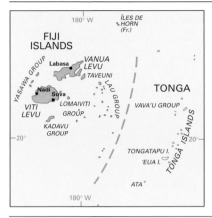

FIJI ISLANDS

VITI LEVU

VANUA LEVU

TAVEUNI

OVALAU

OTHER ISLANDS

Long before the arrival of mass tourism, the Fiji Islands, due to their advantageous geographic location, were a favorite stopover for ships and airplanes traveling between the continents. Today, despite the fact that Fiji far exceeds all other South Pacific island states in its number of visitors, it is never overrun by tourists. Accommodations are available in all price categories, and it is still fairly easy to come in contact with the inhabitants and gain an insight into their daily lives, culture, traditions and customs. The islanders are known for having very open personalities, they are generous, hospitable and smile readily. Their warm greeting, *"ni sa bula vinaka"* (or *"bula"* in short) follows travelers from the time they arrive to their departure.

The Fiji Islands are also rich in all the ingredients of South Seas dreams: gorgeous white sand beaches and iridescent blue lagoons, a fascinating underwater world, lush rain forests and sprawling plantations, isolated mountain reaches and palm-studded islands that might have come straight out of a picture book.

Preceding pages: The sun goes down spectacularly near Suva, Viti Levu. Left: The Nukubati Island Resort on Vanua Levu is an ideal place for enjoying a vacation.

Viti, Feejee, Fidji, Fiji...

The land area of the Fiji Islands – officially known as the Republic of Fiji – (5624 square miles/18,400 sq km) includes 320 islands, approximately 150 of which are inhabited. They are spread out between 15° and 22° south latitude and 177° west and 174° east longitude. The international dateline (coinciding with the 180° meridian) runs through the island of Taveuni. However, in order to avoid two different time zones within the Fiji Islands, the date line was officially "moved" to the east of Fiji. This made life a little easier on this sprawling archipelago.

The islands' geology is influenced by a volcanically active subduction zone. According to the scientific world, the oldest rock formations date to the late Mesozoic Era (around 20 million years ago). Volcanic eruptions, the buckling and settling of the earth's crust and erosion have produced varied climatic conditions and a landscape full of contrast. Rain forests cover the humid southeast slopes of the larger islands, while grassland and scrub characterize the dry northwestern slopes.

The main island, Viti Levu (large Viti) with more than 3950 square miles (10,400 sq km) accounts for more than one-half of

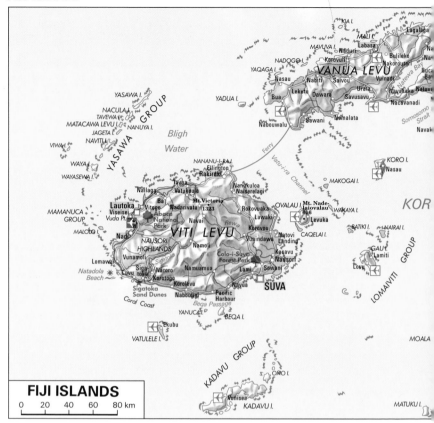

FIJI ISLANDS

0   20   40   60   80 km

Fiji's total land area. The second largest island, Vanua Levu (large land) covers just over 2000 square miles (5500 sq km), more than a quarter of the area. Small island groups account for the rest.

Climate

The Fiji Islands are located in the southeast trade winds zone and are swept by steady breezes from the east throughout the year. Occasional cyclones and hurricanes occur between November and March. The leeward slopes of the higher islands, Viti Levu, Vanua Levu and Taveuni, have a lower annual rainfall (Nadi, 69 inches per year/1800 mm) than the windward sides (Suva, nearly 120 inches

per year/3100 mm). The difference in precipitation on the lower-lying islands is negligible. Although temperatures vary little throughout the day or at various seasons of the year, the difference is more noticeable in dry areas than in humid ones. The average annual temperature at sea level is between 73 and 75° F (24 and 25° C) in all areas. In the cooler months, between June and August, overnight temperatures can fall to approximately 63° F (17° C) – which increases the sales of winter jackets and sweaters!

Mynah Birds at Breakfast

Two kinds of bats and three species of flying fox (one of which is indigenous)

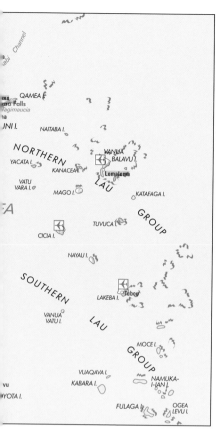

gecko, two kinds of iguanas (*Brachylophus facsiatus* and *B. vitiensis*) deserve special attention. Since their nearest relatives live in Central America, it is unknown how iguanas got to Fiji. Perhaps, as some suggest, their nest floated to Fiji on a raft of debris.

Twenty-three of Fiji's 60 land and freshwater birds are indigenous. Colorful parrots still inhabit the remoter forested areas. Mynah birds (*Acridotheres tristis* and *A. fuscus*) have developed into pests over the years. These incredibly bold and shameless birds were brought to the islands from India in the 19th century to combat insects in the sugar cane fields. They are easily recognized by the yellow spots on either side of the eyes (common mynah) and the tuft of feathers above the bill (jungle mynah). Because mynah birds know the value of a good breakfast, visitors are sure to spot one of them sooner rather than later pecking away at a meal set on a terrace.

The mongoose (*Herpestes auropunctatus*), imported in 1883 to combat rats on the sugar cane plantations, also wreaked havoc on native animal life. The islands' amphibian, reptile and bird population suffered especially, but the number of rats did not seem to decline.

In 1936, the sugar cane toad (*Bufo marinus*) was imported from Hawaii as yet another attempt at controlling insects that damaged the sugar cane. They had no natural enemies and increased so rapidly that they live all over today.

Vegetation

Fiji's vegetation is closely related to the plant life of Malaysia and New Guinea. Many species originated in Australia or New Caledonia. Thirteen of the circa 450 known plant species are indigenous. Vegetation on the humid windward slopes is in itself varied and differs significantly from the plant life of the dry leeward slopes. Thick rain forests cover

are the only mammals native to the Fiji Islands. Some household pets are found in the wild.

Of the seven species of snakes, two live exclusively on land. One, *Ogmodon vitianus*, a 15-inch-long (40 cm) snake, a poisonous relative of the cobra family, has not been sighted for quite a while, and some scientists conclude it may be extinct. The other is the Pacific boa *(Candaio bibroni)*. The five species of water snakes include the *Lauticauda colubrina*, recognizable by its alternating light and dark horizontal stripes. It is more poisonous than any land species in the world. Fortunately it is only aggressive when it feels threatened. In addition to some types of skink (*Scincidae*) and

the moist zone. It is possible that forests once covered the dry zone as well, but slash and burn agriculture and the resulting erosion of the fertile topsoil eventually transformed the landscape into grass and scrub land.

Sugar Sweet Islands

The driving force behind Fiji's economy are the families of Indian descent; something that the native Fijians themselves are none too happy about, even though – or maybe because – doing business is not exactly a talent the Fijians have in their blood.

The sugar industry remains the single most important element of the economy of the Fiji Islands, even if this dominant position may soon fall behind tourism,

Above: A large proportion of the people on the Fiji Islands are of Indian origin. Right: One of the main economic pillars of the economy is the sugar cane industry.

fishing, forestry and gold mining, which are all gaining in importance.

Small holdings owned by Indian families are gradually transforming the sugar cane agriculture that was introduced to the islands in the 19th century: in 1990, there were about 22,000 sugar cane planters, very few of whom were actually Fijians. The sugar industry accounts for about 35 percent of Fiji's total exports. The textile industry accounts for almost 20 percent and gold for over 10 percent. The fishing industry has been on the upswing since the 1980s.

Pine reforestation of the dry zones produces enough wood for Fiji's domestic needs, plus a surplus for export. Although a large part of the profits still leave the country, tourism has increased and is now one of the main factors effecting the islands' economy. Fiji has chosen to go the way of gentle "eco-tourism." In 1996 more than 400,000 visitors came to Fiji, which has now replaced French Polynesia as the number one tourist destination in the South Seas.

Before the Europeans

Scientists agree that Fiji's first settlers arrived at least 3500 years ago. Where they actually came from is still a mystery, however. According to one legend, Lutunasobasoba and Degei, two deified chiefs from Tanganyika in Africa, came to western Viti Levu where they founded the village Vuda. Their descendants now are believed to live in Viseiei and its neighboring villages. A great flood came and carried the inhabitants to the other islands.

Archeologists have been able to dig up evidence that there have been settlements in the Sigotoka valley and the island of Lakeba since circa 1500 B.C. It is also clear that Fiji has long lived under Polynesian influence. This is especially true of the Lau island group which was ruled for several centuries by Tonga chiefs. Their huge war canoes could even reach and conquer far off islands like Rotuma. Tonga kings valued Fijians for their talents as artisans and warriors.

Many of the double-hulled canoes that later sailed under the Tonga flag were actually built on Fiji.

Fijians and their Enemies

A great deal of information about the social structure and way of life of the inhabitants of Fiji before the arrival of Europeans has survived.

A rigid caste system determined by birth regulated each person's social position and duties in the community. The chief was entitled to tribute. His power was absolute and he could decide whether his subjects lived or died. Fijians worshipped hundreds of gods and deified ancestors. It is false to assume from their gentle natures that the Fijians were a peaceful bunch of people living in a kind of paradise. A very strict system of rituals and taboos determined the course of their day to day existence. Even minor violations of the laws of the land were often punished by death. Important events called for human sacrifice.

When chiefs or honored warriors died, their wives were killed or buried alive with them. Wars were frequent and often accompanied by great cruelty. In many tribes, killing an enemy, whether man, woman or child, was part of the initiation rite into manhood. The enemies they killed were often eaten; prisoners of war were sometimes cruelly tortured before being "prepared" (which often meant being roasted alive). Such cruelty was the reason that many warriors, women and children were quick to choose suicide over surrender.

All in all, very few islanders in those days managed to die of old age. War canoes were often launched on ramps made up of live Fijians. When new temples or houses for the rulers were being built, Fijians who volunteered to hold the corner

Above: The Sigatoka Valley was already settled around 1500 B.C., according to archeologists. Right: A painting by R. Dodd (1790) depicting Captain Bligh being thrown off the "Bounty" during the famous mutiny.

posts were often buried alive supporting them. The dedication ceremonies culminated in a banquet in which slaughtered Fijians were one of the culinary delicacies.

Discoverers, Merchants and Missionaries

The first European to set eyes on the Fiji Islands was Captain Abel Tasman, a Dutch explorer whose ship landed on Taveuni in 1643. Captain James Cook discovered some of the islands tucked away in the far eastern reaches of the group in 1774. Captain Bligh, who, following the mutiny on his ship *Bounty*, was put out to sea in a lifeboat in 1789, sailed past the two main islands and was pursued by hostile Fijians in war canoes on his way to Timor.

In 1800, the American Schooner *Argo* ran aground on a reef near Lakeba (Lau island group). Most of the crew managed to make land safely but cholera had broken out on board and soon the epidemic spread to Lakeba and other islands, killing thousands of Fijians.

A seaman who reached Australia told of the great forests of sandalwood on Fiji – news that spread rapidly and brought swarms of merchants and adventurers to the islands. Within ten years the supply of sandalwood was exhausted. For a short time the trade in sea cucumbers (*holothuria, bêche-de-mer*), regarded as a delicacy in the east, flourished.

Two missionaries from Tahiti, members of the London Missionary Society, reached Fiji in 1830. Five years later, the first Methodists settled in Lakeba. The missionaries were not immediately successful. In 1854, they achieved an important breakthrough when Ratu Seru Cakobau, an influential chieftain from the small island of Bau, converted to Christianity. In the years that followed, his power grew and his followers named him *Tui Viti*, King of Fiji.

The Europeans also wanted something from him. As a ruler he was, in their eyes, responsible for his subjects and thereby also for payments of damages that they caused. American Consul John Brown Williams demanded payment of US $43,000 as compensation for damages resulting from arson and theft. Cakobau appealed, without success, to the British Crown, offering the United Kingdom the Fiji Islands in return for payment of his debt. In 1867, the same year Cakobau crowned himself King of Fiji, Thomas Baker, a missionary working inland on Viti Levu, was killed and eaten. Following a period of political unrest in which local chieftains, European settlers and invaders from Tonga jostled for power, Britain took up Chief Cakobau's offer. The Fiji Islands were declared a British Crown Colony in 1874.

Arrival of Foreign Workers

In the 1860s workers were needed for the growing number of cotton plantations on the islands. Slave traders, called "blackbirders," brought in thousands of workers from other Pacific islands.

Cotton proved to be uneconomical, and coconut palms and sugar cane replaced the cotton plantations. In 1875, a measles epidemic killed 40,000 Fijians, reducing still further the number of workers needed to operate the plantations. Between 1879 and 1919 some 60,000 contract workers from India came to Fiji. According to the terms of their contracts, they could either settle in Fiji or return to India at their own cost after five years of labor. Those who had worked ten years on a plantation had a right to free transportation home. About two-thirds of the contract workers decided to remain. The high birth rate of the Indians, along with the high death rate of the Fijians, who fell victim to European diseases, eventually gave the Indians a population majority over the native Fijians. At the same time, cultural and religious differences kept the two groups from merging into a homogeneous society.

Independence

On October 10, 1970, the Fiji Islands gained their independence from Great Britain. Three parties made up the political landscape in the 1987 elections: the up to then ruling *Alliance Party* (primarily made up of Fijians), the *Federation Party* (made up of Indians) and the *Labor Party* (mixed). When a coalition of the Federation and Labor Parties won control, Indian politicians took up important positions and traditional Fijians began to worry about the loss of their heritage, because Indians already controlled the economy. Lieutenant Sitiveni Rabuka, supported by the right nationalist *Taukei* movement, seized power in a military coup on May 14, 1987. Finding the provisional government ready for compromise, Rabuka staged a second coup in September of the same year and also took

Above: The ritual of drinking kava (here in Nadi, Viti Levu) is one of the significant moments in social life on the Fiji Islands.

control over government-owned businesses. On October 7, 1987, he declared Fiji a republic. The country lost its membership in the Commonwealth. At the end of the year, Ratu Sir Penaia Ganilau was appointed president and Ratu Sir Kamisese Mara became prime minister.

The first free elections after the coup were held in 1992, following an amendment to the constitution guaranteeing the Fijians – regardless of other political circumstances – a majority in the Parliament and the Senate. Sitiveni Rabuka, who had staged the coup in 1987, came out the winner and became the new prime minister. In 1997, Rabuka went to London to negotiate the reinstatement of the monarchy on Fiji.

Kava, Meke and Walking on Fire

Yaqona, the national drink, made from the extract of the root of the native *kava* plant (*piper methysticum*), a member of the peppermint family, is without doubt among the most important things in the life of a Fijian. Kava is drunk on many Melanesian and Polynesian islands, but nowhere else in the Pacific basin does drinking kava occupy such an important place in day to day life.

Dried kava root, or instant kava in powdered form (called *grog*) is available at all local markets and in many stores. The roots are ground in a mortar; the powder is then tied into a cloth and the liquid extracted by wringing the cloth in a large water-filled wooden bowl (*tanoa*). The resulting gray-brown liquid is poured into a communal coconut shell (*bilo*) and passed around.

The taste takes some getting used to – kava also leaves a light felt-like coating on the tongue. Imbibing large amounts has a sedative effect: the limbs become heavy but the drink does not affect cognitive faculties. Kava is an important means of communicating. It is drunk preferably in the company of relatives, friends or guests and on special occasions where it is part of a ceremony with clearly defined steps and procedures.

No visit to a family or village should pass without a gift (*sevusevu)* of kava root, given with both hands, to the head of the family or the chieftain and accompanied by a short speech of introduction. Customarily the men, according to their rank, then sit in a circle on straw mats. The visitor is assigned a place. They then sit Indian-fashion with legs crossed; women tuck their legs to one side – only then can preparation of the kava drink begin. Before taking the coconut shell the participant is expected to clap once with cupped hands and then take the shell with both hands, drink it in one gulp and then clap three times with cupped hands. Many tourist hotels hold kava ceremonies, a good opportunity for visitors to familiarize themselves with the procedure.

Presentations of traditional dances (*meke*) should also not be missed. The dancers are accompanied by the rhythmic beat of slit drums (*lali*), hollow bamboo tubes slammed against the earth, and by singers. The dances illustrate scenes out of Fijian legends. V*akamalolo* is the women's dance. Wrapped in tapa cloth, the seated women swing rhythmically to the beat of the drums.

Fire walking – where men walk barefoot over heated stones – is practiced by Indians as well as native Fijians. The actual ritual came from India and is part of the celebrations that take place at Hindu temples once a year, in honor of the goddess Kali. Fijian fire walkers come from the island of Beqa, but today they present their fire walking ceremony exclusively in Viti Levu hotels.

The Fijian People

Fifty percent of the inhabitants of the islands are Fijians. They are Melanesians, but the Polynesian influence is sometimes hard to overlook. Indians make up 45 percent of the population and are found mainly in cities and on the larger islands where sugar cane is grown. A typical Indian flair marks many towns.

Chinese, Europeans and other Pacific islanders make up the remaining five percent. The total population is approximately 800,000. Christians (mainly Protestants) are the largest religious group, followed by Hindus and Moslems.

Language

Methodist missionaries who came to Fiji in 1835 were responsible for developing the written Fijian language. Their valuable dictionary and grammar book was only published 15 years later, however.

Maps still bear contradictory spellings for place names because the written and spoken languages have yet to be reconciled. So, for example, b is pronounced mb: b = mb (bula = mbula), d = nd (nadi = nandi), g = ng (Korotogo = Korotongo), q

= ngg (yaqona = yanggona, Bequ = Mbengga), c = English "th" (Cakobau = Thakombau).

Most Indians in Fiji speak Hindi, Urdu and English. English is the second official language, and travelers who speak it should have no difficulty making themselves understood.

VITI LEVU

The Southern Part of the Island: From Nadi to Suva via Queen's Road

The view from the airplane as it approaches Nadi is sobering: the relatively dry west side of the main island bears witness to intensive agricultural use. In all directions the view encompasses sugar cane fields and dry grass-covered

Above: The landscape around Mount Evans Range in the vicinity of Nadi is stark and daunting. Right: The Hindu temple of Sri Siva Subramaniyam Swami in Nadi.

hills. To the west of Nadi, the tiny islands of the Mamanuca group, outlined with the thin white line of their sand beaches, is barely visible in the blue sea.

The **International Airport** is located about 6 miles (10 km) northeast of Nadi. Before turning onto the main thoroughfare, Queen's Road, the road from the airport crosses the railroad track that, at harvest time, is busy with trains carrying sugar cane to the refinery in Lautoka. The section of the road leading to the city is lined with hotels, restaurants and supermarkets.

A left-hand turn leads to the eastern mountainous region known as the **Nausori Highlands** (up to nearly 3500 feet – 1076 m – high).

Shortly before coming to the bridge that leads directly into the city center, a street turns to the left leading to the **Denarau peninsula**. The beautiful **Sheraton Royal Denarau Resort** (formerly Regent of Fiji) and the **Sheraton Fiji Resort** have settled there on a sandy stretch of beach. The peninsula also has an 18-

hole golf course. Boats leave from the **Denarau Marina** to the exciting Mamanuca island group west of Nadi (more on page 113). The place tends to be overrun with tourists.

The city of **Nadi** (approximately 11,000 inhabitants, mainly Indians) has little to offer tourists: souvenir shops, clothing, shoe and secondhand shops line the main street. Everywhere signs advertising duty-free goods tempt shoppers. Beware, the prices have very little resemblance with "duty-free." The colorful **fruit and vegetable market** is at its radiant best on Saturdays. A little bit to the south of it is an art and **handicraft market**. The rainbow-hued Hindu temple, **Sri Siva Subramaniyam Swami**, built in 1994, is at the southwestern edge of the city and well-worth visiting.

A new road now heads straight south from the airport, by-passing Nadi, so it is no longer necessary to drive through the city. It leads through a hilly landscape of small scattered sugar cane farms. In the distance the grass and scrub covered mountains of the highlands are clearly visible. The Fijians call this land, once covered with forests, *talasiga* (burnt earth). With the help of international organizations, parts of the *talasiga* have been successfully re-forested within the last few decades.

The largest hotel of the Fiji Islands, the **Fijian Resort**, is circa 28 miles (45 km). southeast of Nadi on the small island of **Yanuca**, which is joined to the main island by a bridge. The hotel management has leased the island from the neighboring town of Cuvu. On a hill to the left of the bridge that connects the island to the main road, is the village Methodist church. The station of the **Coral Coast Railway**, a railroad once used to transport sugar cane, is in the curve of the road. Now the rebuilt narrow-gauge railroad is used to transport day trippers to **Natadola Beach**, 10 miles (16 km) away, where a small luxurious resort awaits them. The train wanders through villages and presents spectacular views. The long white sand beach that stretches from Na-

tadola to the village of Sanesana is a true paradise for sun worshippers.

Some kilometers from the Fijian Resort there is a fork in the road that leads to the **Pacific Green** furniture factory. Australians began making furniture out of coconut palm wood in the early 1990s. The project is interesting and successful. Visitors are welcome.

Just before reaching Sigatoka two unpaved roads toward the south veer off to the right to the **Sigatoka Sand Dunes** (about 2 miles/3 km). The dunes, which have since been designated as a national park, are more than 60 feet (20 m) high and can only be reached by foot. After about 15 minutes the path opens to the breathtaking panorama of the wild, winding coast and the delta of the **Sigatoka River**.

Above: Sigatoka Valley is famous for its ceramicware. Right: Japanese tourists enjoy some of the pleasures of speed boating in the waters off the Denarau peninsula.

The beach stretches on for more than a mile (2 km) where experienced surfers, body surfers and windsurfers can ride the waves. Lapita ceramics and 2000-year-old burial stones have been found on this coast.

Sigatoka is a simple small town with a colorful Indian-Fijian market at which local produce but no art objects are offered. An impressively narrow bridge (with only one auto lane and the tracks for the sugar cane train) crosses the Sigotoka River, which, a short way from its estuary, is very broad.

Roads into the **Sigatoka Valley** branch off on both sides. Tobacco, papaya, okra, eggplant and other crops are grown on the fertile alluvial plain. This is the only region in the Fiji Islands where the inhabitants work intensively with clay and produce beautiful ceramics, a fairly good source of local cash. You can purchase their wares in many of the valley villages.

The road to the right follows the river and is paved part of the way. It soon opens to a stunning view of the valley. A

short way down the road at the foot of **Tavuni Hill** is the village of **Naroro**. The limestone hill was actually built up as a fort in the 18th century. There are many complexes of this type in the Sigatoka Valley, but this is the only one which has been restored and is open to visitors. The road ends about 50 miles (80 km) inland at **Namoli**.

The picturesque **Coral Coast**, which has been developed for tourism, begins east of Sigatoka. The road travels through small villages. The mountain slopes are increasingly covered with thick growths of rain forest as you go along. The Coral Coast offers a choice of good hotels, beaches and water sports at **Korotogo**, **Korolevu** and **Naboutini**.

Before the road reaches Pacific Harbour it offers glimpses of two islands from various places along the way. The small island is **Yanuca** (not to be confused with the island of the same name which is the site of the Fijian Resort Hotel). The other is **Beqa**, home to Fiji's fire walkers.

Pacific Harbour, which rests upon a beautiful white sand beach, was built by a Japanese company in 1988 as a vast recreation and vacation center with its own airport, accommodations in various price ranges, and a broad spectrum of water sports and golf.

Everything seems to have taken on larger-than-life proportions, like the beautiful **Cultural Center and Market Place** complex, an open-air museum designed as a traditional Fijian village on a small island. "Fijian warriors" ferry visitors to the island. Various stops along the way through the village offer glimpses into the manufacturing of native handicrafts, and take an interesting and evocative look at pre-European life on the islands. In the afternoons, fire walkers stage their show or dancers perform the traditional dances (*meke*).

Farther down, the road plunges into the broad plain of the Navua River, where rice is grown. Majestic banyan trees (*Ficus bengalensis*) dominate the landscape with increasing frequency. The

lively market town of Navua lies on the east bank of the river. It is the departure point for organized boat and rafting trips to downstream villages. One particularly adventurous tour passes through a gorge with rushing white waters, and then crosses some hair-raising rapids to reach **Namuamua**; it also includes the dangerously narrow **Navua Gorge**.

The road to Suva winds farther northeast. After about a 20-minute drive, just a short way from Lami, is the **Orchid Island Cultural Center**, an open air museum where Fijian traditions and art work are presented. Visitors also have the opportunity to learn about the native fauna and flora.

Lami, a suburb of Suva, is the site of the **Raffles Tradewinds Hotel**, built on a photogenic bay. Its floating restaurant offers a good place to take a lunch-time break.

Above: The gaily decorated graves in the cemetery of Suva, a peculiar attraction on Queens Road.

Suva – the Colorful and Lively Capital

Suva is the largest city in the South Pacific, and one of the most important commercial and harbor cities in the South Seas. It is home to approximately 150,000 people. A modern city has sprung up within the last 15 years, with skyscrapers, a spacious indoor market, stores selling a broad range of merchandise and luxurious residential neighborhoods.

But much of the city's old charm remains intact, and it is easy to imagine how this cosmopolitan city with, its jumble of architectural styles, slowly evolved. Suva is not a tourist city and few vacationers visit it.

Until 1882 Levuka, on the island Ovalau, was the capital of Fiji. Soon it became clear that the island was too small and lacked a good enough harbor to be a colonial capital. Plans to move the capital to Suva began in 1877 after two Australian merchants offered the government

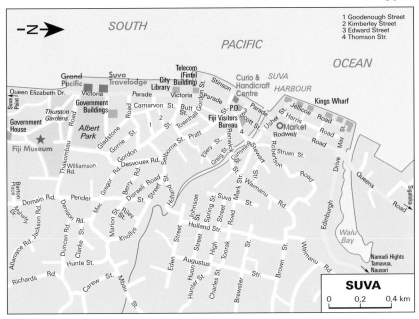

half of their extensive land holdings as a gift under the condition that the new capital be built there. Suva was then still but a gathering of a few small houses. All attempts to plant sugar cane had failed: the sugar mill had closed and the land was considered virtually worthless.

The first three sights here contrast sharply with each other: a large **cemetery** is situated at the edge of the city on Queen's Road – a few of the newer graves are decorated with colorful plastic flags, flowers and *tapa* fabric (made of bark fiber and also called *masi*); the **Royal Suva Yacht Club**, a bit further south to the right, provides a perfect place to have a drink with a yacht captain; the colonial-style **jail**, built in 1913, is directly across the street in a part of the city dominated by industrial compounds and harbor facilities.

At the next traffic circle **Edinburgh Drive** veers to left into the island's interior, eventually coming to the city of Nausori, about 12.5 miles (20 km) away. At the **Fiji Institute of Technology** a

road to the left crosses Princess Road and enters the high plateau called **Namadi Heights**. Its elegant neighborhood, **Tamavua**, offers a beautiful view of the Bay of Suva.

The inner city of Suva is best investigated on foot, which gives you ample time to spot little details of Fijian life. Any itinerary you plan should involve at least a nice stroll through the picturesque **market** on Usher Street, especially good on Saturday mornings when crowds push their way among stands piled high with goods. On the ground floor of the covered market fresh seafood is sold, along with native and imported fruits and vegetables. The upper floors sell vast quantities of spices, legumes, such as beans of all kinds, great bundles of tobacco and kava.

The **Curio and Handicraft Center** is about 270 feet (300 meters) to the south in the building complex on Stinson Parade. The small stands sell carvings, straw mats, hats, bags, *tapa* fabric and souvenir shells of all kinds. In the South

Seas it is not customary to barter, but the Fijians have taken a hint from the Indians when it comes to doing business. The authorities warn visitors to be wary of fly-by-night peddlers who try to sell tourists souvenirs of shoddy quality and dubious origin. It usually takes a firm "no" to discourage them, but if that doesn't work, a mention of the police will.

Edward Street heads inward from the handicraft center to the **General Post Office**. The **Fiji Visitors Bureau**, in a pretty colonial building from 1912, is adjacent to it. The bridge on Thomson Street provides a nice view of the colonial style **arcades** (1912) at Nubukabu Creek. **Cumming Street** forks off to the right, and presents row upon row of duty-free shops.

Above: The sentinel at Government House in Suva offers a particularly good subject for a photographer. Right: The old colonial houses with their arcades grace the inner city of Suva.

Suva's oldest and main street, Victoria Parade, runs southward from the Visitors Bureau. Several interesting colonial buildings on the seaward side of the street are significant from an architectural and historical point of view. The **Fintel Building** (dating from 1926) now houses Fiji's telecommunications company.

The **Ming Palace Restaurant**, built in 1904, was formerly the city hall. American millionaire industrialist Andrew Carnegie donated money that helped build the **City Library** in 1909.

South of the **Suva Travelodge** is the building of the legendary **Grand Pacific Hotel** which, until it closed in the early 1990s, offered visitors a nostalgic glimpse into the romantic past of South Seas travel. Since the building changed ownership, two if its wings have been razed. It now awaits restoration.

Statues of two famous Fijians, Ratu Sir Cakobau and Ratu Sir Lala Sukuna, decorate the monumental **Government Buildings** (1939) on the other side of the street. **Albert Park**, a large open area

where sporting competitions, public festivities and fairs are held, lies to the south. Every year some time toward the end of August the entertaining *Hibiscus Festival* is held there.

The **Fiji Museum** is situated in **Thurston Gardens**, a beautifully planted botanical garden featuring tropical trees and flowers, just south of Albert Park. The museum is one of the important stops on a tour of Suva. Its exhibits of Fijian pre-European and early European history are not only interesting, but are very well presented as well. A small shop sells a selection of publications and souvenirs, while the upper stories display masterworks of *tapa* fabric.

At Thurston Gardens, **Victoria Parade** becomes **Queen Elisabeth Drive**. A short distance to the south is the entrance to **Government House**, which was built in 1928 and serves as the residence of Fiji's head of state. A soldier, wearing an elegant white skirt and red tunic, stands guard at all times and remains impervious to the plethora of silly remarks made by tourists day in and day out. The changing of the guard takes place daily at noon, but is especially interesting on the first Friday of the month, when it gets a little musical assistance.

The street leads to **Suva Point**, with another stunning view of the sea. The **House of Parliament** (1992), on Ratu Sukuna Road, presents an interesting blend of modern and traditional architectural styles.

The south side of Suva has been taken over by schools, clubs and elegant villas housing politicians and expatriates, foreign employees, consultants and a bevy of business people.

To the east, at **Laucala Bay**, are the city's **National Stadium** and the campus of the **University of the South Pacific** (USP). Twelve Pacific member states support the university, which was founded in 1968 and which has branches on a number of islands. More than 2500 students attend classes on campus, and 6000 others complete correspondence courses.

The Northern Part of the Island: From Suva to Nadi on Kings Road

Kings Road, which stretches for more than 180 miles (290 km) along the east and north coasts of Suva into western Viti Levu, has very little traffic. It is about 70 miles (110 km) longer than Queens Road, the southern route. More than 30 miles (50 km) of the road between Korovu and Rakiraki are unpaved and covered, for the most part with gravel. Kings Road is a must for nature lovers. It traverses a varied landscape and passes through delightful villages where traditional style houses *(bure)* still remain.

The most-traveled section, between Suva and the town of Nausori, has experienced a building boom during the last

Above: A house (bure) thatched in traditional style. Right: The dream of any visitor to the South Seas – white beaches, palms, and a light breeze to take the edge off the heat (Nananui-Ra Island).

15 years. Whoever has sufficient time to spare should take the somewhat longer road that goes from Suva via Princess Road toward the northeast to Savanti and then turns east to Nausori.

Shortly before reaching Sawani, it is worth taking extra time for an excursion to **Colo-i-Suva Forest Park**, at about 600 feet (200 m) above sea level. The rain forest, just a short way from the main highway, is in a protected area. The entrance to the park is at the **Forestry Station**. Various trails wind through mahogany forests and thick vegetation, interrupted by small waterfalls and crystal-clear pools in which a refreshing swim is always welcome.

Nausori is a small town on the **Rewa**, Fiji's largest river. Except for the longest bridge, a colorful market and Suva's airport (2 miles/3 km to the southeast), Nasori has little to offer tourists. Sugar cane was planted in the area in the 1950s, but proved less lucrative than in the drier areas of the island. Now the fields are used for planting rice, making this the

country's largest irrigated agricultural project. Rice is hulled and polished on site. King's Road continues north along the east coast. **Korovou**, a small center for dairy products developed after World War One, lies some 18 miles (30 km) down the road.

Just past Korovou a small road bears right to **Natovi Landing**, where ships dock on their way to and from the islands of Ovalau and Vanua Levu. King's Road heads toward the interior at Korovou and doesn't return to the coast again until **Nanukuloa** on Viti Levu Bay. It then continues to hug the coastline.

The walls of the Catholic church in the village of **Naiserelagi**, south of Nanukuloa, were painted in 1962 by artist Jean Charlot. The fine frescos, inspired by Fijian motifs, and the impressive rendering of the "Black Christ," certainly merit a stop.

The center of the pretty little town of **Rakiraki** lies less than a mile (1 km) from King's Road. About 3 miles (5 km) before the town a road forks off toward

Ellington Wharf. From there it is possible to reach Vanua Levu and the restful island of **Nananui-Ra**, where white sand beaches, coral reefs, mangrove trees and nature trails make it a perfect place to escape from the rest of the world for a few days. Accommodations are limited, so it is best to make reservations before going.

Rakiraki is situated on the northern tip of the island, about halfway between Suva and Nadi. King's Road to the west is, from this point, paved and therefore very easy to drive. The road passes the sprawling meadows of **Yaqara Cattle Ranch**, Fiji's largest producer of beef. The land which is near the Nasivi River covers more than 17,000 acres (7000 hectares).

The Island Highway branches off just over a mile (2 km) before **Tavua** and turns southwest into the interior. The forestry station at 2800 feet (900 meters) altitude at **Nadarivatu** makes an ideal starting point for hiking trips into the mountains, including **Mount Victoria**

(also called Tomanivi), Fiji's highest peak (4000 feet/1323 m). The area affords spectacular views of the surrounding countryside.

The road proceeds through **Navai** and **Koro-ni-O** (to the right is the **Monasavu Dam**) and Sawani to Suva. A four-wheel-drive vehicle is needed to pass this stretch of road.

The **Emperor Gold Mine** is in **Vatukoula**, which is located 5 miles (9 km) inland from Tavua. Strip mining and underground tunnels are both used to extract the precious metal.

The poor working conditions and low pay prompted the 1500 mine workers to stage strikes and massive protests in the recent past. Taking a walk through the mines is possible, but tours must be booked at least one week in advance

Above: The market of Lautoka is fun and also gives a good overview of the region's products. Right: Splendid orchids can be seen in the Garden of the Sleeping Giant.

(Emperor Gold Mine, Public Relations Officer, Tel: 680477, Fax: 6807772). A road from Vatukoula leads back to the island highway.

Just over 18 miles (30 km) farther down Kings Road you'll discover the Indian sugar town of **Ba**, which nestles under the shade of mangrove trees at the estuary of the Ba River. The mosque and small market are just in front of the bridge.

Lautoka, on the west coast, is an important business center and Fiji's second-largest city, with 35,000 – mostly Indian – inhabitants. Adherents of several religions, however, live peacefully together here: alongside various churches there are, for example, the **Sikh Temple**, the attractive **Jame Mosque** and the massive **Sri Krishna Kala Temple**. The large, busy market brings together buyers and sellers from the entire region. In the "crushing season" railroad cars and trucks line up in front of the **Lautoka Sugar Mill**, which went into operation in 1903 and is still in use today. Ships sail from Lautoka to the

islands of the Mamanuca and Yasawa groups (see page 113).

Abaca National Park is approximately 7.5 miles (12 km) inland from Lautoka. Nature trails provide an opportunity to learn the native fauna and flora, and bubbling waterfalls offer an opportunity to cool off.

According to legend, the first Fijians are supposed to have landed near **Vuda Point**, where they founded a settlement. Archeologists have found no evidence to support this legend.

The beautiful, large, traditional house (*bure*) at Viseisei, a little way further east, is impossible to ignore. It belongs to the former Prime Minister Timoci Bavadra, who was overthrown in the military coup of 1987. The **Garden of the Sleeping Giant** is a little over 3 miles (5 km) farther, off to the left. It is an orchid garden, created by the late American actor Raymond Burr. A circular path leads through the garden and past exhibits of native plants, as well as imported orchids.

VANUA LEVU

Although tourism is already highly developed on Viti Levu, the neighboring island of Vanua Levu still has idyllic scenery, romantic bays, deserted coconut studded beaches, untouched villages and extremely friendly Fijians.

Running parallel to the north coast is one of the longest barrier reefs of the South Seas. Sugar cane is the principle crop of the dry northwest region. An unbroken chain of mountains, reaching nearly 3000 feet (1000 m), runs the length of the island down its center. The southeast is more humid and is covered with thick tropical vegetation. This is where the copra plantations are.

The ferries from Viti Levu arrive at **Nabouwalu** on the southwest tip of the island (simple accommodations, post office). From there, roads branch off to Labasa and Savusavu (also reachable by bus). On the way to Labasa, a path a few miles northeast of **Lekutu** leads from the road to **Naselesele Falls**, which lies in a

lush green setting – a perfect spot for a quick swim.

The small town of **Labasa**, heavily influenced by its Indian population, is the sugar and commercial business center of the north. It is situated in the delta of the river of the same name.

For tourists there is little to see there with the exception of the sugar mill constructed in 1894 just over one mile (2 km) to the east of the town. The restaurants are good and the shops in the town are inviting. Boats drop off surfers and divers at the magnificent **Great Sea Reef**, near Kia Island in the northwest.

The Cross Island Road connects Labasa with the sleepy little town of **Savusavu** on the beautiful bay of the same name in the south (bus service). The town center consists of one shop-lined street

hugging the bay. The many colonial-style houses evoke the by-gone era when Savusavu was an important maritime commercial settlement and its harbor was commercially significant.

The town has been experiencing an ever-increasing flow of visitors in the last decade because it offers a beautiful setting and a safe anchorage for yachts. First-class diving is found nearby. Left, under the **Hot Springs Hotel**, are natural **hot springs**, used by some families for cooking.

Other spots on Vanua Levu also show evidence of geophysical phenomena that attest to the island's volcanic activity. Just a few hundred feet from the hot springs is the **Copra Shed Marina**. The recently renovated building complex includes the **Yacht Club** and the **Captain's Cafe**, which serves pizza and is popular with young people. The terrace of the café provides one of the world's greatest views.

A few miles to the west, outside the city, is a **copra mill** that is open to visitors. Anyone wanting to make an excursion from Savusavu should drive northwest past the village of **Urata** to the end of the bay and then get on the Cross Island Road toward the interior. Soon the road climbs higher, and breathtaking views appear out of the emerald green tropical rain forest.

Another stretch of road offering superb scenery is the circa 50-mile-segment (77 km) called the Hibiscus Highway, which begins at the airport and follows the coconut-palm-studded southern coast of the peninsula to **Natuvu** on Buca Bay. The highway ends at the old missionary station of **Napuka** on the eastern point. From **Buca Bay** a ferry crosses over to the islands of Kioa and Taveuni.

TAVEUNI

Taveuni, which measures only 25 by 6.5 miles (40 by 11 km), is called the

Above: Crossing the sea to Taveuni. Right: A diver meets a cuttlefish during an underwater expedition off Taveuni, which is considered a top diving area.

"garden island" because of its lush flora, rain forests and coconut groves. A chain of high mountains runs down the island's middle. Two of the peaks rise more than 3500 feet above sea level (1200 m). The fertile volcanic soil and high annual rainfall have assured Taveuni rich vegetation and a flourishing agricultur-based economy. At one time cotton, coffee and cacao were planted in great quantities. Today, copra is the principle crop. The interior still shelters plant and animal species that have become extinct on other islands.

Experienced scuba divers find this a diving paradise; it is considered to be among the world's best. The fabulous **Rainbow Reef** in the Somosomo Strait between Vanua Levu and Taveuni is nearly 20 miles long (30 km), and is known for its strong and dangerous currents. A number of diving schools offer courses and organize dives.

There is no road that circles the entire island. The wild south coast is impassable. **Matai Airport** is in the extreme north, the ferry port is on the west coast at **Waiyevo**, the administrative center of the island. Less than a mile to the south of the town (1 km) a monument and a colorful road sign mark the location of the International Dateline (180° meridian). For practical reasons – in order to avoid different time zones within the Fiji Islands – the official dateline has been moved east to bypass Fiji.

Several miles further south is the **Wairiki Catholic Mission** with its old stone church. The 3824-foot **Des Voeux Peak** (1195 m) is a day's round-trip journey on foot from Wairiki. It is also reachable by jeep and offers a grandiose panoramic view.

At the Garden Island Resort in Waiyevo a side street turns off to the right of the main road to the **Sliding Rocks** of **Waitalava** (the sign says Waitalava Estates). The smooth natural rock formations are formed like slides and bathers can slip down them into the river.

The largest urban center on the northwest coast is **Somosomo**. A strenuous

day trip with incredible views takes sightseers to **Lake Tagimaucia**, a crater lake situated about 2500 feet above sea level (830 m). It is advisable to make the trip with a guide.

Tagimaucia, by the way, is a native plant that only grows on Taveuni and on Vanua Levu. It is a vine with large red and white clusters of flowers.

The east coast of the island is famous for its spectacular scenery. **Bouma Falls** is a 44-foot waterfall (14 m) that drops into a crystalline pool, the perfect spot for a refreshing swim. **Tavoro Forest Park**, a bit further south, features more waterfalls, opportunities to swim and trails through the rain forest. The **Lavena Coastal Walk** (an entrance fee is charged) offers superb beaches and a spectacular coastline for hiking.

Above: A bird's-eye view of Turtle Island, one of many in the Yasawa archipelago.
Right: Enjoying a romantic dinner for two on one of the Yasawa islands.

OVALAU

The egg-shaped 39-square-mile (100 sq km) main island of the Lomaiviti group is just 15 minutes away by plane from Suva's airport in Nausori. It is well worth a day trip. Ships depart from Natovi Landing (northeast of Korovou). The volcanic island has exciting scenery, high mountains (**Mt. Nadelaiovalau** stands at a proud 1900 feet/616 m) and an agreeable climate.

In the east is Levuka, a town built on a narrow strip of coast. White settlers built the town in the 1830s and by the 1870s it had grown into a busy wild-west-style boomtown populated by seamen, traders and plantation owners. With the signing of the colonial agreement between the British and King Cakobau in 1974, Levuka became the capital of the Fiji Islands until 1882, when it was moved to Suva.

Today **Levuka** is a quiet town of 1700 inhabitants and beautifully preserved colonial houses which evoke the town's

history. The **Sacred Heart Church** was built in 1858, the same decade as the **Royal Hotel**. The building now housing the **Levuka Community Center** along with the museum and library, was built in 1878, and the **Levuka Public School** first opened in 1879. In the old colonial **Ovalau Club**, a letter from Count Felix von Luckner, who became famous in World War One as the "Sea Devil," hangs on the wall. Many other grand old houses decorate **Mission Hill** and enjoy a panoramic view.

South of Levuka, in **Navosa**, a monument marks the spot where the colonial contract between Fiji and Great Britain was signed in 1874. In the nearby village of **Draiba**, a trail bears off to the right through an idyllic forested area to the **Lovoni Valley** in the interior (four to five hours; it is advisable to take a guide).

OTHER ISLANDS

Mamanuca Group: The Mamanucas are wonderful, palm studded coral islands with powder white sand beaches and turquoise blue lagoons – just as promised in South Seas travel brochures. With their location, west of Nadi and Lautoka, they are naturally very popular, fully developed for tourism, and often crowded. Luxury island resorts guarantee the comfort of their guests and provide a full range of excellent opportunities for divers, snorkelers, surfers and deep-sea fishing enthusiasts.

Yasawa Group: The archipelago, named after one of its northernmost islands, stretches like a string of pearls over 50 miles (80 km) northwest from Viti Levu. It consists of six larger and ten smaller islands, and countless tiny islets. The mountains reach a surprising height; on Waya, for example, 1800 feet (570 m). The picturesque deserted bays and lovely sandy beaches make this group the favorite destination of cruise ships (for example, *Blue Lagoon Cruises* out of Lautoka). In addition to two luxury resorts there are numerous simple accommodations.

113

Kadavu Group: The long drawn-out island group, reachable by plane or ferry from Suva, lies about 55 miles (90 km) south of the capital. Its main island, giving the group its name, is **Kadavu**. Mountains reaching up to 2500 feet (800 m), traditional Fijian villages, attractive beaches and a magnificent diving area make the islands ideal for South Seas getaways. Their major attraction is the **Great Astrolabe Reef**, with its coral formations, underwater caves and varied sea life. It encloses nearly 20 miles (30 km) of the northern part of the archipelago. Roads are unknown except on parts of Kadavu and **Ono**, the second-largest island. The largest city, **Vunisea**, where there is an airport and hospital, is located on the narrowest part of the island. The **Matana Resort** is near **Brue**, somewhat north, on a wonderful beach. Another great beach is located to the south at **Muani**. There are accommodations in various price ranges, but there are no banks, and buses do not service the area.

Lau Group: The island group in the east of the country stretches from north to south. The remote archipelago consists of some sixty islands, of which only about half are permanently inhabited. For centuries the group was under Tongan rule, and it still bears the signs of Polynesian influence. The two largest islands, **Balavu** and **Lakeba**, are reachable by plane from Suva.

The long drawn-out island of **Vanua Balavu** (northern Lau), with its green hills and beautiful palm-bordered beaches, is simply breath-taking. **Lomaloma** offers a choice of accommodations, including a friendly traditional "rest house" and a luxury resort.

The almost round, fertile volcanic island of **Lakeba** (southern Lau) has limestone caves. Several gorgeous beaches line the west coast, the best of which are in **Nukuselal**. In **Tubou**, a government guest house provides overnight accommodations, but advance bookings are requested.

FIJI ISLANDS
Country code: 679. No area code.
Traveling In and Out
West Europeans, North Americans and citizens of Commonwealth states need a passport valid for at least three months and an ongoing ticket. Airport tax is F\$ 20 when departing. Int'l flights: Fiji Asia, Australia, New Zealand and the USA. Nadi airport is located about 6 miles (10 km) north of the city. Various smaller South Seas airlines fly to other islands. The Visitors' Bureau at the airport is helpful for information. Taxis are cheap; fares are posted in the arrivals building.
Currency / Money Matters
The currency is the Fiji dollar (F\$): US \$1 = about 1.80 F\$. Common credit cards and traveler's checks are generally accepted in tourist areas.

VITI LEVU – NADI REGION
Accommodation
LUXURY (over F\$ 200): **Sheraton Fiji Resort**, Denarau, Tel: 750777, Fax: 750818, 300 rooms, suites. **Sheraton Royal Denarau Resort**, Denarau, Tel: 7500 00, Fax: 750259, 285 rooms. **Sonaisali Island Resort**, about 6 miles (10 km) southwest of Nadi on a private island, Momo Bay, Tel: 720411, Fax: 720392, 41 rooms, bungalows, water sports, marina. *FIRST CLASS (F\$ 100 to 200):* **Fiji Mocambo Hotel**, Queens Rd. bet. the airport and the city, Tel: 722000, Fax: 720324, 128 rooms. **Raffles Gateway Hotel**, opposite the airport, Tel: 722444, Fax: 720620, colonial-style house, 93 rooms. *MODERATE (F\$ 50 to 100):* **Club Fiji Beach Resort**, agreeable complex 2.5 miles (4 km) northwest of Nadi, Wailoaloa Beach, Tel: 702189, Fax: 702324, 24 bungalows, dorm, restaurant, pool, water sports. **Dominion International Hotel**, Queens Rd. bet. the airport and the city, Tel: 720255, Fax: 720187, 85 rooms, travel agent, friendly. **Rosie's Serviced Apartments**, Queens Rd. between the airport and the city, Tel: 722755, Fax: 722607, 8 modern apartments, ideal for families, travel agent. *BUDGET (under F\$ 50):* **Hotel Kennedy**, Kennedy Ave., Nadi, Tel: 664011, Fax: 661773, 30 apartments, rooms, dorm, pool, restaurant. **Nadi Hotel**, Koroivolu St., Tel: 700000, Fax: 700280, pleasant hotel in the city, pool. **Sandalwood Inn**, Queens Rd. between the airport and the city, Tel: 722044, Fax: 720103, 25 rooms, pool, restaurant.
Restaurants
Chef's the Restaurant, Tel: 703131, Sagayam Rd., off main road, international, Nadi's best. **Hamacho Yakitori**, Tel: 720252, Queens Rd., bet. the airport and the city, Japanese. **Maharaja Restaurant**, Tel: 722962, Queens Rd., 1.5 miles (2.5 km) from the airport, Indian. **Mama's Pizza Inn**, Tel: 700221, Main St., near the bridge, Italian.

THE SOUTH
QUEENS ROAD: NADI – SUVA
Accommodation

LUXURY (over F$ 200): **Fijian Resort**, 28 miles (45 km) southeast of Nadi near Cuvu, Tel: 520155, Fax: 500402, 364 rooms. **Natadola Beach Resort**, 22 miles (35 km) southeast of Nadi, Tel: 721001, Fax: 721000, 10 suites. **Warwick Fiji**, Korolevu, Tel: 530555, Fax: 530010, 288 rooms, suites. *FIRST CLASS (F$ 100 to 200):* **Hideaway Resort**, west of Korolevu, Tel: 500177, Fax: 520025, 56 bungalows. **Pacific Harbour International Hotel**, Pacific Harbour, Tel: 450022, Fax: 450262, 84 rooms. **The Naviti Beach Resort**, west of Korolevu, Tel: 530444, Fax: 530343, 140 rooms. **The Reef Resort**, 5 miles (8 km) east of Sigatoka, Tel: 500044, Fax: 520074, 72 rooms.

MODERATE (F$ 50 to 100): **The Crow's Nest**, near Sigatoka around Korotogo, Tel: 500230, Fax: 520354, 18 bungalows, dormitory, good restaurant. *BUDGET (under F$ 50):* **Coral Coast Christian Camp**, just to the east of Pacific Harbour, Tel: 450178. **Seashell Surf & Dive**, 20 miles (32 km) south of Nadi, Momi Bay, Tel: 720100, Fax: 720194, 28 rooms, bungalows. **Tabua Sands Beach Resort**, around Korolevu, Tel: 500399, 31 rooms, bungalows. **Tubakula Beach bungalows**, near Korotogo, Tel: 500097, Fax: 340236, 27 bungalows, dorm. **Vakaviti**, 6 miles (9 km) east of Sigatoka, Tel: 500526, Fax: 520319, 6 rooms, dorm.

SUVA REGION
Accommodation

LUXURY (over F$ 200): **Toberua Island Resort**, 19 miles (30 km) east of Suva on a small coral island, Tel: 302356, Fax: 302215, 14 bungalows, gourmet cuisine, water sports, good for children. *FIRST CLASS (F$ 100 to 200):* **Best Western Berjaya Hotel**, corner of Malcolm/Gordon St., Tel: 312300, Fax: 305442, 56 rooms. **Raffles Tradewinds Hotel**, in the suburb of Lami west of Suva, Tel: 362450, Fax: 361464, 108 rooms, seafood restaurant. **Suva Travelodge**, Victoria Parade, Tel: 301600, Fax: 300251, 131 rooms, pool. *MODERATE (F$ 50 to 100):* **Capricorn Apartment Hotel**, 7 St. Fort St., Tel: 303732, Fax: 303069, 34 studios, apartments, pool, family resort. **Southern Cross Hotel**, 63 Gordon St., Tel: 314233, Fax: 302901, 34 rooms, good restaurant. *BUDGET (under F$ 50):* **Outrigger Apartment Hotel**, 349 Waiman Rd., Tel: 314944, Fax: 302944, 20 rooms, pool, pizza restaurant. **Tanoa House Hotel**, 5 Princess Rd., suburb of Samambula (near Fiji Institute of Tech., bus), Tel: 381575. Good guesthouse with garden. **Tropic Tower Apartments**, 86 Robertson Rd., Tel: 313855, Fax: 304169, 34 apartments, pool, families.

Restaurants / Nightlife

CHINESE: **Lantern Palace**, 10 Pratt St., Tel: 314633. **Ming Palace**, Victoria Parade, Old Town Hall, Tel: 315111. *EUROPEAN:* **Cardo's Chargrill & Bar**, Regal Lane, Tel: 314330. **Aberdeen Grill**, Noble House, Bau St., Tel: 304322. *INDIAN:* **Curry House**, Victoria Parade, Old Town Hall Building, Tel: 313000. **Curry Place**, Pratt St., Tel: 313885. *ITALIAN:* **Papa La Pizza**, Outrigger Apartment Hotel, Waimanu Rd., Tel: 314944. *MALAY:* **Kampong Ku**, Berjaya Hotel, Tel: 312300. *SEAFOOD:* **The Galley Floating restaurant**, on the Stinson Parade, Tel: 313626. *VEGETARIAN:* **Hare Krishna**, Pratt St., Tel: 314154.

The best known nightclubs on the island are: **Lucky Eddie's** (also for gays) and the fine **Urban Jungle**, both at 217 Victoria Parade; **Traps**, 305 Victoria Parade, with live jazz. A favorite discothèque is the **Golden Dragon**, 379 Victoria Parade. Around the corner is the more quiet **O'Reilly's Pub**, 5 MacArthur St. **Bali Hai**, Rodwell Rd., is mainly frequented by the locals; **Chequers**, 127 Waimanu Rd., live music on weekends. The last two establishments mentioned become somewhat rowdy later on in the night.

THE NORTH
KINGS ROAD: NADI – SUVA
Accommodation

LUXURY (over F$ 200): **Mokusigas Island Resort**, on Nananu-i-Ra island, Tel: 694449, Fax: 694404, 20 bungalows, restaurant, scuba diving, PADI course, picture-book beach. *FIRST CLASS (F$ 100 to 200):* **Mediterranean Villas**, Vuda Point, Tel: 664011, 6 villas, Italian restaurant. **Bekana Island Resort**, Bekana Island off Lautoka, Tel: 665222, Fax: 665409, bungalows, dormitory, pool, water sports. **Waterfront Hotel**, Marine Drive, Lautoka, Tel: 664777, Fax: 66 5870, 43 rooms, pool. **Wananavu Beach Resort**, Volivoli Rd., Rakiraki, Tel: 694433, Fax: 694499, 14 bungalows, dormitory, water sports. *MODERATE (F$ 50 to 100):* **Anchorage Beach Resort**, between Viseisei and Vuda Point, Tel: 662099, Fax: 665571, rooms, dormitory, pool. **Rakiraki Hotel**, Kings Rd., Tel: 694101, Fax: 694545, 36 rooms, restaurant. *BUDGET (under F$ 50):* **Cathay Hotel**, Tavewa Ave., Lautoka, Tel: 660566, Fax: 660136, 44 rooms, pool, friendly. **Lautoka Hotel**, 2 Naviti St., Tel: 660388, Fax: 660201, 38 rooms, restaurant, nightclub, pool. **Ba Hotel**, 110 Bank St., Tel: 674000, Fax: 670559, rooms, pool, restaurant. **Tavua Hotel**, Tel: 680522, 11 rooms. **Charley's Place**, Nananu-i-Ra island, Tel: 694676, 4 bungalows, dormitory, friendly family enterprise. **Kon Tiki Lodge**, Nananu-i-Ra island, Tel: 694290, 9 bungalows, dormitory, ideal for backpackers.

VANUA LEVU
Accommodation

LUXURY (over F$ 200): **Cousteau Fiji Islands Resort**, 4 miles (6 km) southeast of Savusavu, Lesiaceva Point, Tel: 850188, Fax: 850340, the resort of the oceanographer Jean-Michel Cousteau, 20 bungalows, excellent restaurant, water sports, underwater photography, ecological tours. **Moody's Namenalala Island Resort**, southwest of Savusavu, Tel: 813764, Fax: 812366, elegant, quiet, 5 romantic bungalows, scuba diving, bird-watching. **Namale Resort**, on a copra plantation 6 miles (9 km) east of Savusavu, Tel: 850435, Fax: 850400, 9 bungalows on a white sand beach, gourmet cuisine, friendly management. **Nukubati Island Resort**, 25 miles (40 km) west of Labasa, Tel: 813901, Fax: 813914, 4 bungalows, full board, 7 day minimum, no children. *FIRST CLASS (F$ 100 to 200):* **Kontiki Resort**, on Hibiscus Highway 9 miles (15 km) east of Savusavu in a coconut palm forest, Tel: 850262, Fax: 850355, 16 bungalows, restaurant, pool, golf, tennis, marina, diving, nature paths. *MODERATE (F$ 50 to 100):* **Savusavu Hot Springs Hotel**, up on a hillside with a view over the bay, pool, Tel: 850195, Fax: 850430, 40 rooms. *BUDGET (under F$ 50):* **Savusavu Holiday House**, Nasekula Rd., just below the Hot Springs Hotel, Tel: 850216, 10 rooms, dormitory. **Buca Bay Resort & Yacht Club**, Natuvu, Tel: 880370, rooms, dormitory, restaurant, hiking, bird watching. **Grand Eastern Hotel**, Gibson St., Labasa, Tel: 811022, Fax: 814011, 27 rooms.

Restaurants / Nightlife

Savusavu has simple Chinese and Indian restaurants. **Captain's Café**, Copra Shed marina, Tel: 850511, pizza. For a drink, sometimes dancing on weekends: **Planters Club**.

Water Sports / Boats / Excursions

Water-skiing, diving, sailing, windsurfing: offices are located in the complex in the yacht harbor **Copra Shed marina**, Savusavu. **Eco Divers**, Tel: 850122, Fax: 850344, also make arrangements for excursions on land.

TAVEUNI
Accommodation

LUXURY (over F$ 200): **Forbes' Fiji Island**, Laucala Island east of Taveuni, Tel: 880077, Fax: 880099, 5 bungalows, minimum 3 days. **Matagi Island Resort**, private island 6 miles (10 km) northeast of Taveuni, Tel: 880260, Fax: 880274, 10 bungalows. *FIRST CLASS (F$ 100 to 200):* **Dive Taveuni**, just south of the airport, Tel: 880441, Fax:

880466, 6 bungalows, closed February/March. **Maravu Plantation Resort**, just south of the airport, Tel: 880555, Fax: 880600, 10 bungalows in a plantation, restaurant, pool. **Qamea Beach Club Fiji**, on an island about 3 miles (5 km) east of Taveuni, Tel: 880220, Fax: 880092, 11 bungalows, water sports, tours. *MODERATE (F$ 50 to 100):* **Garden Island Resort**, Waiyevo, Tel: 880286, Fax: 880288, 30 rooms, dormitory, pool, restaurant, water sports, tours. **The Palms-Soqulu Plantation Homestead**, west coast, south of Wairiki, Tel/Fax: 880241, 5 rooms. *BUDGET (under F$ 50):* **Kaba's** Motel & Guest House, Somosomo, Tel: 880233, Fax: 880202, 10 rooms.

OVALAU
Accommodation

BUDGET (under F$ 50): **Mavida Guest House**, Beach St., Levuka, Tel: 440051, colonial flair, 13 rooms, dormitory. **Royal Hotel**, Langham St., Levuka, atmospheric house in colonial style (1852), Tel: 440024, 15 rooms, bungalow, dormitory, friendly service. **Ovalau Holiday Resort**, Vuma, 3 miles (5 km) north of Levuka, Tel: 440329, 7 bungalows, dormitory, camping, rock beach, good restaurant, pool. **Rukuruku Resort**, northwestern coast, Tel: 444329, 6 bungalows, dormitory, restaurant, good campgrounds, black sand beach. **Leleuvia Island Resort**, Tel: 313366, 22 bungalows, dormitory. Coral island with sand beach and palms south of Ovalau. Scuba diving. A favorite with the backpacking crowd, a little on the loud side.

MAMANUCA ISLANDS

All resorts offer water sports.

LUXURY (over F$ 200): **Castaway Island Resort**, Galito Island northwest of Malolo Island, Tel: 661233, Fax: 665753, 66 bungalows, good for children. **Mana Island Resort**, northwest of Malolo, Tel: 661210, Fax: 662713, 160 bungalows, rooms, large complex, restaurants, shows, PADI scuba diving center. **Musket Cove Resort**, Malololailai Island, southeast of Malolo Island, Tel: 662215, Fax: 662633, PADI course. **Naitasi Resort**, Malolo Island, Tel: 669178, Fax: 669197, 38 rooms, local cuisine, riding, Kayaking, nature paths. **Sheraton Vomo Island Resort**, between Lautoka and Waya Islands, Tel: 667955, Fax: 667997, 30 villas. **Tokoriki Island Resort**, north of Mana Island, Tel: 661 999, Fax: 665295, 19 bungalows. **Treasure Island Resort**, about 11 miles (17 km) southwest of Lautoka, Tel: 666999, Fax: 666955, 67 beach bungalows. *FIRST CLASS (F$ 100 to 200):* **Beachcomber Island**, west, near Treasure Island, Tel: 661500, Fax: 664496, 19 bungalows, open dormitory, buffet meals, relaxed atmosphere, a favorite of the young solo traveling crowd. **Matamanoa Island Resort**, between Mana and Tokoriki Islands, Tel: 660511, Fax: 661069, 26 beach bungalows. **Plantation Island Resort**, Malololailai, Tel: 669333, Fax: 669200, 110 rooms, bungalows.

YASAWA ISLANDS
Accommodation
LUXURY (over F$ 500): **Turtle Island Lodge**, Nanuya, Tel: 663364, Fax: 665044, 14 bungalows, sports, water sports, hiking, all-inclusive resort, eco-logically-orientated, very expensive, only for couples. **Yasawa Island Lodge**, Yasawa Island, Tel: 663364, Fax: 665044, 16 bungalows, full board, water sports.
MODERATE (about F$ 40-100): **David's Place**, Tavewa Island, Tel: 663939, 9 bungalows, dormitory, camping, full board, small shop, very friendly and familiar atmosphere. **Octopus Club Fiji**, Waya Island, Tel: 666337, Fax: 666210, nicely managed by Ingrid and Wolfgang Denk, 3 bungalows, half-board, sports, Snorkeling along the white sand beach. **Dive Trek Nature Lodge**, Wayasewa Island, Tel: 720977, Fax: 720978, 10 bungalows with bath, dormitory, nature paths, PADI certification course, recommendable ecological resort.

LAU / KADAVU
Accommodation
LAU: *LUXURY (over F$ 200):* **Kaibu Resort**, Kaibu island, Northern Lau, west of Vanua Balavu, Tel: 880333, Fax: 880334, 3 bungalows, minimum 6 nights, no children. Water sports, gourmet cuisine. **Lomaloma Resort**, on the tiny island of Yanuyanu near Lomaloma, Vanua Balavu, Tel: 880446, Fax: 880303, 7 bungalows, full board, children from 12 onward. *BUDGET (under F$ 50):* **Government Rest House**, Tubu, Lakeba island, reservations: Lau Provincial Office, Tel: 42090, ext. 35.
KADAVU: *LUXURY (over F$ 200):* **Malawai Resort**, on a plantation 9 miles (15 km) east of Vunisea, Tel: 520102, Fax: 361536, elegant bungalows in colonial style, full board, minimum 3 days, scuba diving, sailing on the open seas.
MODERATE (F$ 50 to 100): **Dive Kadavu Matana Resort**, Drue, 4 miles (6 km) north of Vunisea, Tel: 311780, Fax: 303860, bungalow, dormitory, water sports, white sand beach. **Nukubalavu Adventure Resort**, northeast tip near Kavala Bay, Tel: 520089, Fax: 303160, bungalows, dormitory, camping, scuba diving, tours, 1.25 mile (2 km) sand beach. Boat transfer from Vunisea airport.
BUDGET (under F$ 50): **Albert's Place**, Langalevu, northeast tip, Tel: 302896, 15 romantic bungalows, camping, scuba diving, very good food. Boat transfer from Vunisea airport.

General Information
Cruises / Charter Boats
MAMANUCAS / YASAWAS: **Beachcomber Cruises**, Tel: 661500, Fax: 664496. **Blue Lagoon Cruises**, Tel: 661622, Fax: 664098. **Captain Cook Cruises**, Tel: 701823, Fax: 702045.
SUVA: **Nai'a Cruises**, Tel: 450382, Fax: 450566, also diving. **Tradewinds Marine**, Tel: 361522, Fax: 361035. *TAVEUNI:* **Tropical Dive Enterprises**, Tel: 880260, Fax: 880274, diving. **Sea of Legra Cruises**, Tel/Fax: 880141.

Car Rentals / Charter Flights / Tours
CAR RENTALS: **Avis**, Tel: 722233, Fax: 720482. **Budget**, Tel: 381555, Fax: 302450. **Hertz**, Tel: 723466, Fax: 302748. **Thrifty**, Tel: 722935, Fax: 722607. **Beware!** Traffic on Fiji drives on the left-hand side, British style!
AIRLINES: **Air Fiji**, Tel: 313666 / 722521. **Island Air**, Tel: 722371. **Sunflower Airlines**, Tel: 723016, Fax: 723611. **Turtle Airways**, Tel: 722389. **Vanua Air**, Tel: 313726, Fax: 313902. *HELICOPTERS:* **Island Hoppers**, Tel: 720410, Fax: 720172. *TOURS:* Details at the Visitors Bureau located at the arrivals building of Nadi airport. Excursions and flights to other islands with overnight stays and special tours (for example trekking in the highlands, visit to the Abaca National Park, excursions on the river and in jet boats): **Natural Tours Fiji**, Tel: 721937. **Rosie the Travel Service**, Tel: 722935, Fax: 722607. **South Pacific Tours**, Tel: 720673, Fax: 720719. **Sun Tours Fiji**, Tel: 722666, Fax: 720075.

Culture / Festivals / Museums
Bula Festival, Nadi, in July. **Hibiscus Festival**, Suva, Aug. **Sugar Festival**, Lautoka, in Sept. **Fijian Cultural Center**, Pacific Harbour, Tel: 450177, Fax: 450083. **Fiji Museum**, Thurston Gardens, Suva, Tel: 315944. **Garden of the Sleeping Giant**, Tel: 722701. **Orchid Island Fijian Cultural Center**, 6 miles (10 km) west of Suva, Tel: 361128.

Business Hours
Banks: Mon-Thu 9:30 a.m.-3 p.m., Fri till 4 p.m.; Nadi airport open 24 hours. **Offices**: Mon-Thu 8 a.m.-4:30p.m., Fri till 4 p.m. **Shops**: Mon-Thu 8 a.m.-5 p.m., Fri till 6 p.m., Sat till 1 p.m. **Post Office**: Mon-Fri 8 a.m.-4 p.m., Sat 8 a.m.-noon.

Electricity / Photography
Electrical current is 240 V – 50 Hz. Film is not expensive and is widely available in shops.

Tourist Information
Fiji Visitors Bureau, GPO Box 92, Suva, Tel: 302433, Fax: 302751, 300970, Thomson St. Opposite the post office. **Tourism Council of the South Pacific**, 343-359 Victoria Parade, PO Box 13119, Tel: 304177, Fax: 301995. **24-hour service** within Fiji: Tel: 0800-721721 (toll-free).

SAMOA

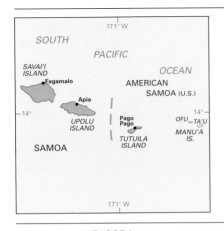

SAMOA

UPOLU

SAVAI'I

AMERICAN SAMOA

TUTUILA

MANU'A

SAMOA

The Samoan islands consist of an archipelago stretching from west-north-west to east-southeast. Independent Samoa is made up of the two largest western islands, Savai'i and Upolu. The islands of the eastern archipelago, Tutuila and the Manu'a Group (which includes the islets Ofu, Olosega and Tu'a) belong to the United States of America. The islands are known for their scenic beauty. The traditional ways of the islanders and their social structures have been, on the whole, very well preserved, making Samoa a unique vacation destination.

With its thick tropical rain forest, coconut plantations, waterfalls and crater lakes, broad white sand beaches and turquoise-colored lagoons, Samoa lives up to the image of a South Sea paradise as dreamed by many travelers. The black lava fields on the volcanic island of Savai'i evoke the power of the sometimes active volcanoes on the island. Round or oval open houses, called *fale*, still stand in many villages and offer a rare glimpse into the traditional family life of the Polynesians.

Preceding pages: Joy of life can be danced out (Upolu, Samoa). Left: Luxuriant vegetation around the Sopo'aga waterfall, Upolu.

American Samoa is every bit as scenically exciting as its sister state to the west. The American way of life, however, has left its mark on the islands at the expense of traditional Polynesian culture and customs.

Humidity, Heat and Lush Greenery

After Hawaii, the Samoan islands, with their total area of 1189 square miles (3130 sq km), are the largest island group of Polynesia. Savai'i, the westernmost and largest island, with an area of nearly 650 square miles (1700 sq km), is still volcanically active. Its volcano, Matavanu, last erupted in 1905 and 1911, covering large areas of the island with lava and transforming the lush tropical scenery into a bizarre moon-like landscape. On Upolu, the neighboring 423-square-mile (1115 sq km) island, all the volcanic craters have been extinguished. Tafua, the more than 2000-foot-high (669 m) volcanic cone with its 359-foot (110 m) deep crater, stands isolated on the western side of the island. Lanotoo has a beautiful crater lake 2240 feet (700 m) above sea level.

American Samoa is geologically older and is characterized by steep mountains and cliffs. The most impressive are on the Manu'a Islands. Samoa has fertile vol-

121

canic soil, but the thick cover of tropical vegetation in many areas has been severely damaged by tropical storms that have swept the islands in recent years.

The natural fauna indigenous to Samoa is very limited. The only reptiles to have reached these Pacific islands are skinks, geckos and Pacific boas. The only native mammal is the flying fox (*Pteropidae*), which is threatened with extinction.

The climate is tropical. The maximum temperature varies between 80 and 90° F (27 and 32° C) on a monthly average. The average annual rainfall on the windward slopes exceeds 190 inches (5000 mm). In Apia and Pago Pago, the principle cities of both island states, the annual precipitation has been recorded between 107 and 134 inches (2800 and 3500 mm). Statistically, rain occurs year-round, once every other day on the average – which is no reason to avoid visiting the islands.

Cradle of Polynesia?

Polynesian legends tell of brave ancestors who made their way from a far off land and settled new islands. But Samoans are the only people to tell another story: they believe their archipelago is the cradle of Polynesia and are firm in the belief that the volcanic island of Savai'i is the *Hawaiki* described in the creation legend as the place where god first created Polynesian life.

Lapita ceramic shards excavated on the islands, however, show that Samoa was first inhabited only about 2800 years ago. One thing is certain: in the early days of its existence there were frequent contacts among the island states of Fiji, Tonga and Samoa. These sometimes took the form of wedding celebrations and at other times bitter warfare.

Right: Going to mass on Sundays is an important social event in Apia.

The first European to come to Samoa was the Dutch captain Jacob Roggeveen, who sailed to the Manu'a Group in 1722. In 1768, the French explorer Antoine de Bougainville reached the islands and named them the *Îles des Navigateurs* in honor of the impressive seamanship of the native inhabitants.

Samoa is Built upon God...

"Samoa is built upon God," is what is written in Samoa's constitution. A trip through the towns and villages of the islands indeed reveals many churches. In 1830, John Williams of the London Missionary Society landed on Samoa with eight lay preachers, but the islanders only gradually got a taste for Christianity. Today, 50 percent of all Samoans belong to the Congregational Church, 22 percent are Catholic, 15 percent Methodist and 8 percent are Mormon. Religion is an important factor in Samoan life. Prayers are said every evening in most families. In some communities the inhabitants go to several church services on Sundays.

In the rigid social structure of the old days, the missionaries found fertile ground for planting their Christian beliefs. The new religion swiftly took root and is still evident today. Long before the advent of Europeans, Samoans lived in extended families (*aiga*) under the authority of a *matai*, who served as both head of the family and chieftain. Even today, this authority is unquestioned – in everything ranging from arbitration in family disputes to the distribution of land. Private ownership and private life is virtually unknown. Whoever earns money must support the entire family; sometimes even the entire village.

Younger Samoans are increasingly critical of this system. They are torn between the traditional social structure that allows no criticism and the glittering temptations of Western-style life. Often these seemingly irreconcilable conflicts

drive them to leave Samoa, or in some cases to take their own lives. The high rate of suicide among teens and young people in their twenties is one of the few secrets and represents the dark side of Samoa's sunny isles.

In the Interest of Great Powers

In the 19th century, England, the United States and Germany all had economic interests in Samoa. The islands were one of the most important trading centers in the Pacific. Godeffroy & Sohn, a Hamburg company, opened a branch office in Apia in 1855, their first step toward the vast holding that would later constitute their South Seas financial empire. In the 1870s many European traders, Germans in particular, bought land from the chieftains and started coconut plantations. When the Samoans showed themselves reluctant to work on the plantations, the Europeans brought in labor from China and Malaysia. Hundreds of Europeans then lived in Apia.

The second half of the 19th century was marked by civil war over control of the islands. The foreign powers supported the strife amongst rival chieftains. The German Trade and Plantation Company (*Deutsche Handels- und Plantagengesellschaft*, or DHPG) withdrew its support from the quarrelsome King Malietoa Laupepa and sought out a new ruler more to their taste. Reaction from Samoans, the British and Americans was immediate. In March 1889, as a hurricane approached the island, the harbor of Apia held three German, three American and one British war ship. Only the British ship managed to sail out to sea in time. The others sank in the harbor or were smashed against the reef. Sobered by the loss of men and ships, the three powers signed the Treaty of Berlin in June, 1889, agreeing to joint control of Samoa.

On November 7, 1899, another agreement called for the partition of the islands. Great Britain gave up its claim to Samoa and got the Solomon Islands and Tonga instead. East Samoa, with its shel-

German rule. In 1909, its leaders were deported to the Mariana Island of Saipan along with the members of their families. Despite these political traumas, however, Samoa's short German interlude was crowned with economic success. The colony's chief source of revenue was copra, followed by cacao.

In 1914, at the beginning of World War One, German Samoa fell to an expedition corps from New Zealand without a shot being fired. All assets of the German Trade and Plantation Company were confiscated. German government representatives were either deported or taken as prisoners of war. German civilians had the choice of leaving or staying in Samoa. Today, the telephone book shows many German names, indicating that many chose to remain.

In 1918, the *SS Talune* from Auckland arrived in Samoa via Fiji. The flu epidemic on board soon spread throughout the island killing 7000 to 8000 people before it abated. About 20 percent of the population died.

The New Zealand administration, in the eyes of many Samoans and resident Europeans, discredited itself through its interference in village affairs. It made itself especially unpopular by refusing to recognize the traditional titles of the Samoan chieftains. By the end of the 1920s, the *O le Mau* movement arose to fight for wider autonomy and eventually independence for Western Samoa.

Following the Japanese attack on Pearl Harbor, Hawaii, the United States, in 1942, suddenly stationed 12,000 soldiers on Samoa. This changed the Samoan way of life irreparably, but allowed many businessmen an opportunity to increase their income.

After the Second World War, the United Nations placed the islands under its protection. Preparations for eventual independence slowly began.

On December 31, 1961, the church bells of Western Samoa rang to announce

tered harbor of Pago Pago, went to the United States. Western Samoa fell under German colonial rule. The German flag was hoisted over the island on March 1, 1900. The border between the two colonial powers stood at 171° longitude west.

The Long Way To Independence

In many ways, the government led by Dr. Willhelm Solf (between 1900 and 1912) and Erich Schultz (1912-1914) set the example in the Pacific. Solf attempted to preserve the Samoan way of life and culture. The first public school, hospital and road were built.

But repression also existed: Samoans were obliged to plant a certain number of coconut palms per year and to pay a pro capita tax. They were not allowed to enter a hotel, nor to drink alcoholic beverages. By 1905, the *Mau a Pule* movement had formed in opposition to

Above: A traditional dance being performed at the Pacific Art Festival (Upolu).

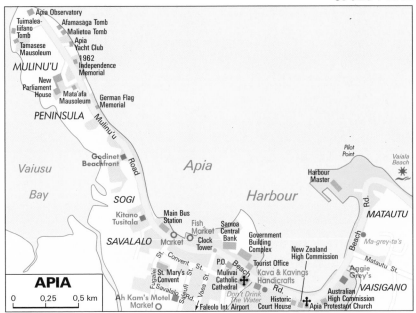

Apia Observatory
Tuimalea-liifano Tomb
Afamasaga Tomb
Malietoa Tomb
Tamasese Mausoleum
Apia Yacht Club
MULINU'U
1962 Independence Memorial
New Parliament House
Mata'afa Mausoleum
German Flag Memorial
PENINSULA
Mulinu'u
Vaiusu Bay
Godinet Beachfront
Road
Apia
Pilot Point
Vaiala Beach
Harbour Master
SOGI
Harbour
Kitano Tusitala
Main Bus Station
Fish Market
Samoa Central Bank
Government Building Complex
MATAUTU
Beach Rd.
SAVALALO
Market
Clock Tower
New Zealand High Commission
Ma-grey-ta's
Convent St.
P.O.
Tourist Office
Matautu St.
Fugalei St.
St. Mary's Convent
Savalalo Rd.
Saleufi St.
Vaea St.
Mulivai Catholic Cathedral
Kava & Kavings Handicrafts
Beach Rd.
Don't Drink The Water
Aggie Grey's
Ah Kam's Motel
Market
Faleolo Int. Airport
Historic Court House
Australian High Commission
Apia Protestant Church
VAISIGANO

APIA

0   0,25   0,5 km

independence. Samoa became the first Pacific Island group to gain independence.

The head of the parliamentary democracy is Malietoa Tanumafili II, a post he holds to the end of his life. At first only *matais* (chieftains or heads of families) could vote. In 1991, universal suffrage was granted. Since 1997, Western Samoa has been known simply as Samoa.

UPOLU

Apia – Charming Little Capital

Apia, the capital of Samoa, has about 35,000 inhabitants. The main street, which begins on Apia harbor, is Beach Road. On Beach Road, toward the city, is **Ma-grey-ta's** beer garden (short for "Mama Grey, thanks"), where a refreshing stop and a cool glass of local beer is called for. The beer garden, under German management, brews and serves its own Vailima beer. Next to the bridge over the Vaisigano River is a legendary hotel of the South Pacific, **Aggie Grey's Hotel**. Aggie Grey, the charming, lively daughter of a New Zealander father and Samoan mother opened a tavern in 1930 on this location. During World War Two it became the regular drinking hole of American GIs stations on Samoa. Later it turned into a favorite meeting place for Hollywood stars like Gary Cooper, Raymond Burr and Marlon Brando. Even the British royal family dropped in for drinks. Although the tiny tavern has now become a worldly hotel, its familiar atmosphere remains. Mondays the hotel holds a *fiafia*, a native festival with a buffet dinner and performances of local dances. A bit farther down the road is the wooden **Congregational Church**, which was badly damaged in the latest hurricanes. It has since been repaired. Some of the last remains of John Williams, the missionary who fell victim to cannibalism on Vanuatu in 1839, are buried in the churchyard.

Further west on Beach Road is the **Australian High Commission**, the **New**

Zealand High Commission (on the opposite side of the street an obelisk commemorates the unfortunate John Williams) and a fairly dilapidated building dating from the colonial era. On 'Ifi'Ifi Street, which turns away from the coast, is the police headquarters. Every day, Monday through Friday, at 7:45 a.m., an impressive spectacle occurs in front: the police corps, marching to the snappy rhythm of a brass band, goes from the new government building to the police station to raise the flag.

Souvenirs are plentiful at **Kava & Kavings**, a bit further west on Beach Road. The owner, Harry Paul, has gathered together an excellent – albeit expensive – selection of Samoan handicrafts and carvings. Paul is also an expert on Samoan culture and is the best person to

consult for related questions. Your purchase can be celebrated in the bar next door, which is appropriately named **Don't Drink the Water**. Down the road is the true symbol of Apia, the **Catholic Cathedral** (1905), with its two monumental white towers. Across from it is the **Tourist Bureau**.

Two buildings on the spit of land west of the harbor have left a questionable impression on Apia: the **Samoa Central Bank** (from Beach Road outward, left) and the **Government Building** (right). Not only do these constructions have obvious technical and aesthetic failings, but their method of financing became a political scandal. Originally, the buildings were meant as a gift from the People's Republic of China. In fact, as it turned out, the gift was really a loan. The Samoans good-naturedly figured that the project would yield well-paying and much-needed jobs, but were disappointed when Chinese workers arrived in Apia to do the construction work themselves. The punchline to this peculiar tale is that

Above: Law and order? The police force in Apia on its daily musical beat. Right: The clock tower in Apia keeps the memory of those who died in World War One alive.

the buildings were erected on a landfill and have already started sinking.

The **post office** across the street sells the colorful Samoan postage stamps that are so much in demand by collectors. The English-style **clock tower**, just off Vaea Street, is an unusual monument: it commemorates the Samoans who lost their lives in World War One. Shops and a small shopping center have grown up around it.

A bit further on, near the water, is the **fish market**, where freshly-caught seafood is sold every morning. In the old market hall, just 150 feet away (50 m), is the **flea market**. In addition to clothing, it sells beautiful hand-woven straw mats and sea shells. On the seaward side of the market a number of street food stalls have gathered.

The **fruit and vegetable market**, a potpourri of sound, color and exotic smells, is three blocks further toward the city center between Saleuefi and Fugalei streets. Many families from distant villages remain at the market until all of their wares are sold. For this reason the market is often open nights. During the day it is not unusual to see the sellers taking a nap among their merchandise, especially during the warmest hours at midday. Mothers brush insistent flies from their babies; and travel-weary farmers sit sipping their coffee or cocoa.

Mulinu'u Road follows the water and eventually comes to the **Mulinu'u Peninsula** and the **Kitano Tusitala Hotel**, the second-largest hotel in Samoa. The peninsula is also the site of both the old and new **Parliament** building (1972), the **federal court**, the **Apia Yacht Club**, the weather station in the **Apia Observatory**, built by the Germans in 1902, and a series of **chief's graves** and **monuments**. Two of the monuments commemorate German, English and American soldiers and civilians who died in the bay of Apia (see page 123) during the hurricane of 1889. Another monument honors the raising of the German flag on March 1, 1900. The **Independence Memorial** is a tribute to Samoa's independence.

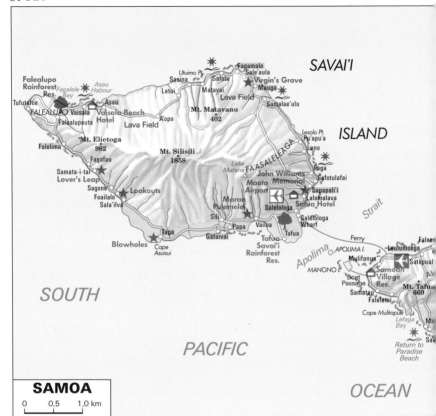

The **Papase'ea Sliding Rocks**, southwest of Apia, are a delight for children and adults alike. You can take either a bus or a taxi there (but be prepared to pay an entrance fee). A trail just over a mile long (2 km) leads to the smooth, natural water slides down which bathers hurtle into natural rock pools filled with refreshing water.

Upolu's Gorgeous West

It is not difficult to see Upolu in one day's drive, but several days should be set aside in order to get to know the island properly.

The stretch of road between Apia and the **Fale'olo International Airport**

leads from village to village and church to church. Some villages have two or three houses of worship, which is necessary to serve the multi-religious communities, not only on Sunday, but every day. Many houses have graves in front of them where children play or dogs nap in the afternoon sun.

Although cemeteries do exist on Samoa, beloved relatives and friends are often buried at home, following an ancient tradition, near their families and loved ones, instead of being tucked away in some distant parcel of land. The number of steps on a grave indicates the importance of the occupant. In the village of **Malie**, for example, you can see the high grave of Malietoa Moli, a "paramount

128

The coastal road continues to the westernmost point of Upolu, where the **Samoan Village Resort** is found. A few hundred yards further on there are boats to the island of **Manono** just beyond the coast. The island, with its 1500 inhabitants, is relatively heavily populated but has lost nothing of its beauty. It has no streets, no shops, no accommodations for tourists. A white sand beach and crystal-clear lagoon await day-trippers who've made their way to the island. The coastal road ends slightly more than 6 miles (10 km) southwest at Samai.

A road to the right at **Leulummoega** leads to the interior. After five miles (8 km) southward, Alafa'alava Road appears on the left and continues all the way back to Apia. The interior of Upolu is fertile and offers a glimpse of many tropical crops: bananas, taro, yams, manioc, cacao, coffee and breadfruit trees.

The road along the coast to the southwest continues through the district of **Lefaga**, with its immaculate white beaches. Snow-white sand bays alternate with the gray-black of solidified lava fields. The crystal-clear water is too tempting to resist, but caution should be taken. There are dangerous currents.

The most famous beach on the island is called **Return to Paradise Beach**. It is named after James Mitchener's eponymous novel that was made into a movie in 1951, starring Gary Cooper and Roberta Hayes. Unfortunately, this and the neighboring beaches – like quite a lot on Samoa! – were badly damaged in the most recent hurricanes.

Great swimming is to be found several miles away from the main road at **Manureva Beach** (a road sign points the way). As is often customary in the South Seas, villagers charge a small fee for swimming, and use of the picnic area and outhouse on the beach.

Back on the main road, driving east, the next village is **Lotofaga uta**, which is in a region containing some of the is-

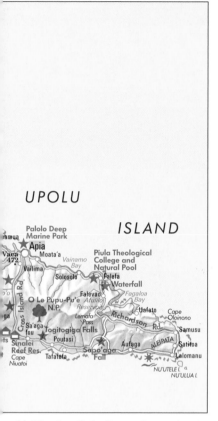

chief," who died after a short reign in 1860. In **Leulumoega** the very fine architecture of the **Congregational Church** merits attention.

The region from the airport to the ferry port at Mulifanua, from where ships leave for Savai'i, is filled with coconut plantations. The plantations, some dating back to German colonial rule, stretch out as far as the eye can see. The road continues southwest along the seashore through small neat villages and offers glimpses of the tiny islands of Manono and Apolima. **Apollima** is formed from a crater broken open on its northern side. A narrow passage leads into the only bay on the island, and further on to the island's village, where about 100 people live.

land's most beautiful scenery. Its inlet, protected by a split of land, resembles an idyllic lake.

A bit further to the east is **Coconut Beach Resort**, a relatively expensive American hotel situated on a rather average sand beach.

At the **Sinalei Reef Resort**, a small first-class resort, it is well worth your while to stop off for a refreshing cocktail, and to watch the sunset from here in grand romantic style.

The Cross Island Road

The Cross Island Road begins just beyond the village of **Maninoa** and meanders through the interior, eventually reaching the capital city Apia and cross-

ing the island, as its name indicates. The well-maintained road climbs steeply into the mountains, shaded on its left side by massive teak trees (*Tectona grandis*). The tall trees are easy to spot by their huge oval leaves. Their wood is very coveted by shipbuilders and wood carvers alike.

You will come across the **Tiavi** or *Papapapaitai* waterfall just before reaching the pass. It crashes down from a cliff more than 300 feet (100 m) high. A lookout platform near the road affords a good view and shelters visitors from the spray.

After the pass there is an unpaved road to the left that leads to **Lake Lanoto'o**, in the crater of the extinct volcano. It is a good one-hour hike from the end of the road to the lake. The lake is untouched and is full of goldfish, one of the rarely-visited attractions of Upolu. The main road leads back to Apia past the farm of the Grey family and the **grave of Aggie Grey**, which is daily decorated with fresh flowers. Visitors are welcome.

Above: Return to Paradise Beach, Upolu's most famous strip of real estate. Right: Robert Louis Stevenson's old residence in Vailima has been turned into a museum honoring the great author.

Oceania's only **Bahai Temple** is five miles (8 km) from Apia on the left side of the road. The Bahai religion, which was founded by Baha 'Ullah (1817-92) in Iran, honors gods of all religions and preaches friendship and peace among all of mankind. The dome of the temple soars more than 90 feet (30) skyward. The nine sides of the temple represent the nine predominant religions of the world. Adherents of all religions are invited to pray at the temple.

Soon afterwards, the peak of **Mt. Vaea**, the 1500-foot (470 m) "city mountain" of Apia, comes into view. A few hundred yards further on is a small company called **Island Styles** that specializes in the manufacture of silk-screened fabrics with wonderful traditional designs, as well as clothing made from them. It also sells fragrant coconut oil soap, fruit wine and liquor.

The suburb of **Vailima** is the capital's most well-to-do residential neighborhood. The road is bordered with beautifully-decorated villas.

The blue roof of the **Robert Louis Stevenson** house is hard to miss. The former home of the Scottish novelist and poet has been enlarged since his death and has since been taken over by the Mormons. Stevenson was already a famous literary personality when he moved to Vailima in 1890. The reason for this unusual displacement was that he hoped the warm humid tropical air would alleviate the symptoms of, if not cure, his tuberculosis.

The wooden colonial-style house was renovated in 1994 in honor of the 100th anniversary of Stevenson's death. It contains a small but interesting **museum**, and sells many of his works, including the best-selling *Treasure Island*, in paperback version in many languages. It is in his best-known book that one finds some of his most interesting and rough-cut language, borrowed from the tough seafarers of that era.

Stevenson earned the love of the Samoans for his understanding, friendliness and enthusiastic devotion to the preservation of Samoan culture. They called him *Tusitala*, which translates appropriately as "the story teller." Stevenson's last wish was to be buried at the summit of Mount Vaea, and it was scrupulously respected.

When his wife Fanny, who was called *Aolele* by the Samoans, died in 1914 in California, her ashes were returned to Samoa and buried next to her husband on the mountain.

Stevenson's grave lies at the end of a 45-minute trail through the lush rain forest. A poem that he wrote is engraved on his tombstone:

Under the wide and starry sky,
Dig my grave and let me lie.
Glad did I live and gladly die,
And I laid me down with a will.

This be the verse you grave for me:
Here he lies where he longed to be;
Home is the sailor, home from the sea,
And the hunter home from the hill.

Upolu's Watery East

The entrance to the **Palolo Deep Marine Reserve** is less than one mile (one km) from Aggie Grey's Hotel on the east side of the harbor peninsula, north of Vaiala Beach.

The way to the marine reserve is well signposted, so you should have no trouble finding it. This protected area along a reef just off the coast is perfect for snorkeling and swimming. Twice a year, when the Palolo reef worm rises to the surface of the water, natives come here with lanterns and nets on long poles to scoop up the "caviar of the South Seas." With any luck visitors might be offered an opportunity to try this local delicacy.

Right: Agricultural pursuits – a young man with his harvest of coconuts on Upolu.

The road proceeds along a stretch of dark and wild but extremely photogenic coast, and finally arrives at **Solosolo**, home of the **Piula Methodist Theological College**, the first Methodist Missionary School in Samoa.

Swimming is possible in a natural fresh-water pool that is found right on the coast (a fee is charged). Visitors in cars may park at the entrance to the church grounds. The road turns toward the island's interior, and a few hundred yards/meters later comes to a rather low but impressive waterfall.

After the town of **Falefa**, which translates as "four houses," the road turns south and begins its steep climb up to **Lemafa Pass**. Just before the pass there is a superb view of the coconut plantations that stretch out as far as the eye can see.

As you approach the top of the ridge, you can still see the extensive damage caused by the violent hurricanes *Ofa* and *Val*, which struck the island in 1991 and 1992 respectively. The once thick tropical rain forest has been thinned out, palm trees decapitated, and other trees now stripped of their branches stand like ghosts against the sky.

Beyond the pass the road first comes to the internationally-financed **Afulilo Reservoir**. The road then splits: the right fork travels south to **Sopo'aga Falls**; the falls are visible from a small botanical garden (nominal entrance fee).

The left fork that branches off behind the reservoir is Richardson Road, a well-improved road that will take you to **Samusu** and on to the beautiful coastal area of **Aleipata**. Picturesque villages and beaches dot the coast, and a host of small, jewel-like islands are sprinkled all along the offshore area.

The largest island, **Nu'utele**, is quite high and is uninhabited. People only go to Nu'utele in order to harvest coconuts and to fish.

In the 1970s, a group of American businessmen came up with the idea of

building a large hotel complex on the island, but the chieftain's advisory committee held a meeting on the proposal and ultimately turned the lucrative lease offer down.

Foreigners, by the way, are not permitted to purchase land on Samoa but may only lease it long term. Samoans are also restricted in the acreage they are allowed to possess. They are only authorized to buy land in the greater area of Apia and in some areas of former trading stations.

Along the coast small huts (beach *fales*) are available for rent at very reasonable prices. These traditional little huts are ideal for enjoying a sheltered picnic or for an overnight stay. The beaches at Aleipatas are considered by many to be among the most beautiful in Samoa and the calm sea is great for swimming.

The South Coast Road now follows the south coast – as the name indicates – toward the west. After some 19 miles (30 km) it reaches the **O Le Pupu-Pu'e Na-**tional Park, a protected area where, with a little bit of luck, you might be able to spot the elusive flying fox *(Pteropidae)*. Numerous marked trails for hiking lead through the park.

Togitogiga Falls, a 10-minute walk from the parking lot, is a perfect place for a rest stop or a cool swim. About 6 miles farther (10 km) the Cross Island Road (already described) turns off to the right and leads to Apia.

THE VOLCANIC ISLAND OF SAVAI'I

The volcanic island of Savai'i rises straight out of the water 12.5 miles (20 km) from Upolu. According the Samoan legend, Savai'i is the mythical *Hawaiki*, the original homeland of all Polynesian tribes.

A trip to Samoa would not be quite complete without a visit to Savai'i and its numerous sightseeing possibilities, including the famous and bizarre black lava fields. A ferry leaves from Mulifanua

(Upolu) two or three times a day to Salelolga, the business center of Savai'i. The trip across lasts about one hour. Please note that only a limited number of rental cars can be brought over from Upolu and public bus service is irregular, which means transportation could be a problem. A half- or full-day tour of the island is recommended. Many hotels on Savai'i offer tours and organize rental cars.

The road that circles the island is paved except for a stretch on the north coast between Sasina and Asau, where it turns into a bumpy gravel strip. Most of the unpaved side streets and paths into the interior come to a dead end. In the east, a road in poor condition runs for about 20 miles (35 km) into the island's interior, almost parallel to the coastal route, and connects the towns of Sapapali'i and Samalae'ulu.

Above: The magnificent blowholes of Taga, on Savai'i, pump spray up to a height of almost 260 feet (80 m).

The island excursion begins at **Salelologa Wharf**, where the ferry docks and circles the island in a counter-clockwise direction. The village of **Sapapali'i** is approximately 6 miles away (10 km). A monument across from the church is yet another commemoration of John Williams, the missionary who fell victim to cannibals in the Fiji Islands.

Fa'asaleleaga, a name given to the entire eastern region, is characterized by picturesque stretches of coastline offering superb surfing and snorkeling, white sand beaches and enchanting villages. It is an area in which the island's population is heavily concentrated. It is also where most of the hotels are found.

The next 12.5 miles (20 km) or so of road lead through a heavily forested area. Whoever has the time should not miss a chance to hike along one of the few paths that lead down to the coast and to discover some of the fantastic deserted black lava sand beaches.

A short way beyond the village of **Samalae'ulu** is the island's most recent lava field. **Mt. Matavanu**, a nearly 1300-foot (402 m) volcano, erupted in 1905 and again 1911, spewing out molten lava that burned a path almost ten miles long (15 km) to the coast. The molten rock cooled into bizarre formations and delicate lacy patterns. The gray-black strips of hardened lava contrast strikingly with the lush green of the tropical vegetation that surrounds them. In many places *nonu* (*Morinda citrifolia*), a traditional Polynesian medicinal plant, has reestablished itself on the slopes. Its fruit is edible but tasteless. Savai'i's volcano is still active, but there is no indication that another eruption will be occuring any time soon.

On the right side of the main road the village of **Mauga** grew up at the edge of a secondary crater. The road proceeds to the north coast through an area devastated by lava. Shortly before reaching **Sale'aula**, the road passes a monument known as the **Virgin's Grave** which, although in the path of the lava flow, was miraculously spared. The family to whom the grave belongs lives in the small valley beyond and charges a token fee for visiting the last resting place of the novice. A rough path leads to the Methodist church, less than 500 feet (150 m) further west, which was never fully completed. It too, escaped the devastating lava flow. The path to the church is not marked and it is advisable to find a local guide to lead the way.

The road follows the north coast to **Sasina**. The gravel roadbed from Sasina to Asu is a real challenge. A much wider lava field, stemming from an 18th-century eruption of **Mt. 'Elietoga** (3142 feet/982 m) appears beyond Letui. **Asau**, a pretty village on a beautiful bay, is a favorite anchorage for visiting yachts. The town offers shopping and overnight accommodations. The sawmill in the village processes tropical wood and has been the cause of protests by the ecologically-conscious villagers.

The **Falealupo** peninsula forms the northeastern tip of Savai'i, which is, according to ancient beliefs, the departure point for souls on their way to *Polotu*, the world of the dead. Today, it is the perfect spot to enjoy one of the region's spectacular sunsets. Unfortunately, tropical storms *Ofa* and *Val* also cut a swath of destruction through the **Fallelupo Rain Forest Reserve**. In order to quickly replant the forest, fast-growing eucalyptus trees were planted – a poor substitute for the tropical hardwoods that the storms destroyed.

Near the town of **Falelima** on the wild, rocky southwest coast, a natural stone arch bears witness to the primeval force of the surf. The white monument beside the road honors a shark that, according to local legend, promised to protect the village. The road continues for another 12 or so miles (ca. 19 km) skirting a steep cliff that drops dramatically to the sea, offering grandiose views over the South Pacific.

Fagafau, a tiny bay filled with foaming surf, stands at the foot of the cliff. It is known as **Lover's Leap**, named not after the tragic end of an unhappy couple, but rather, commemorating a desperate mother and her child who are believed to have jumped from the spot. They were not killed but, according to legend, swam away after turning into a sea turtle and a shark. Another bay on the island is also known by the same name.

Taga, a village on the southeast coast, lies another 48 miles (30 km) further on. A foot path leads off to the right through the wild scenic landscape of **Cape Asuisui** to the **Alofaaga Blowholes**. Water fountains shoot heavenward with immense force through the blowholes, lava pipe-like formations known as *pupa* in the Samoan language. The water pillars sometimes reach a height of nearly 260 feet (80 m). Near Gataivai, a river (with the largest volume of water on Samoa) empties into the sea in several waterfalls.

The **Letolo Plantation**, in the district of Palauli, is at the end of a road leading to the left. In the middle of the coconut plantation, before the village of Vailoa, are the archeological remains known as **Pulemelei Mound**. Many consider this to be the largest pre-European monument in Samoa. The road leading to the site is unfortunately only passable by four-wheel-drive vehicle. The earthworks structure surrounded by stones is built up in steps, and measures 160 by 192 feet (50 by 60 m) and is more than 30 feet (10 m) high. Nearby are graves and smaller platforms and ramparts. The meaning of the structures has not yet been explained. It is believed to be an ancient cultic center of some sort. Archeological excavations are underway, but there are no guided tours. Visitors have to ask permission at the farm house to be allowed onto the site.

At **Maota Airstrip**, about 3 miles (5 km) from the road to the ferry dock at Salelolga, a road to the right leads to the **Tafua Savai'i Rain Forest Reserve**. Given time before the ferry leaves, it makes a worthwhile side trip into nature. At any rate, passengers wishing to return to Upolu should be at the ferry dock in time because reservations are not always honored and cars are loaded on a strictly first-come first-served basis.

AMERICAN SAMOA

Following the partition of the Samoan Islands in 1900, East Samoa fell under the jurisdiction of the American Ministry of the Navy. Since 1951, it has been administered by the US department of the Interior. In the 1960s, large sums of money from the USA flowed into the island state to finance the building of schools, streets, houses, two tuna fish processing plants and a hospital. Illiteracy declined and an excellent system of health care developed. At the same time, the rise in the standard of living to closer

approximate that of the American mainland also caused the deterioration of native culture and customs.

American Samoa has developed into a shopping paradise for the relatively poorer Western Samoans who cross over to the US islands to shop. Clothing is especially cheap. The people of American Samoa are so dependent on their higher standard of living that when given a chance for reunification with Western Samoa in 1966, they voted to remain a territory of the United States. Today, some 45,000 inhabitants live in American Samoa. Agriculture and the fishing industry have progressed to the point that they now supply local needs and produce a surplus for export. Nonetheless, many native inhabitants are dependent upon money from expatriate relatives, or from US government financial help.

The hopes of building a solid tourist industry have not proved successful. The main island, Tutuila, is not serviced by international airlines, and the neighboring islands in independent Samoa, with their original character intact and a new airport in Faleolo, have proven much more attractive to tourists.

TUTUILA

Hamburgers in Paradise

The 53-square-mile (137 sq km) island is not only the largest of American Samoa's seven islands, it is also the most populated. But its most astounding statistic is that Tutuila has the greatest concentration of burger and fast-food restaurants in the entire South Pacific.

Pago Pago Harbor, the name that applies to the entire bay, is located on a deep inlet approximately in the middle of the long narrow main island, Tutuila. The city of **Pago Pago** lies at the innermost part of the bay. The island's largest sports facilities are built on landfill within its limits. It also marks the beginning of the

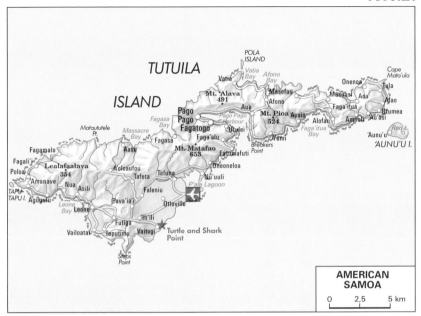

coastal road to Fagasa Bay. The two fish packing plants on the north side of the bay are primarily used to process tuna. (guided tours are possible).

A cable car travels from Utulei (daily from 8 a.m. to 4 p.m.) on the southern side of the bay to the 1571-foot (491 m) **Mt. 'Alava**. The top yields a spectacular panoramic view that assures that all is well in the island world.

The harbor dozes in its natural bay, but the idyllic view is an illusion: at ground level it is apparent that the water of the harbor is polluted; piles of garbage and the ever-present smell of fish detract from the dreams you may have entertained of a South Sea paradise.

The actual capital city of Tutuila is **Fagatogo**. The former **Governor's House**, built in colonial style in 1903, is across from the neo-Samoan Rainmaker Hotel on Goat Island Point. Only the garden of the Governor's House is open to visitors. The **Jean P. Hayden Museum**, a bit farther west on the main street, is devoted to the cultural history of old Samoa and to its handicrafts, of which the museum has a rich and varied collection. **Fono Maota**, the local parliament built in 1973, stands just next door. The building presents an exciting combination of modern and traditional elements in its architecture. The police station and post office, along with other important bits of officialdom, are in the center of Fagatogo. The **open market** and bus station are about 800 feet (250 m) to the west.

Sadie's Restaurant is a couple of hundred yards farther. Sadie Thompson's zest for life was immortalized by British writer Somerset Maugham, who spent some time in Pago Pago en route from Tahiti to Hawaii. The food at Sadie's is good, although somewhat expensive. The Sunday brunch is legendary.

The East of Tutuila

There is no road circling the island. Flights are possible to either the eastern or western parts. With a rental car, both tours are possible in one day.

East of Pago Pago a steep road to the north coast branches off at the village of **Aua** and leads to the villages of **Afono**, less then 2 miles away (3 km), and **Vatia**, just over 4 miles (7 km) away. Rainmaker Pass, at an altitude of 832 feet (260 m), offers a fantastic view of the bay of Pago Pago and the coastline.

Mt. Pioa, also called Rainmaker Mountain by the locals, is 1677 feet (524 m) high. Clouds are not exclusive to **Rainmaker Mountain**. Pago Pago enjoys ample rainfall and even the highest mountain on the island, the 2089-foot (653 m) **Mount Matafao**, is involved in the rain-making process.

The northwest coastal road ends in Vatia Bay. This unspoiled coastal region was set aside as the **National Park of American Samoa** and is an excellent place for hiking.

The idyllic village of **Vatia** has a beautiful beach. The land framing the west side of the bay reaches deep into the sea. At its tip is a tiny islet called Pola. The crenellated point of land is aptly named Cockscomb Point. Its steep cliffs harbor colonies of sea birds.

Traveling southeast from Pago Pago the street passes Breaker's Point and continues to Avaio. A beach named after its entry fee, **Two Dollar Beach**, is popular with locals as well as tourists.

A small excursion to the northeast coast is possible from **Faga'itua** (a left turn a short distance after the village). At the end of the road the pretty little village of **Masefau**, on the bay of the same name, is too tempting to pass up. **Sa'ile-le's** sandy beach is one of the most attractive beaches on the island. The main street follows the south coast to the east. A short distance farther, the tiny inhabited islet of **'Auunu'u**, with an area of just over one square mile (3 sq km) comes

Right: Fagatogo Bay before the backdrop of the Rainmaker Mountains, American Samoa.

into view. Ferry boats shuttle regularly to the small boat harbor in **'Au'asi'**. **'Auunu'** is volcanic in origin. Its crater is difficult to reach through a swampy area. Numerous eels crowd **Red Lake**, in its center.

The last part of the coastal road is especially beautiful. It ends about 2.5 miles (4 km) from 'Au'asi, in **Tula** near **Cape Mata'ula**, the easternmost point of the island.

The West of Tutuila

Leaving 'Utulei the road follows the coast to the southwest, then turns inland into a stretch bordered by shopping centers and restaurants, to **Nu'uuli** in the interior of the island.

The town marks the beginning of the largest level area of the island which also includes the industrial region of Tafuna and, further south, the **International Airport**. The rather unattractive settlement called **Ottoville**, southwest of the airport, has some delightful surprises in store for art lovers: the **Holy Family Church**, completed in 1994, was decorated by Samoan artists who designed the stained-glass windows and created the wood carvings. Especially interesting is the painting of the Holy Family on a Samoan beach by painter Duffy Sheredi. Not far from the church is a small but lovingly-designed **historical park**.

Lava Lava Golf Course, a bit farther west, welcomes paying guests. Behind the village of **'Ili'ili**, a road to the left leads to **Turtle & Shark Point**. According to a local legend, a shark and a turtle appear at the point, drawn by the sound of children singing. The village of **Vaitogi** and the picturesque coast are worth going out of your way to see.

Southwest from Nu'uuli, through the interior of the island, it is also possible to reach the north coast by taking a road from **Pava'ia'i**. A short way past the village of **A'oloaufou**, a road that is slip-

pery in parts leads to **Massacre Bay**. The name dates to 1787, when the French captain La Pérouse engaged in a bloody battle with the islanders. Twelve of his crew and 39 Samoans lost their lives in the encounter. The enchanting sandy beach near the tiny settlement of **Aasu** is perfect for whiling the hours away.

Back in Pava'ia'i, the road continues to **Futiga**. Less than a mile (1.5 km) behind the village, a secondary road turns off to the left to **Steps Point**. The main road continues to **Leone**, the former capital of Tutuila. A monument in front of the imposing **Congregational Church** honors missionary John Williams. Past **Leone Falls** the road arrives at the wild southwest coast where heavy waves make the beach a paradise for surfers. Beyond the village of **'Amanave**, the road is passable only by four-wheel-drive vehicles.

MANU'A ISLANDS

The Manu'a Archipelago, about 60 miles (100 km) east of Tutuila, is made up of the three small islands of **Ofu**, **Olosega** and **Ta'u**. Ofu and Ta'u have their own airports. Olosega is connected to Ofu by a bridge. The islands' landscapes are marked by high mountains. **Mount Lata**, on Ta'u, at over 3000 feet (995 m), is the highest point in American Samoa. Steep, almost perpendicular cliffs soar dramatically over 1000 feet (350 m) into the air.

The wide white sand beaches, including **South Ofu Beach**, are among the most beautiful in the South Pacific. Water sports enthusiasts will be delighted with the diving and swimming in the Manu'a islands.

The famous American anthropologist Margaret Mead lived for a time in **Luma** on Ta'u. In 1925, she began the field work that eventually made her famous. Her first book, *Coming of Age in Samoa*, documented the development of native children through adolescence and began a life-long career of examining the lives of women and children among primitive peoples.

139

SAMOA
Country code: 685. No area code.

Traveling In and Out
Via American Samoa, Australia, Hawaii, Los Angeles, Fiji, Tonga and New Zealand. The national airline is Polynesian Airlines (Tel: 21261, Fax: 20023). Bus service and a few taxis (about W$ 35) shuttle to Apia (22 miles/35 km). It is advisable to book space ahead of time. Taxis are by and large inexpensive in Samoa, but you should negotiate the fare ahead of time. The airport of Fagalii near Apia is the departure point for flights to Savai'i and Pago Pago. Airport tax W$ 20 on departure.

UPOLU – APIA REGION
Accommodation
A *fale* is a Samoan-style house, some are well furnished, others are very simple.
FIRST CLASS (US$ 80 and above): **Aggie Grey's Hotel**, Tel: 22880, Fax: 23626, on the east side of the harbor, 154 air-conditioned rooms/fales/ suites, restaurant, bar, pool; legendary, impeccably managed hotel, informal atmosphere. **Hotel Kitano Tusitala**, Tel: 21122, Fax: 23652, at the start of the Mulinu'u Peninsula, 94 air-conditioned rooms, restaurant, bar, pool, tennis.
MODERATE (US$ 30 to 80): **Hotel Teuila**, Vaitele St., Tel: 23959, Fax: 23000, 13 air-conditioned rooms, restaurant, bar. **Fehmarn Island Hotel**, Falealili St, Moto'otua, Tel: 23301, Fax: 22204, 54 air-conditioned rooms with a kitchen alcove, restaurant, bar, pool, tennis. **Le Godinet Beachfront Hotel**, Mulinu'u Peninsula, Tel: 25437, Fax: 25436, 10 air-conditioned rooms. **Pasefika Inn**, Tel: 20971, Fax: 23303, air-conditioned rooms, communal kitchen, diving center. **Vaiala Beach Cottages**, Vaiala, Tel: 22202, Fax: 22008, 6 bungalows with kitchen alcove. *BUDGET (under US$ 30):* **Ah Kam's Motel**, Savalalo Rd., Tel: 20782, Fax: 20886. **Betty Moors Accommodation**, Matautu St., Tel/Fax: 21085, 13 rooms, communal bath. **Olivia's Accommodation**, Matautu, Tel: 23465, Fax: 24092, 6 bungalows with kitchenette/dormitory, communal kitchen. **Seaside Inn**, Matautu, Tel: 22578, Fax: 22918, 15 rooms, restaurant, bar. **South Sea Star Hotel**, Alafua, near University of South Pacific, Tel/Fax: 21667. **Samoan Outrigger**, Vaiala Beach, Tel/Fax: 20042, rooms/dormitory, communal kitchen.

Restaurants / Nightlife
CHINESE: **Treasure Garden**, Fugalei St. *INTERNATIONAL:* **Sails**, Beach Rd., offers excellent fish dishes. **Le Godinet**, in the hotel by the same name on Mulinu'u Peninsula, Tel: 23690. *ITALIAN:* **Giordano's Pizzeria**, near the Fehmarn Hotel. *SAMOAN:* There are a number of restaurants, in the hotels as well, weekly Polynesian Buffet.

Don't Drink the Water and **Otto's Reef**, both located on Beach Rd., are good bars for a drink. **Ma-Grey-Ta's Beer Garden** on Beach Rd. In the east is somewhat more relaxed. The most popular disco is **Mt. Vaea Club**, Vaitele St.

UPOLU – OUTSIDE APIA
Accommodation
FIRST CLASS (US$ 80 and above): **Coconuts Beach Club**, south coast, 30-minute drive from Apia, Tel: 24849, Fax: 20071, 20 rooms/fales, restaurant, bar, pool, water sports (incl. diving). **Sinalei Reef Resort**, south coast, 30-minute drive from Apia, Tel: 22880, Fax: 23626, 20 villas, restaurant, bar, pool, tennis, 9-hole golf course. *MODERATE (US$ 30 to 80):* **Samoan Village Resort**, 6 miles (10 km) west of Faleolo International Airport, Tel: 20749, Fax: 45554, air-conditioned 2-room fales with kitchenette, restaurant, bar, pool. **Vava'u Beach fales**, south coast, Tel: 20954, Fax: 22680, fales with kitchenette. *BUDGET (under US$ 30):* **O Le Satapuala Beach Resort**, nearly a mile (1 km) from the airport, Tel: 42212, Fax: 42386, fales with kitchenette.

Aleipata district in particular has many beach fales, little open huts without furnishings costing about US $10 per person per night.

SAVAI'I
Accommodation
MODERATE (US$ 30 to 80): **Lagoto Beach fales**, Fagamalo, Tel: 21724, Fax: 20886, 4 bungalows with kitchen. **Safua Hotel**, Lalomalava, 4 miles (6 km) north of the ferry, Tel: 51271, Fax: 51272, 10 fales, meal times. **Savaiian Hotel**, Salelogoga, Tel: 51206, Fax: 51291, 6 air-conditioned rooms. **Savaiian Ocean View**, Salelologa, Tel/Fax: 51258. **Siufaga Beach Resort**, Faga, Tel: 53518, Fax: 53535, 6 fales with kitchenette. **Stevenson's at Manase**, 40-minute drive from the airport/ ferry embarkation on the north coast, Tel/Fax: 58219, 28 air-conditioned rooms, suites, villas, restaurant, bar, water sports. **Vaisala Beach Hotel**, Vaisala, Tel: 22027, Fax: 23396, 35 rooms. *BUDGET (under US$ 30):* **Taffy's Paradise Inn**, Salelologa, Tel: 51321, 7 rooms.

General Information
Excursions
All-day excursions to Aleipata on the southeast coast, to the southwestern coast and to the islands of Manono and Savai'i. Half-day excursions as well. Small agencies such as Samoa Sunshine Trips and Eco-Tour conduct special tours that are very attractive and interesting. **Annie's Tours**, Tel: 21550, Fax: 20886. **Eco-Tour Samoa**, Tel/Fax: 25993. **Island Hopper Vacations**, Tel: 26940, Fax: 26941. **Janes Tours & Travel**, Tel: 20218, Fax: 22680. **Moana Tours**, Lalomanu, Aleipata, Tel: 22790,

Fax: 22480. **Oceania Travel & Tours**, Tel: 24443, Fax: 22255. **Pacific International Limited**, Tel: 23 225, Fax: 21944. **Retzlaff's Tours**, Tel: 21724. **Safua Tourist Travel**, Savai'i, Tel: 24262. **Samoa Scenic Tours**, Tel: 26981, Fax: 26982. **Samoa Sunshine Trips**, Tel/Fax: 26189. **Schuster Tours**, Tel: 23014, Fax: 23636. **Vaisala Hotel Tours**, Savai'i, Tel: 58016, Fax: 58017.

Rental Cars / Airplane Charters

CARS: **Apia Rentals**, Tel: 24244, Fax: 26193. **Budget**, Tel: 20561, Fax: 22284. **Funaway Rentals**, Tel: 22045. **Mt. Vaea Rentals**, Tel: 20620, Fax: 20886. **Pavitt's U Drive**, Tel: 21766, Fax: 24667. **Samoa Sunshine Reisen**, Tel/Fax: 26189. *BICYCLES:* **Rainforest**, Tel: 25030. *MOTORCYCLES:* **Tulei's Bike Rental**, Tel: 24145. *HELICOPTERS:* **Pacific Helicopters Limited**, Tel: 20047.

Sports

GOLF: **Royal Samoa Country Club**, Tel: 20210. *DIVING:* **Samoa Marine**, Tel: 22721, Fax: 20087. **Pacific Quest**, Tel/Fax: 24728. **Sqvama Divers**, Tel: 24858, Fax: 23853. *RIDING:* **Moana Tours**, Lalomanu, Aleipata, Tel: 22790, Fax: 22480. *SQUASH:* **Apia Squash Courts**, Tel: 23780. **Heem's Squash Courts**, Tel: 20183. *SURFING:* **Samoa Surf Tours**, Tel: 26377. *TENNIS:* Public courts located in **Apia Park**.

Festivals / Events

There are a number of holidays including: **Independence Day** (June 1st-3rd) and the **Teuila Festival** (first week in September). The larger hotels and some of the bars offer a **Fiafia**, a Samoan dance performance, once a week. The Wednesday show in Aggie Grey's Hotel in Apia is the most famous.

Business Hours

Banks: Mon-Fri 9 a.m.- 3 p.m., Sat 9 a.m.-noon. **Offices**: Mon-Fri 8 a.m.-noon and 1 p.m.-4:30 p.m. **Shops**: Mon-Fri 8-12 p.m. and 1:30-5 p.m., Sat 8-12:30 p.m.. **Post**: Mon-Fri 8 a.m.-3 p.m.

Currency / Electricity

CURRENCY: Tala (W\$) and Sene. US \$1 is equal to about 2.50 W\$. *ELECTRICITY:* 240 V - 50 Hz.

Tourist Information

Samoa Visitors Bureau, G.P.O. Box 2272, Beach Rd., Apia, Tel: 20180, Fax: 20886.

AMERICAN SAMOA

Country code: 684. No area codes.

Traveling in and out

International flights to Hawaii (Hawaiian Airlines, Tel: 6991875, Fax: 6991282), to Samoa and Tonga (Samoa Air, Tel: 6999106, Fax: 6999751). Samoa Air also connects to the islands of Ofu and Ta'u in the Manu'a Group.
No airport taxes on departure.

TUTUILA
Accommodation

Only a few rather expensive accommodations are available. *MODERATE (US\$ 30 to 80):* **Apiolefaga Inn**, Masepa, Tel: 6999124, 27 rooms, bar, pool. **Barry's B&B**, Leone, Tel: 6995113, Fax: 6339111, 5 rooms, kitchen available, hot showers, garden, friendly, recommendable. **Motu o Fiafiaga Motel**, Pago Pago, Tel: 6337777, Fax: 6334767, 12 rooms (some are noisy), good restaurant. **Rainmaker Hotel**, Goat Island Point, Tel: 6334241, Fax: 6335959, 184 air-conditioned rooms, restaurant, bar, pool.

Restaurants

INTERNATIONAL: Food is good (expensive too) in **Sadie's Restaurant** west of the market in Fagatogo as well as in the restaurant of the Rainmaker Hotel. In Pago Pago: **Soli & Mark's Restaurant** and the **Pago Pago Bay Restaurant**. *ITALIAN:* **Paisano's Pizzeria Deli**, Matu'u, south of Fagatogo, terrific pizzas and sandwiches. *KOREAN:* **Seoul Restaurant**, Anua, opposite the fish factory. *SAMOAN:* **Taima's Palace**, near the airport.

MANU'A ISLANDS
Accommodation

MODERATE (US\$ 30 to 80): **Ta'u Motel**, Ta'u, Tel: 6773155, 9 rooms. **Vaoto Lodge**, Ofu, Tel: 6999628, 10 rooms. *BUDGET (under US\$ 30):* **Don & Ilaisa**, Olosega, Tel: 6335841, 6 rooms. **Fitiuta Lodge**, Ta'u, Tel: 6335841, 8 rooms.

General Information
Sports

GOLF: **Lava Lava Golf Course**, 18 holes. *DEEP-SEA FISHING:* **American Samoa Game Fishing Association**, Tel: 633459. *DIVING:* **Dive Samoa**, Tel: 6332183.

Excursions

Pleasure Tours & Travel, Tel: 6992675. **Royal Samoa Tours & Travel Agency**, Tel: 6335884, Fax: 6331311.

Car Rentals

Avis Travel, Tel: 6994408. **Pavitt's U Drive**, Tel: 6991456. **Royal Samoa Tours & Travel Agency**, Tel: 6335884, Fax: 6331311.

Business Hours

Banks: Mon-Fri 9 a.m.-4 p.m. **Offices**: Mon-Fri 9 a.m.-5 p.m., lunch breaks are taken! **Shops**: Mon-Fri 8 a.m.-noon and 1:30-4:30 p.m., Sat 8 a.m.-12:30 p.m. **Post Office**: Mon-Fri 8 a.m.-4 p.m., Sat 8:30 a.m.-noon.

Currency / Electricity

CURRENCY: US dollar (US\$).
ELECTRICITY: 110 V- 60 Hz.

Tourist Information

American Samoan Office of Tourism, P.O.Box 1147, Pago Pago, Tel: 6331091, Fax: 6331094.

TONGA

TONGATAPU

'EUA

HA'APAI ISLANDS

VAVA'U ISLANDS

Unlike the neighboring island nations, Tonga retained its sovereignty over the centuries. It also constitutes the last monarchy in the South Sea region, under the current king Taufa'ahau IV.

Tourism is one of Tonga's most important sources of income, which is not surprising given the country's highly varied and relatively untouched natural treasures. Moreover, even early visitors to the area were impressed by the extraordinary hospitality of the natives; Captain Cook went so far as to dub the islands the "Friendship Islands." Yet Tonga is not a big tourist destination in comparison to Fiji, Tahiti and other South Sea islands.

Here Today...

The kingdom of Tonga is composed of three larger island groups: Tongatapu in the south, Ha'apai in the middle of the larger island group, and Vava'u in the north. The small Niuas island group, with the volcanic islands Niuafo'ou, Niuatoputapu and Tafahi, adjoins the archipelago in the far north. Tonga extends from about 18° to 20° southern longitude and

173° to 176° western latitude. Its total area comprises more than 139,000 square miles (360,000 sq km), yet the actual land area within the archipelago amounts to a much more modest 266 square miles (690 sq km) divided among about 170 islands, of which 36 are inhabited.

The 99-square-mile (257 sq km) main island of Tongatapu is a flat, raised coral island. In contrast, the neighboring island of 'Eua has a mountainous appearance. Most of the Ha'apai Islands are coral islands with white (and usually secluded) beaches. Many of the western islands (e.g., Tofua) are volcanic in origin, and volcanic activity still occurs there now. The Vava'u Islands are high coral islands covered with thick tropical vegetation.

The Tonga Islands lie directly above a subduction zone. Earth's tectonic plates slide over one another at a rate of over 3 feet (1 m) per year. One result of this geological activity is that Tonga's eastern trench is over 34,449 feet (10,500 m) deep. Colossal rises and depressions occur in this region, a phenomenon which proved confusing for European captains in the days of the discovery voyages. A small island might disappear under the surface of the ocean and be consequently erased from the nautical charts – only to reappear several years later as a nearly 100-foot-high (30 m) island.

Preceding pages: Waiting patiently for the bus to come in Nuku'alofa. Left: Bringing home the bacon, Tongan style.

145

Climate

The trade winds assure a pleasant visit to Tonga. About 98 inches (2500 mm) of annual precipitation falls on the Vava'u Islands in the north, while the temperatures and humidity decrease somewhat as one moves southward – especially on the flatter islands. By way of example, Tongatapu receives about 59 inches (1500 mm) of precipitation annually.

The warmest and rainiest period is from December to March. Tornadoes often develop as well. Temperatures can reach up to 80-82° F (27-28° C) during the day, while seldom dropping below 68° F (20° C) at night. The cooler part of the year, from June to September, presents a favorable comparison with daytime temperatures of up to 71-73° F (22-23° C), and nighttime lows around 62° F (17° C). The best time for travel here is from April to October.

Above: The volcanic isle of Tofua. Right: The coat of arms of the kingdom of Tonga.

Godly Rulers

The first settlers presumably arrived here from neighboring island groups west of Tonga about 3500 years ago. These new residents fed themselves with sea creatures, turtles and birds; they also kept hens and pigs. Ceramic shards from the Lapita culture date to circa AD 200.

A tightly organized societal structure already existed in Tonga before the European era. The nation's ruler, the *Tu'i Tonga*, was a descendent of the gods. For many centuries the *Tu'i Tongas* represented the most expansive political power in western Polynesia. With enormous fleets of canoes (each canoe holding up to 200 warriors) they controlled not just nearby archipelagoes like Samoa and large parts of Fiji; their reign extended as far as the Solomon Islands.

According to tradition, the 24th Tu'i Tonga – who occupied the position of ultimate temporal and religious power – gave up the worldly power to his brother in 1470, thereby creating the royal line of

Tu'i Ha'atakalaua. A further royal line, the *Tu'i Kanokupolu*, arose through another division of rulership in about 1600; it gradually surpassed the other two and developed into the actual ruling family.

Dangerous Hospitality

The Dutch sea captains Schouten and Le Maire were the first Europeans to set eyes on the island of Niue (which at that time belonged to Tonga), in the year 1616. Captain Abel Tasman followed, arriving at Tongatapu in 1643, while Captain Cook first had contact with these islanders in 1773. Impressed by the orderly life on the islands, the willing obedience which the subjects here showed their king, and the friendly welcome bestowed upon strangers here, Cook waxed enthusiastic over the "Friendship Islands."

Ironically, this very hospitality was once employed for less than friendly ends. Magnificent feasts with martial exhibitions, dances, theater, music and extremely sumptuous meals were held for visitors. It is not hard to see how captain Cook and his men were nearly lured into an ambush at one of these luxurious feasts; the plan only failed when tactical problems arose.

Missionaries and Kings

The first ten missionaries of the London Missionary Society landed on Tonga in 1797. Three of them were eaten, six were able to flee, and one was "converted" by the islanders: he married three wives, was tattooed, and became an advisor to the king of Ha'apai. The Methodists, who arrived in 1826, were more successful in their preaching.

Starting in 1787, bloody civil wars shook Tonga; rival rulers struggled for decades, trying to get the upper hand. Taufa'ahau, the king of the Ha'apai Islands, was converted to Christianity in 1831, and became the ruler of the Vava'u

Islands. As King George Tupou I, he succeeded the *Tu'i Kanokupolu* on Tongatapu in 1845, becoming the powerful autocrat of a united Tonga. In 1862 he abolished serfdom, and in 1875 he gave the country its first constitution. King George Tupou I ruled until 1893.

The Tongan rulers avoided the colonial power plays of larger countries through a series of savvy diplomatic moves. The missionary Shirley Baker, who attained the rank of prime minister under King George Tupou I, concluded treaties of friendship with Germany (1876), England (1879) and the USA (1888). A protectorate treaty with Great Britain followed early in the 20th century, guaranteeing the continuance of local governmental autonomy; this occurred during the reign of the exceedingly popular Queen Salote Tupou III, who was a granddaughter of George Tupou I. This stately monarch – well over 6 feet tall (2 m) – was crowned in 1918 at the age of 18. When she died in 1965, the people of Tonga wore black for six months; male tourists were even re-

quired to don black ties during this period.

Under Salote Tupou III's son, King Taufa'ahau Tupou IV, the country achieved full sovereignty in 1970; Tonga has been an independent Commonwealth state since then. The king has three sons and a daughter, and will probably be succeeded by the crown prince Tupouto'a. Tonga's government is absolutist to this day. The king personally names the members of his cabinet and most of the members of parliament; all these tend to come from his inner family circle.

At the same time, a growing opposition is demanding greater democratic rights for the people.

To Every Citizen His Land, to Every Religion Its Church

The 36 inhabited islands are home to about 110,000 people of Polynesian de-

Above: Tongan women in their Sunday best.
Right: Vanilla, a top export commodity.

scent. Many of the younger generation have moved to the cities in an attempt to get away from village life with its partly traditional, partly Christian way of life. Especially Tongatapu appears to embody a desirable Western lifestyle. There are other reasons for the emigration from the Ha'apai islands: no more new land is available for agricultural use. Many of the islanders attempt to get a better education at one of the missionary schools, since there is a high unemployment rate here. At the same time, Tongatapu is essentially full to the brim with a population of 70,000.

All land belongs to the royal family; a part of it is administered by other noble families. Every citizen over the age of 16 is entitled to the use of an approximately 8-acre (3.3 ha) piece of viable land as well as of an additional plot near a city or village; this is a basic right in the constitution. Yet the king has long been incapable of accomplishing this praiseworthy social measure; the waiting list is much too long due to rapid population growth.

148

Seventy-five percent of Tonga's population is Methodist. The various smaller denominations, such as the Free Wesleyan Church of Tonga, the Free Church of Tonga and the Church of Tonga have arisen through church schisms, but not from actual differences in belief. About 15 percent of the population is Catholic, and 8 percent is Mormon.

Let the Gourd Times Roll

Officially speaking, Tonga receives between 40,000 and 50,000 visitors per year; of these, about 10,000 to 15,000 can be considered "real" tourists. The latter represent an important economic factor for the island kingdom, since its income from tourism is already almost twice as high as its total export income.

Coconut oil, vanilla and vegetables are among Tonga's agricultural export products; in addition, the sales of gourds to Japan have experienced an unexpected upswing since 1990. The government does indeed make a constant effort to woo foreign investors with temporary tax exemptions and other benefits. Yet national law also stipulates that land may not be owned by foreigners here, and 51 percent Tongan ownership of every business enterprise is also required. These limitations scare many potential investors away.

Foreign economic aids are very important to the country. Bank transfers from Tongan nationals who have immigrated to New Zealand, the USA or Australia represent an important additional source of income for many families here.

TONGATAPU

The Capital Nuku'alofa

Nuku'alofa means "residence of love." The kingdom's capitol city is located on the north coast of the island of **Tongatapu**, and numbers 30,000 inhabi-

tants. Its most prominent buildings are the large churches and the Victorian **Royal Palace** west of the Vuna Wharf. This handsome white palace with its red roof was in fact prepared in New Zealand; it was then assembled here in 1865-1867 by Edward Becker, the director of the Tongan branch of the Hamburg trading company Goddefroy & Sohn (the upper veranda was added in 1882). The royal family now lives in Kauvai (see page 152); the palace is not open to visitors.

The best way to photograph the palace is from the seaward gate in the west, on which the resplendent royal coat of arms is displayed. The three stars represent the country's three island groups; the three sisters stand for the three royal families, while the dove and the crown respectively symbolize peace and the monarchy. "God and Tonga are My Inheritance" is the royal motto.

Moving from this gate alongside the palace toward the center of the city on Vaha'akolo Road, one sees the **Vilai Army Barracks** (the headquarters of the

149

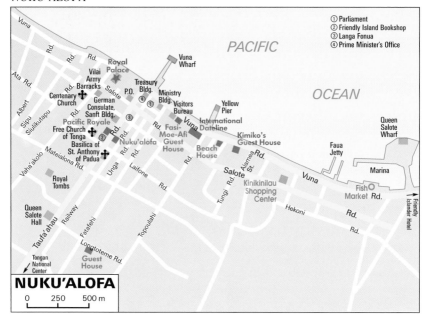

Key:
① Parliament
② Friendly Island Bookshop
③ Langa Fonua
④ Prime Minister's Office

NUKU'ALOFA

0   250   500 m

Tongan army) on the left. Shortly after this, the gigantic **Centenary Church** (1952) of the Wesleyan Church of Tonga, on the right, is not to be overlooked. This church has room for about 2000 worshipers, and the king and queen are frequent participants in its Sunday services.

If one leaves Vaha'akolo Road a short stretch further, turning left onto Laifone Road, one soon reaches the monumental church building of the **Free Church of Tonga**. Across from this are the **Royal Tombs**, the burial place of the royal family, which have been made inaccessible to visitors by a broad stretch of grass. The royal tombs have been located here since 1893.

The **Basilica of Saint Anthony of Padua** rises imposingly above the intersection of Laifone Road and Taufa'ahau Road. Completed in 1980, this church has attracted the attention of connois-

seurs thanks to its pagoda-like architecture. Astonishingly enough, both a library and a Japanese restaurant have been opened in the lower story of the building. The restaurant is so popular at lunchtime that you must sometimes wait a while for a table.

The main shopping street, Taufa'ahau Road, offers a pleasant constitutional back to the seaside. The **Langa Fonua**, a cooperative of village women, sells Tongan handicrafts at astonishingly low prices. Especially beautiful items include painted bast (*tapa*), woven articles, mats, baskets and bags. The **Friendly Island Bookshop**, also on the same street (in the Tungi Arcade), offers the latest publications about the South Seas and Tongan music and literature.

The **German Consulate** (*Deutsche Honorarkonsulate*) is somewhat hidden away in the back yard of the Sanft Building on Taufa'ahau Road, but is easily recognizable by the German eagle emblem. The philatelic bureau, with its collection of South Sea postage stamps, which are

Right: The Victorian Royal Palace, a colonial jewel located in Nuku'alofa.

coveted by collectors of stamps, is situated on the second floor of the **post office**; across from this building is the **Prime Minister's Office**.

Parliament House, built in 1894, is located one block further east on Railway Road; this building was also constructed in New Zealand and then transported to Tonga. Fruits and vegetables are hawked nearby at the colorful **Talamahu Market**.

Freshly caught fish and all kinds of sea animals are offered at the **Vuna Wharf**. This was formerly the main landing place for large ferries and cargo ships; these operations were moved to the new **Queen Salote Wharf**, east of the Faua Jetty, in 1966.

The **Treasury Building** stands opposite the Vuna Wharf, directly on the sea; this building formerly served as the municipal post office. The bus stop for long-distance buses is also located at the Vuna Wharf.

The government-owned **International Dateline Hotel** is located a bit further to the southeast. It is the best and most atmospheric hotel on Tongatapu.

Boats headed for the offshore islands and 'Eua depart from the **Faua Jetty**, which is a yachting and fishing harbor located about 1000 yards (1 km) from the city center.

Tongatapu: The "Holy Island of Tonga"

The most important sights on Tongatapu lie east of Nuku'alofa. Yet there is another absolute "must" for visitors in an outlying district to the south of the city: the **Tongan National Center**, which is reached via Taufa'ahau Road. Its culture center, built on the **Fanga'uta Lagoon** (across from the Vaiola hospital) in 1988, offers an informative exhibition about Tonga cultural history, as well as demonstrations of traditional handicrafts, such as wood carving, tapa production, weaving, etc.

The Tongan women possess considerable abilities in the area of handicrafts.

151

Among the most beautiful of their skill-fully-made woven articles are the baskets which they make from hibiscus bast and the ribs of coconut palm leaves, and often adorn with decorative patterns.

A selection of these high-quality objects is for sale in the little souvenir shop; it also has a good selection of typically Tongan carving work using wood, coral and bone. It's a good place, too, to enjoy some Tongan cuisine. Chicken in coconut milk and freshly caught fish are to be had, cooked in an earth oven and served on a banana leaf. To top it all off, the islands' natives perform their traditional dances in the adjacent amphitheater.

Yet another attraction are the exotic plants, such as vanilla (*vanilla planifolia*), kava (*piper methysticum*), the annatto tree (*bixa orellana*) and paper mulberry (*broussonetia papyrifera*), which are to be found in the well-tended gardens here.

The street continues circling the lagoon; almost 2 miles (3 km) to the south and inaccessible to the public, the residence of Crown Prince Tupouto'a is enthroned on a hillock. Across from it, two white tiger sculptures guard the home of Princess Pilolevu.

In **Vaini**, a street branches off to the left onto a peninsula, and continues on to the **Fanga Kakau Lagoon**. After 2.5 to 3 miles (4-5 km) comes the royal residence in **Kauvai** at the peninsula's eastern tip. Or head eastward on the main road (Hahake Road) from Vaini, the street to the airport and to Oholei Beach on the southeast coast forks off to the right near **Malapo**.

Three miles (5 km) further along Hahake Road, in the direction of Mu'a and Ha'amonga, the **Captain Cook Monument** reminds us of the famous seaman who landed here in 1777. The back of the monument bears an inscription commemorating the visit of the British Queen Elizabeth "11" (this number was unfortunately inscribed instead of "II"). The

TONGATAPU

mighty banyan tree under which Cook supposedly took repose has unfortunately been felled. A pleasant view of the mangrove-trimmed bay is to be had from Cook's landing place.

Shortly after this, comes **Mu'a**, which was the island kingdom's capital city until 1799 (there are regular bus connections from Nuku'alofa to Mu'a). A large fortress, which was probably built before 1650, formerly stretched over a considerable area here; today only some remnants can still be discerned. The fortress was built in the shape of a horseshoe so that the kingdom's war canoes could be more easily brought into the boathouses. The dozens of **'Otu Langi** – graves of the kings and their families – are much more

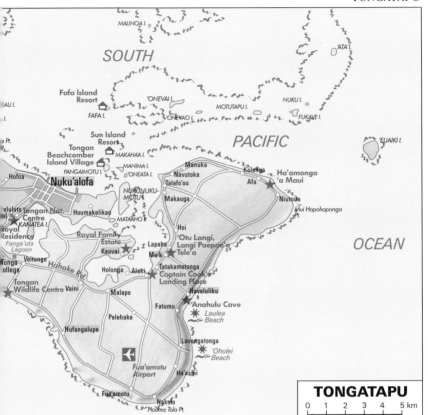

impressive; these take the form of graded platforms and are found all around Mu'a. The Catholic graveyard, containing one large coral-enclosed terraced tomb and two smaller tombs, is on the right at the town entrance. Many of the modern tombs are colorfully decorated, and they are often bordered with empty bottles, which provides protection from erosion of the coral sand, from the wind and from the free-ranging pigs that lounge about here.

The **Langi Paepae'o Tele'a**, a well-kept monumental grave dating back to the 15th century, lies somewhat hidden a bit further along the Hahake Road; a turnoff leaves the main road opposite the Free Wesleyan Church (as marked by a traffic sign). Blocks of coral rock were carefully joined together to border this tomb. Beside it towers the three-stepped, pyramid-shaped **Langi Namoala**. No particulars are known about the contents of the graves; archeological excavations are forbidden here in order to ensure the peaceful rest of the departed.

Just outside the village of **Afa** on the northeastern tip of the island, an imposing trilithon meets the eye: the nearly 17-foot (5m) tall **Ha'amonga 'a Maui** ("the burden of the god Maui"). Two standing stone blocks and a perpendicular block mounted on top of them together form a gate. The heaviest of the stones is estimated at 55 tons. The origin of this ancient Tongan masterpiece is the subject

153

of numerous legends. One of these reports that the gate was built by the 11th Tu'i Tonga, King Tu'itatui, between AD 1100 and 1200. Another maintains that the king erected the gate as an admonition for his two sons, in order to prevent them from quarreling; the monument was designed to bring home the idea that the two sons were tied together by familial bonds – as symbolized by the perpendicular stone. Yet another theory claims that the trilithon served as a gate to the formerly prominent city of Heketia. Perhaps this peculiar archway also aided astronomical calculations. As King Tupou IV argued in 1967, the chiseled lines on the upper stone block, as well as two later markings, point in the direction of the sun's rising and setting at the exact moment of the equinoxes (to get to the trilithon, you can board the public bus toward Niutoua.

Above: The trilithon of Ha'amonga 'a Maui – source of many legends. Right: Ginger when it blooms.

Strolling onward toward the ocean, you soon reach an upright ashlar; this large cut stone functioned as King Tu'itatui's throne **Maka Fakinanga**. According to legend, the king supervised the building of the stone gate, and perhaps also of the city of Heketa, from here. As several hill dwellings and a royal tomb attest, Heketa served as the seat of the Tu'i Tonga before this was moved to Lapaha. The lack of a safe anchoring place for canoes was certainly one of the reasons for the change of royal residence.

There are streets leading from Mu'a to the island's east coast (2 miles/3 km) to the village of **Haveluliku**, with the **'Anahulu Cave** on the coast (one possible route passes Captain Cook's landing place). The exploration of 'Anahulu Cave's multi-sectioned network of stalactite caverns should be left to experienced spelunkers. Diving schools offer scuba diving tours. The first cave is easily accessible and contains a fresh-water pool suitable for swimming; one must first ask permission from the family in Haveluliku, which is in charge of admission to the cave. **Laulea Beach** starts somewhat further south; a long, marvelous sand beach bordered with coral rocks extends from there to **'Oholei**. Bathing is a difficult proposition in the shallow water here, but a walk along the beach is always worthwhile.

The road proceeding southward from here is bad, but certainly still passable. Picturesque hamlets are to be seen along the way to the village of **Fua'amotu** near the international airport. From here, one can continue along the coast in a westerly direction to "the doves' haven," **Hufangalupe** – which is also reachable from the northern part of the island, where a turn-off from the Hahake Road near **Vaini** heads southward. A street sign points out a path several hundred yards in length, leading to a spectacular point of interest: the blowholes. Over a stretch of several miles, frothy fountains shoot skyward through hundreds of holes in the coral rock coastline – quite a singular natural occurance. A former cave in the cliffs here, whose roof has collapsed, looms up as an imposing rock tower – only the entrance has remained as a rock bridge. Two paths lead to the left away from the coral rock bridge. The first path is sometimes difficult to discern; from the end, one has a splendid view of the surf. The second and better-trodden path leads to a rather dangerous rock ledge.

The inviting **Tongan Wildlife Center** (Tel: 23561) is located a few miles from here. Founded in 1990 by workers from the German bird sanctuary in Walsrode, the Wildlife Center doesn't just exhibit rare and endangered bird species of the Pacific; the birds are also bred and then released in order to increase non-captive populations. Among these species are the nearly extinct malau and the colorful pompadoured parakeet.

Shortly after this, a sign pointing left indicates the way to the **Keleti Beach Resort**. This rather run-down facility is

nevertheless quite suitable for taking a little break and enjoying a lovely view of the coast. A change of ownership has taken place and renovation is planned; yet the hotel has unfortunately lost its pleasant bathing inlet as a consequence of the last large hurricane.

The village of **Houma** lies about 4 miles (7 km) further along the southwest coast. A sign points to the impressive blowholes (also called "arrows of the chief") a few hundred yards from the road. Starting from the parking area, the most photogenic of these "arrows" are to be found about 100 yards to the right. Well-preserved fossils of coral colonies are also discernible on the pointy and impassable coral stone here. The coast features several miles of these natural fountains; the surf presses water into caverns and small caves which are located at sea level, and the water pressure empties these cavities out again through outlets in the porous stone.

Six miles (10 km) further to the northwest, the island tapers off into a cape.

The village of **Kolovai**, located near the beginning of the cape, is famous for its colonies of flying foxes. During the day, hundreds of these rusty-brown animals hang in the beachside casuarina trees; at night they fly over the island in search of food. Being vegetarians, these flying mammals mainly eat mangos, papayas and bananas. The flying foxes are under the official protection of the royal family, and it is forbidden to hunt them. If the island's natives find them in the fields or plantations, however, the hapless animals tend to be caught and prepared for food, including such dishes as bat curry.

In back of the flying fox colony, a street heads left to the **Good Samaritan Inn** on the other side of the cape. This hotel offers simple *fales* for lodging, and the little restaurant is ideal for a midday break. One can't swim in the ocean, however, due to the shallow water.

Above: The brilliant underwater world of the Ha'atafu Beach Reserve. Right: Fishermen on the island of 'Atata.

Near the furthest northern point of the island, the splendid colors of the undersea world enchant visitors to the **Ha'atafu Beach Reserve**, a maritime wildlife sanctuary. At the island's northern extremity, the **Missionary Landing Monument** honors the Methodist pastors John Thomas and John Hutchinson.

Enchanting Isles off Nuku'alofa

The offshore islands to the north of Tongatapu are favorite day-trip destinations for the natives here. A pleasant boat ride to one of the smaller vacation islands is especially worthwhile on Sundays, when all of Nuku'alofa is "closed."

The trip to the **Royal Sunset Island Resort**, 6 miles (10 km) northwest of the capitol on the island of **'Atata**, only takes an hour; a small village is also located on this island. The **Fafa Island Resort** (4.5 miles/7 km and about a 45-minute boat ride to the north) is well-suited for a bathing holiday with a relaxed atmosphere. As for the island itself, one can comfort-

ably walk around its circumference in 20 minutes. On the island of **Pangaimotu**, only about 15 minutes from the harbor, the **Tongan Beachcomber Island Village** also awaits its guests. On **Makaha'a Island**, the Australian-run **Sun Island Resort** has a splendid sand beach.

THE ISLAND OF 'EUA

The 33-square mile (87 sq km) island of **'Eua**, located 12 miles (20 km) southwest of Tongatapu, is reachable by aircraft in about 10 minutes; a ferry takes 2 to 3 hours, depending on the sea. Despite being close to Tongatapu, 'Eua is seldom visited; life is quiet, and there is hardly any tourism. In short, this island presents an exceptional opportunity for getting to know unspoiled Tongan life. A day tour can be a fascinating experience; this can be booked in Tongatapu, for example, at Paea Tours (see *Guidepost*, page 162).

In contrast to the main island, 'Eua is mountainous (having an elevation of up to 1253 feet/382 m); it offers breathtaking cliffs, dolinas and limestone caves. Magnificent empty beaches invite sunbathing. Plantations and densely forested areas can be explored on foot or by pony. About 4500 people live on 'Eua.

The ferry moors at **'Ononua** on the west coast. About 1.5 miles (3 km) to the north, the alluring **'Ufilei Beach** awaits the visitor (caution should be exercised here due to the dangerous currents!). A road from **Houma** offers the prospect of a marvelous vantage point in the northern part of the island, as well as some nice scenery along the way. The road proceeds along a forest with young sandalwood trees. At the now completely dilapidated **Anokula Palace**, an incomparable vista unfolds over the glittering ocean from the 394-foot (120 m) cliffs. From here, a road runs southward over mountainous terrain to the **Forestry Reserve**, and continues on to the airstrip.

The dense, emerald-green tropical forest is full of aromatic cedars, fern trees and a world of fantastic avian life. From the main street by **Futu**, in the middle of

the island, an inland path leads through lush vegetation to the Forestry Reserve. At the **Topuva'e 'a Maui**, the highest elevated place on the island, the **Soldier's Grave** monument marks the grave of a New Zealand soldier from World War Two. The hike takes about 3 hours.

Further paths provide access to the eastern part of 'Eua and its dolinas and limestone caves; but you will need an experienced guide. The same applies to exploration of the gigantic yet hidden cavity called **Matalanga 'a Maui**, southeast of **Ha'atua**. Some skill is required to climb down into it. Legend says that Matalanga 'a Maui was created when the god Maui, in a rage over his mother, stabbed the earth with his staff and thrashed violently around with it.

The broad, secluded **Ha'aluma Beach** in the southwest is splendid (but there is also a strong current here). The impressive **Li'angahuo 'a Maui** is a natural

Above: One of the many little uninhabited islands in the Ha'apai group.

158

rock bridge at the southern point of the island. The enraged Maui was at work again here with his staff...

THE HA'APAI ISLANDS

The Ha'apai island group is located ca 93 miles (150 km) north of Tongatapu. Under half of the nearly 40 islands are inhabited, their total population amounts to 12,000. In terms of geology, this island group can be divided into the western volcanic islands on the one hand and the flat eastern coral islands with their unfrequented beaches on the other.

Tofua is the largest of the volcanic islands, having a surface area of 21 square miles (56 sq km). An interesting historical note is that the mutiny on the ship *Bounty* took place near this island in the year 1789. The island can be explored as part of a seaplane tour from Pangai (on the island of Lifuka). Tofua's flat-topped volcano is still active, and can be climbed in about 4 hours from the village of **Manaka** on the east coast. The caldera con-

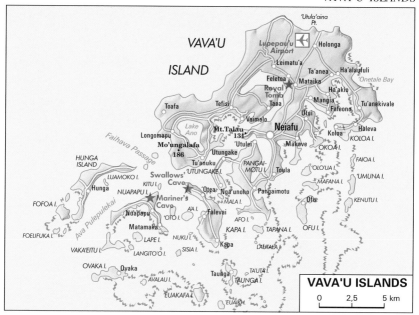

VAVA'U ISLAND

'Utula'oina Pt.
Lupepau'u Airport
Holonga
Leimatu'a
Ta'anea
Ha'alaufuli
'Onetale Bay
Feletoa
Mataika
Ha'akio
Royal Tomb
Tana
Mangia
Faleono
Tu'anekivale
Toafa
Tefisi
Vaimalo
'Utui
Longomapu
Lake Ano
Mt.Talau 131
Nejafu
Koloa
Holeva
Mo'ungalafa 186
'Utulei
Makave
KOLOA I.
HUNGA ISLAND
Utungake
OKOA I.
Tu'anuku
PANGAI-MOTU
'OLO'UA I.
FAIOA I.
LUAMOKO I.
'UTUNGAKE I.
Toula
'UMUNA I.
Swallows' Cave
KITU I.
'Otea
Nga'unoho
Pangaimotu
MAFANA I.
Hunga
NUAPAPU I.
Mariner's Cave
AA I.
MALA I.
Ofa
KENUTU I.
FOFOA I.
Nuapapu
'OTO I.
Falevai
AFO I.
FOELIFUKA I.
Matamaka
KAPA I.
TAPANA I.
OFU I.
VAKA'EITU I.
LAPE I.
NUKU I.
Kapa
LANGITO'O I.
SISIA I.
LAUTALA I.
OVAKA I.
Ovaka
TA'UTA I.
AVALAU I.
Taunga
TAUNGA I.
'EUAKAFA I.
'EUAIKI

VAVA'U ISLANDS

0   2,5   5 km

tains a crater lake suitable for swimming; fissures in the rock here act according to their geological role, emitting smoke and hissing and rumbling. The mountain offers a nice view of neighboring **Kao**, with its own volcano, which is over 3300 feet high (about 1000 meters).

Life on the islands of the Ha'apai archipelago proceeds in idyllic peace and tranquillity. The flat coral island of **Lifuka**, with its coconut palms and plantations, is the main island of the Ha'apai group. **Pangai** is the largest village on Lifuka, with 1500 inhabitants, yet it gives a rather sleepy impression.

There is no disturbing noise or traffic here; on the other hand, there is no nightlife to speak of either. Only a few tourists stray as far as Lifuka, although the Royal Tongan Airlines service the island's airport, **Koulo**, from Tongatapu or Vava'u daily (except for Sundays). Pangai has a bank, a post office, a police station, a hospital, a tourist office and accommodations. A tour of the island is best done by bicycle.

Taufa'ahau (the future King George Tupou I) was born on Lifuka. The first Tongan to be baptized, he underwent that ceremony here under the Methodists in 1831. His later influential advisor, the missionary Shirley Baker, is honored with a monument that stands north of Pangai.

The present king resides in the **King's Palace**, at the southern end of Pangai, while visiting the *Royal Agricultural Show* at the end of the month of September. Palasi Road traverses the island, leading to the east coast where idyllic, secluded sandy beaches await the visitor.

A pier provides a crossing to the neighboring island of **Foa** to the north. On weekdays, buses travel from Pangai to **Faleloa**, the northernmost village of this primarily agricultural island. Nearby is the **Sandy Beach Resort**. Twelve bungalows in splendid surroundings offer an undiluted South Seas vacation to those seeking peace and quiet.

The island of **Uoleva**, which lies across from the southern tip of Lifuka, is easily reachable on foot (wearing shoes!) at low

159

tide. Fantastic snorkeling areas are to be found here. A further island worth visiting is **'Uiha**, which contains the **Royal Tombs** as well as the ancient stone monument known as the **Makahokovalu Ruins**.

THE VAVA'U ISLANDS

The Vava'u island group, with its approximately 50 islands, is located 167 miles (270 km) north of Tongatapu. Only 13 of these raised coral islands (with an elevation of up to 984 feet/300 m) are inhabited, and their total population amounts to about 20,000.

Narrow, fjord-like passages separate these islands, which are among the most beautiful in all of Tonga. They have steep cliffs, white sand beaches, small and tranquil coves, dense tropical vegetation and turquoise lagoons. The abundance of safe natural anchorages make these islands a real sailing paradise.

Above: The harbor of Neiafu in the Vava'u group. Right: Swallow's Cave, Kapa Island.

The Spaniard Don Francisco Antonio Mourelle discovered the group in 1781. He named his anchorage "harbor of refuge," a name it still bears today (Puerto del Refugio). In 1787, the English Captain Edwards arrived here on the *HMS Pandora* on his search for the mutineers from the *Bounty*. Several years later, the tyrannical Finau 'Ulukalala II conquered the island; after the death of his successor, George Tupou I took over the island.

The Island of Vava'u

Neiafu, (pop. 5000) is the economic and cultural center of the nearly 35-square-mile (90 sq km) island of Vava'u. This town and its old wooden buildings radiate colonial charm. The inhabitants are friendly, and the relaxed atmosphere invites the visitor to stay awhile. There is one disadvantage for those who are interested in ancient Tongan culture: relics of the pre-European time, when Neiafu was an important place of worship, are no longer to be found here.

The old harbor of **Neiafu Tahi** has lost its importance since the arrival of the big European ships; the picturesque **Port of Refuge** is one of the best and safest harbors in the entire South Pacific. The **Catholic Church**, built on Palesi Hill (Paris Hill), dates back to the 1850s, whereas the **Free Wesleyan Church** (on Tui Road) with its handsome stained-glass windows was not consecrated until 1970. Several important figures of Tongan life rest in the small **cemetery** on the corner of Naufahu and Pou'ono Roads. These include the daughter of the 35th Tu'i Tonga, as well as two missionaries and a number of European settlers. Several lookout points offer fantastic views: 430-foot (131 m) **Mt. Talau**, west of Neiafu, the **Sia Ko Kafoa** (420 feet/128 m; easily reached from town), the **Toafa Lookout** in the west and the **'Utula'aina Point** (436 feet/133m) in the north.

South of the village of **Longomapu**, a path leads up the **Mo'ungalafa**, Vava'u's highest mountain at 610 feet (186 m). History buffs may want to visit the **grave** of King Finau 'Ulukalala II, located between **Feletoa** and **Mataika**. Peace and quiet can be found at the picturesque bays and beaches in the southeastern and eastern parts of the island; often, these can only be reached on foot or by boat.

Other Vava'u Islands

The islands of **Pangaimotu** and **'Utungake** to the south of Vava'u Island and the small islands **'Okoa** and **Koloa** to the east of it are connected to the main island by means of bridges or piers.

Snorkeling equipment and a bit of nerve are required to see the **Mariner's Cave** on the island of **Nuapapu** (southwest of Vava'u): the approximately 49-foot-high (15 m) cave can only be reached underwater.

Kapa Island lies southwest of Vava'u. But **Swallows' Cave** (at the cliffs at the north tip) is easier to explore than its Nuapapu counterpart. Many islands south of Vava'u have sand beaches and clear water, with good swimming and snorkeling.

161

TONGA ISLANDS
Country code: 676. No area code.
Travel In and Out
International flights to American Samoa, Australia (Sydney), Fiji, Hawaii, Los Angeles and New Zealand (Auckland). Airlines on Tonga: Air New Zealand, Tel: 21646, Fax: 21645. Air Pacific, Tel: 23423. Royal Tongan Airlines, Tel: 23414, Fax: 24056. Polynesian Airlines, Tel: 21565, Fax: 24225. Samoa Air, Tel: 70644, Fax: 70464. The distance from the international airport Fua'a motu (southeast) to Nuku'alofa is about 12 miles (20 km). Many hotels offer transfers, taxis are only available in limited supply. Airport tax on departure is T$ 15.

Traveling in Tonga
Royal Tongan Airlines serves 'Eua and Lifuka (Ha'apai Islands) daily except Sundays, and twice daily the Vava'u group. Ferries shuttle daily (except Sundays) to 'Eua, and twice weekly to Ha'apai and Vava'u.

Business Hours
Banks: Mon-Fri 9:30 a.m.-3:30 p.m., Sat 8 a.m.-11 p.m. **Shops**: Mon-Fri 8 a.m.-1 p.m. and 2-5 p.m., Sat till noon. **Post Office**: Mon-Fri 9 a.m.-4 p.m.

Currency / Electricity
CURRENCY: 100 Seniti equal one Pa'anga, also known as the Tonga dollar (T$). US$ 1 = T$ 1,15. *ELECTRICITY:* 240 V - 60 Hz.

TONGATAPU
Accommodation
MODERATE (T$ 50 to 100): **Friendly Islander Hotel**, 2 miles (3 km) east of Nuku'alofa, Vuna Rd, Tel: 23810, Fax: 24199, 12 rooms with kitchen, 14 air-conditioned bungalows, restaurant, pool, nightclub. **Ha'atafu Beach Motel**, west coast, 2 miles (3 km) north of Kolovai, Tel: 41088, Fax: 22970, 6 bungalows, communal showers, restaurant, water sports. **Hotel Nuku'alofa**, Nuku'alofa, Taufa'ahua Rd., Tel: 24244, Fax: 23154, 14 air-conditioned rooms, restaurant. **International Dateline Hotel**, Nuku'alofa, Vuna Rd, Tel: 23411, Fax: 23410, 76 air-conditioned rooms, restaurant, duty-free shop, pool; the best hotel on Tongatapu. **Kahana Lagoon Resort**, 3 miles (5 km) southeast of Nuku'alofa, Fanga'uta Lagoon, Tel: 21144, Fax: 22330, 12 bungalows, restaurant. **Pacific Royale Hotel**, Nuku'alofa, Taufa'ahau Rd., Tel: 23344, Fax: 23833, 60 air-conditioned rooms, restaurant, pool, nightclub. **Villa McKenzie**, Nuku'alofa, Vuna Rd., Tel/Fax: 24998, 4 rooms, meal times.
BUDGET (under T$ 50): Small guest houses in Nuku'alofa: **Angeles Guest House**, Wellington Rd., Tel: 23930, Fax: 22149, 12 rooms, communal kitchen and baths. **Beach House**, Vuna Rd, Tel: 21060, Fax: 22970, 8 rooms, communal bath. **Kimiko's Guest House**, Vuna Rd., Tel: 21049, 7 rooms,

communal bath. **Sela's Guest House**, Fatafehi Rd., Tel: 21430, 18 rooms some with shower. **Toni's Guest House**, Mateialona Rd., Tel: 21049, 6 rooms, communal shower.
Outside Nuku'alofa: **Good Samaritan Inn**, Kolovai, 11 miles (19 km) west of Nuku'alofa, Tel: 41022, Fax: 41095, beach, but very little swimming possibilities, 12 bungalows, some with kitchen, shower; restaurant. **Heilala Guest House**, Tofoa, 2 miles (3 km) south of Nuku'alofa, Tel/Fax: 23586, 5 rooms, 2 bungalows, communal kitchen and bath.

Island Resorts near Tongatapu
LUXURY (over T$ 100): **Royal Sunset Island Resort**, Atata, 6 miles (10 km) northwest of Nuku'alofa, Tel: 21254, Fax: 21254, 26 two-room bungalows, restaurant, pool, water sports. *MODERATE (T$ 50 to 100):* **Fafa Island Resort**, 4 miles (6 km) north of Nuku'alofa, Tel: 22800, Fax: 23592, 16 bungalows in traditional style, restaurant, water sports without motors; well-tended complex on its own island, good swimming. *SIMPLE (under T$ 50):* **Tongan Beachcomber Island Village**, Pangaimotu Island, over a mile (2 km) northeast of Nuku'alofa, Tel: 22588, Fax: 23759, 6 bungalows, dorm, restaurant, water sports. **Sun Island Resort**, on Makaha'a Island next to Pangaimotu, Tel: 23335, bungalows/dorm, restaurant, water sports.

Restaurants / Nightlife
CHINESE: **Fakalato**, Wellington Rd., in Nuku'alofa. **Hua Hua**, Vuna Rd., near the Dateline Hotel, Tel: 24619. *INTERNATIONAL:* **Seaview Restaurant**, 900 feet (300 m) west of the palace on Vuna Rd., Tel: 21799, is by far the city's best restaurant. **Davina's Restaurant**, in the harbor, Tel: 23385. **Wharfside Restaurant**, in the harbor, Tel: 24084. **The Waterfront**, in the harbor, Tel: 21254. *ITALIAN:* **Fasi-Moe-'Afi Italian Restaurant**, Vuna Rd., near the Dateline Hotel. **Little Italy**, Vuna Rd. *JAPANESE:* **Akiko's Restaurant**, beneath Saint Anthony. The few discos or nightclubs, in which life gets somewhat rowdy at times, either open only weekends or get going late at night: **'Ofa 'Atu Disco**, Friendly Islander Hotel. **Hotel Phoenix**, **Joe's**, Salote Rd. **Top Club**, over Joe's. In the **Ambassador Club**, near the Tongan National Center things are a little quieter, Wed-Sat live music. Ask the locals; they always know what is in.

Excursions / Rental Cars
The larger hotels have travel desks where bookings can be made. For agencies: **Paea Tours**, Tel: 21103, Fax: see Tourist Information. **Paradiseland**, Tel: 24939, Fax: 24977. **Pleasant Tongan Holidays**, Tel: 23 716. **Teta Tours**, Tel: 21688, Fax: 23238. Day-long excursions to offshore islands directly at the resorts. The best partner on 'Eua is Tevita of **Paea Tours**, Tel: 21103. Rides in a **glass-**

bottom boat and *Cocktail Cruises* with **Davina**, Tel: 23385. *CARS:* **Budget**, Tel: 23510, Fax: 24059. **Avis**, Tel: 23344, Fax: 23833. *BICYCLES:* **Niko's Bike Rentals** at the Dateline Hotel.

Water Sports / Boat Charters
DEEP-SEA FISHING: **Tongan Fishing & Sea Tours**, Tel: 237 77. **Royal Sunset Sport Fishing**, Tel: 21254. *SAIL BOAT CHARTERS:* **Royal Sunset Island Resort**, Tel/Fax: 21254. *DIVING:* **Royal Sunset Scuba Diving**, Tel/Fax: 21254. **Beluga Diving**, Tel: 23576.

Cultural Events
Heilalaa Festival (one week) as of July 4th (the king's birthday). **Royal Agricultural and Industrial Show** (end of Sept/beginning of Oct). **Music Festival** beginning of Dec, daily **dance performances** in the evening with dinner: Fafa Island Resort (Mon), Good Samaritan Inn (Fri), International Dateline Hotel (Wed, Sat). Guided tours and dance at the **Tongan National Center** Mon-Fri (2 p.m.).

Tourist Information
Tonga Visitors Bureau, Vuna Road, Nuku'alofa, Tel: 23022, Fax: 23520. Mon-Fri 8:30 a.m.-4:30 p.m., Sat 9 a.m.-1 p.m.

HA'APAI ISLANDS
Accommodation
LUXURY (over T$ 100): **Sandy Beach Resort**, Tel/Fax: 60600, northern end of Foa Island, 12 bungalows on a paradisiacal beach, restaurant, water sports without motors, airport transfer. *BUDGET (up to T$ 50):* **Fifita Guest House**, Lifuka Island, Pangai, Tel: 60175, Fax: 60200, rooms, communal shower, meals, cooking possibilities. **Fonongava-'inga Guest House**, Lifuka, Pangai, Tel: 60038, Fax: 60200, rooms, communal shower and kitchen, meal times. **Niu'akalo Beach Hotel**, Lifuka, over a mile (2 km) north of Pangai, Tel: 60028, Fax: 60200, 16 rooms in bungalows, with and without baths, restaurant, sand beach, water sports. **'Evaloni's Guest House**, Lifuka, Pangai, Tel: 60029, Fax: 60200, rooms, communal shower, meals.

Restaurants
The best food can be had at the **Sandy Beach Resort** on Foa. Reservations are necessary in all accommodations that also serve meals.

Water Sports / Excursions
Watersports Ha'apai, at the Niu'akalo Hotel, Lifuka, Tel/Fax: 60097. **Vava'u Amphibian Air** (see Vava'u) offers tours with hydroplanes from Pangai to the volcanic island of Tofua. Info also available at the Sandy Beach Resort and Royal Tongan Airways Office next to the post office in Pangai.

Rental Vehicles
CARS: Rental cars at **Fifita Guesthouse** in Pangai, Lifuka, Tel: 60175, Fax: 60200.

BICYCLES: Many of the accommodations on the island of Lifuka rent out bicycles.

Tourist Information / Festivals
Tonga Visitors' Bureau, Holopeka Road, Pangai, Lifuka, Tel: 60733.
Ha'apai-Festival, 1st week in June, 3 days.

VAVA'U ISLANDS
Accommodation
MODERATE (T$ 50 to 100): **Paradise International Hotel**, south of Neiafu, Tel: 70211, Fax: 70184, 45 air-conditioned rooms, restaurant, pool, water sports. **Tongan Beach Resort**, 'Utungake, 5.5 miles (9 km) southwest of Neiafu, Tel/Fax: 70380, 12 rooms, restaurant, water sports. *BUDGET (under T$ 50):* **Hamana Lake Guest House**, Tel: 70507, Fax: 70200, in western Neiafu, rooms with communal bath and kitchen. **Hill Top Guest House**, in the southeast of Neiafu with superb view, Tel: 70209, Fax: 70522, rooms, cooking opportunity, communal shower, bicycles, kayaks. **Popao Village Backpackers Resort**, Vaka'eitu Island, Tel/Fax: 70308, bungalows, communal shower. **Vava'u Guest House**, south of Neiafu opp. the Paradise International, Tel: 70300, rooms, communal shower.

Restaurants / Nightlife
INTERNATIONAL: **Ocean Breeze Restaurant**, Tel: 70582, at the Old Harbor southwest of Neiafu, reservations needed. Recommendable restaurants in the **Paradise Hotel**, **Vava'u Guest House** and **Tongan Beach Resort**. Dancing on weekends in the **Paradise Hotel**. Drinks and good vibes: **Vava'u Club** and **Nasaleti Club**; **Bounty Bar**, snacks, live music on Fridays, all three establishments in Neiafu.

Excursions
LAND: **Soanes Scenic Tours**, Tel: 70211, island tours. *AIR:* **Vava'u Amphibian Air**, P. Goldstern, Tel/Fax: 70193, by hydroplane from Neiafu to volcanic Tofua (Ha'apai). *WATER:* Boat excursions: **Hook Up Vava'u**, Tel: 70185. **Niva's Boot Tours**, Tel: 70380. **Soki Island Tours**, Tel: 70576.

Rental Vehicles / Water Sports
CARS: **Coral Cars**, Tel: 70565. **Liviela Taxi**, Tel: 70240. *BICYCLES:* **Chanel Scouts Bikes**, Tel: 70187. *BOAT CHARTERS:* **Sailing Safaris**, Tel: 70441, Fax: 70174. **Sunsail**, Tel: 70211. **The Moorings**, Tel: 70016. *WINDSURFING, SAILING, JET BOATING, KAYAKING:* **Vava'u Water Sports**, Peter Goldstern, Tel: 70193. *DIVING:* **Dolphin Pacific Diving**, Tel: 70507. *KAYAKING:* **Friendly Islands Kayak Company**, Tel: 70380.

Cultural Events
Vava'u-Festival (one week) beginning of May. **Dance performances** with eating: Tongan Beach Resort (Wed), various organizers (Sat).

COOK ISLANDS

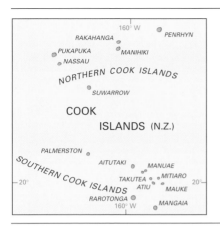

160° W
RAKAHANGA ◦   ◦ PENRHYN
◦ PUKAPUKA   ◦ MANIHIKI
◦ NASSAU

NORTHERN COOK ISLANDS

◦ SUWARROW

COOK

ISLANDS (N.Z.)

PALMERSTON ◦

SOUTHERN COOK ISLANDS
AITUTAKI ◦   ◦ MANUAE
TAKUTEA ◦ ◦ MITIARO
— 20°   ATIU ◦ ◦ MAUKE   20° —
RAROTONGA ◦
160° W   ◦ MANGAIA

RAROTONGA

AITUTAKI AND ATIU

OTHER COOK ISLANDS

Small – but Great – Islands

The enchanting Cook Islands were discovered during the Polynesian migration in the 7th and 8th centuries. In 1824, a Russian map maker reluctantly named them in honor of Captain James Cook. At the end of the 18th century the famous seafarer had discovered these, along with many other island groups, and had marked them on his chart of the Pacific Ocean. But Captain Cook had never mentioned the main island of Rarotonga, nor had he tried to contact the native population.

Cook, who otherwise took great pleasure in his discoveries, seems to have considered these small islands unimportant. Today, they are among the most exciting and attractive tourist destinations of the South Seas. The close contact to the island state of New Zealand has lead to a pleasant mixture of contrasting cultures on the Cook Islands. Natural charm, politeness and a delightful zest for life characterize the people. The islands are also known for their immaculate hotels, ex-cellent restaurants and professional tourist services.

The tiny Cook Islands are divided between the northern and southern archipelago. The total land area is approximately 90 square miles (237 sq km) and is composed of islands scattered over a huge area of 684,000 square miles (1.8 million sq km) of ocean.

The main island Rarotonga, geologically the youngest of the islands, features impressive mountains, some of which rise up to an altitude of over 2000 feet (653 meters), such as Te Manga. The rugged interior is marked by steep slopes overgrown with thick rain forest and the remains of a volcanic crater. Nearer to the coast the tropical vegetation evolves into a fertile belt which was settled by plantations. Rarotonga's exquisite lagoons teem with underwater life and its idyllic palm-bordered beaches have, to a great extent, been spared the ravages of mass tourism.

The tiny 8-square-mile (20 sq km) island, which consists of a tall volcanic section surrounded by coral atolls, is one of the country's favorite destinations for excursions thanks to its spectacular blue lagoon. The northern islands consist primarily of flat coral atolls, while the southern islands rise higher out of the water.

Preceding pages: Muri Lagoon is one of the great spots for swimming and surfing. Left: A lovely young dancer bedecked in Frangipani flowers.

167

Flying Foxes:
The Only Native Mammals

The Cook Islands also exhibit few animal and plant species. The limited surface area of the smaller islands restricts the choice and prevents the spread of flora and fauna.

The fertile soil of Rarotonga, however, supports a great many plant and animal species, particularly birds. Many of the rarer types have found welcome shelter from civilization and other predators in the impassable mountain ranges. The flycatcher has become especially rare and nests only on Rarotonga. All its mammals, with the exception of the flying fox (*Pteropidae*), along with most of its edible and decorative plants, were brought to the island either by the Polynesian settlers or aboard the great sailing ships of the European seafarers

Above: Dense tropical forest covers the slopes of Rarotonga's mountains.

Umbrellas and Sun Hats

All of the islands are in the path of the southeast trade winds which influence the comfortable tropical climate. The average year-round temperature in Avarua is 75° F (24° C). Even in the cooler period, from May to November, the mercury reaches 79° F (26° C) during the day and drops nights to 65° F (18° C). The annual rainfall on Rarotonga is 78 inches (2040 mm), on Pukapuka, in the north, it even reaches 107 inches (2800 mm). Rain showers occur throughout the year, but after a short while a rainbow spreads across the sky announcing the return of the tropical sun. Tropical storms (cyclones and hurricanes) may occur between December and March.

Cook Islands' Maori

The native population, called Cook Islands' Maori, are descendants of Polynesians who intermarried with Maoris from New Zealand. When the first Europeans landed, the entire population is estimated to have been around 20,000. European diseases decimated the population to 8000. In the 20th century, thanks to the increasing birth rate and decreasing death rate, the population has climbed. But after the Second World War, many islanders began systematically to emmigrate to New Zealand. Today, approximately 18,000 people live in the Cook Islands. Some 24,000 in all have emmigrated to New Zealand.

Most islanders are now bilingual. Children learn their native Polynesian language as well as English. Everyone born on the Cook Islands receives New Zealand citizenship automatically, making it easier to work and to receive social benefits from the prosperous island state.

Kiwis, the British and Scandals

The Cook Islands have no clear geographical or historical cultural identity. Who the first settlers were and when they arrived are questions still open to debate. It is generally believed that Polynesians from the Marquesa Islands settled in the southern archipelago about 1500 years ago, and that inhabitants of Samoa or Tonga settled in the north.

The first Europeans to have touched land in the Cook Islands were Álvaro de Mendaña in 1595 and Pedro Fernandez de Quiros in 1606. Both landed on the northern atolls. In 1779, James Cook discovered the islands of the southern archipelago. It was Fletcher Christian and the mutineers of the British ship *Bounty* who actually first reached Rarotonga in 1789.

Missionaries from the London Missionary Society arrived on Aitutaki in 1821. They soon managed to exert their control over all of the island's social and public life, even though political power officially still remained in the hands of the chieftains. As on other Pacific islands, a great number of Cook Islands'

inhabitants fell victim to European diseases. Many islands, especially those in the north, were victimized by "blackbirders," pacific slave traders, who captured countless islanders and shipped them as slave labor to South America.

In 1880, French Polynesia became a colony, causing Britain to fear the growing influence of France in the pacific. The *HMS Hyacinth* was dispatched to the Cook Islands. In 1888, Captain Bourke placed Rarotonga, and then the other small islands, under British protectorate. In 1901, the Cook Islands were administratively joined to the British colony of New Zealand.

In 1965 the country gained its independence. It has full autonomy over its domestic policies; its foreign policies are determined by New Zealand. The government consists of a prime minister and five other ministers who answer to an elected body. The inhabitants are citizens of New Zealand and thereby subjects of Great Britain. All political power is exercised in the name of the Queen of England.

Since independence, the political scene has become extremely volatile. One of the most exciting events was the election scandal involving Albert Henry, Cook Island's first prime minister. Having already been knighted by the Queen, Henry had several hundred of his sympathizers flown in from New Zealand for an "election vacation" at the expense of the state. He won the election but was relieved of his duties a short time later by the High Court. In 1980, one year before his death, the crown also withdrew his title and, with it, the coveted "Sir" before his name.

The planned Sheraton Hotel on Rarotonga also created a whirl of excitement. The super-dimensional complex was never completed and is now a construction ruin in the southern part of the island. In 1996, local authorities finally learned what had long been clear to ex-

the manufacture of textiles, shell jewelry and fruit juices for export to New Zealand. A small but successful pearl and mother-of-pearl industry sprang up on the northern islands of Penryhn and Manihiki. Despite all attempts, however, the deficit in the balance of payments continues to rise and imports exceed exports.

Today, tourism is the country's major industry, with 55,000 visitors annually, most of them from New Zealand and the United States, but also from Europe. The income generated by tourism can, however, only make up a small part of the budget deficit. Without the generous support of New Zealand the standard of living in the Cook Islands would decline.

RAROTONGA

The Capital Avarua

Avarua gives the impression of a sleepy South Sea town rather than a business center. Thanks to its location, it became the capital of the government and administration of the entire island group. The reef surrounding Rarotonga is broken in two places, allowing large ships to enter and requiring the construction of harbor facilities. Freighters and large yachts anchor less than one mile away (one km) at **Avatiu Harbor**, where the water is deep enough to accommodate them. Smaller fishing boats put in at **Avarua Harbor**.

The road into the city passes the colorful stands of **Punanga Nui Market**. In addition to fruits and vegetables, T-shirts, shell jewelry and *pareos* (a kind of sarong worn over the bathing suit) are sold.

A few hundred yards further on, **Ara Tapu**, the main street that follows the coast, begins. Old houses from colonial times stand next to newer buildings. Large businesses, restaurants, banks and travel agencies line the street. During

pert economists in New Zealand: foreign loans had been frozen; the country was bankrupt. Incompetence, ignorance and nepotism had led the Cook Islands to ruin. Drastic steps had to be taken to cut back the budget, especially in the public sector, in the hope of saving whatever could be saved.

Fruits of the Field, Pearls and Tourists

For a long time agriculture was the primary source of income for the population. Crops included taro, bananas, yams, vegetables, arrowroot, oranges and coconuts. Fishing was mainly for personal consumption. Following World War Two, Rarotonga began a moderate program of industrialization that included

Above: A bust of Albert Henry decorated with mussel-shell necklaces (at the Avarua cemetery). Right: Attending a mass at Christian Church on Cook Island is a special experience.

business hours the center is lively, but after 5 p.m. it is completely dead.

Romantic sunsets are best enjoyed at one of the waterside bars and restaurants, such as **Trader Jacks**, where tropical cocktails quench the thirst and the catch of the day teases the appetite.

The gas station and **police station**, where local drivers' licenses are issued, are also on Ara Tapu. Tourists must have a Cook Islands' drivers' license to be able to rent a car or motorbike. Anyone not in possession of a motorcycle license has to take the driving test, which includes a test drive around the block.

Tutakimoa Road turns off from Ara Tapu. Near **CITC**, the island's only department store, is the **Cook's Corner Arcade** and the public bus stop. The "Island Bus" makes a round-trip run every hour on the hour for the clockwise route, and on the half-hour for the counter-clockwise trip.

Further east on Ara Tapu is the **Tourist Information Office** and **Banana Court**, a popular dance club. At the traffic circle, Takuvaine Road on the right leads to the **Philatelic Bureau**, where a large selection of postage stamps and interesting coins are sold. A bit further on is the **Post Office**. At the end of the street is the **Rarotonga Brewery**, where the refreshing local beer, *Cook Islands Lager*, is brewed (tours are available every weekday at 2 p.m., Tel: 21083).

After the traffic circle the coastal road proceeds eastward. On the left side is an attractive restored building. It was erected in 1845 by the London Missionary Society as a schoolhouse, and now belongs to the **Beachcomber Gallery**, which sells beautifully presented local handicrafts and jewelry.

Makea Tinirau Road, which begins across the street from the gallery, is dominated by the imposing **Cook Island Christian Church** (completed in 1853). Sunday services, when islanders don their Sunday best and wide-brimmed straw hats come out of the closets, should not be missed. The cemetery provided the final resting place for missionaries and

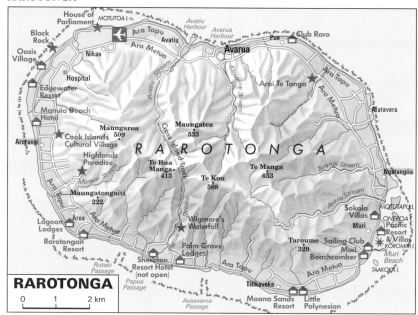

local celebrities. **Albert Henry**'s grave is near the entrance to the church and is marked by a statue of the former prime minister. It is decorated with a genuine seashell necklace and real glasses (for the most part) – presenting a source of apparently irresistible temptation for souvenir hunters.

The grave of American novelist **Robert Dean Frisbie** (*The Book of Pukapuka*) is more difficult to locate. He had lived in the South Seas for 24 years and died in 1948 on Rarotonga. His final resting place is to the right of the entrance in the farthest right-hand corner of the cemetery.

Across from the church is the beautifully-restored **Para O Tane Palace**. In the 19th century Makea Takau Ariki was regent of the Avarua area and resided in the palace. To this day her descendants

Right: Weary travelers from distant lands are given a dancing welcome at Rarotonga's airport.

still live there. The palace is not open to the public. The tiny **Museum and Library of the Cook Islands**, also on Makea Tinirau Road, is worth visiting, however. Its exhibits include a variety of traditional costumes, drums, canoes, shells and historical documents. A bit further south, the **Takamoa Theological College**, built in 1842 by the London Missionary Society, still supplies priests to the island's churches.

Victoria Road, nearly 900 feet (300 m) to the east, is site of the **National Cultural Center**, which opened its doors in 1992. It houses the **National Library**, the **National Museum** with another significant collection of South Pacific artifacts, and an auditorium which can seat up to 2000 spectators. It is here that the annual folklore competition takes place. The statues in front of the building were created by foreign artists.

The **Perfume Factory**, to the west on the old street called Ara Metua, is a good place to shop for locally-produced cosmetics and liquors.

Around Rarotonga

A bicycle or motor scooter are ideal vehicles for exploring Rarotonga, the 25-square-mile (67 sq km) main island, and meeting some of its 10,000 inhabitants. The paved **Ara Tapu** road follows the coast, circling the island (20 miles/32 km). Of course, the trip by car is faster and more comfortable.

There are no passable roads into the interior, but the **Ara Metua**, which runs parallel to the Ara Tapu but further inland, still follows its ancient course. The road was formerly surfaced with crushed coral and is said to have been built about 1000 years ago. The Ara Metua winds through areas that are intensively cultivated, past colorful gardens and plantations and presents the island from a very different perspective than the coastal road.

Taking the *Circle Island Tour* counter-clockwise (west of Avarua), a number of large trees soon come into view on the right-hand side of the road soon after leaving Avatiu harbor. Among them are Barringtonia (*Barringtonia asiatica*), a large tree bearing interestingly-shaped fruit and bizarre flowers looking like the bristles of shaving brushes. Formerly the pits were dried and ground to make a sort of fish poison, which was tied into a piece of cloth and lodged into a coral crevice beneath the surface of a calm lagoon. A little while later, the numbed fish would rise to the surface and could be gathered up with little effort. The poison did not affect human beings so the fish were safe to eat. Today, fishing with Barringtonia poison is forbidden throughout the South Pacific.

Just over one mile (2 km) to the west is **Rarotonga Airport**. Less than a mile (one km) further down the coast stands the **House of Parliament**. It is possible to go and watch parliament in session from a visitors' gallery (February-March and July-September, Tel: 26500). Soon the end of the landing strip, which reaches almost to the coastal road, comes in sight.

173

Just beyond the **Rarotonga Golf Club** (nine holes, open Monday through Friday for visitors) is a black lava stone formation called **Black Rock**. It is a mystical place where, prior to Christianity, Rarotongans believed the souls of the dead began their journey to the original home of the dead, *Avaiiki*. The sea at Black Rock is perfect for swimming. A few hundred yards farther along, a side road leads to the hospital. **Hospital Hill**, a five to ten minute walk from the parking lot, offers a spectacular view of Arorangi.

In former times the **Arorangi District** had a great deal of political power. It was where the missionaries founded their first village. Today, the west side has become the focus of the island's tourist industry and that is where many of the large hotels and a selection of smaller inns have opened for business.

Above and right: Activities and sights in the Cook Islands Cultural Village – a meal prepared in an earth oven and a carved wooden statue.

Sparkling white sand beaches stretch out in both directions, but swimming, especially at ebb tide, is barely possible owing to the sharp coral reefs.

The **Cook Islands Cultural Village**, an open air museum, which should not be missed, is less than 4.5 miles (7 km) from the center of Avaruas on the Ara Metua. Reconstructed Polynesian houses and guided tours give a lively impression of the culture of the Cook Islands. A traditional pit barbecue in an earth oven is accompanied by South Sea dances. The *Tamure*, once forbidden by the missionaries, is an erotically charged dance for couples. It is indeed quite difficult to leave such an exciting place and continue the tour.

Back on the coastal road, less than a mile away (one km) two old buildings merit closer inspection. The colonial style **Timomana Palace** (also known locally as **Au Maru**), a lovingly-restored wooden house was once the residence of the great chieftain Tinomana who was baptized by Papeiha, a Tahitian missionary who eventually became his son-in-law. **The Cook Island Christian Church** next door was built in 1849. Papeiha is buried in its cemetery. A monument marks his grave. Attending a mass here is also an interesting social experience.

Further south, a road forks off to the left and leads to the **Highland Paradise** (Tel: 20610), a botanical garden with an archeological complex that lies on a slight elevation.

The **Rarotongan Resort**, farther south, was renovated in 1997. It was the first large hotel on the island and catered well to its illustrious guests long before tourism became established in the area. At the resort, the coastal road nears the water and the view skims the trees of the steep mountains at the island's interior.

The construction ruin of the Sheraton Resort Hotel is for most Rarotongans the embodiment of national and international nepotism. The construction, begun in 1989, will almost certainly never be completed.

In **Titikaveka**, the southernmost community on the island, is a delightful coral block church built in 1841. **Muri**, the village less than 2 miles (3 km) away, embodies everyone's South Seas dream: a white sand beach, shimmering blue-green lagoon with a tiny coral atoll in the distance. Even Rarotongans appreciate the good swimming and wide selection of water sports, especially windsurfing, available at Muri Beach.

A street follows the southern bank of the **Avana Stream** inland. The path along its bank provides a good opportunity for an extended hiking tour into the interior. **Ngatangiia** (or **Avana**) **Harbor**, north of the estuary, now provides a good anchorage for yachts and fishing boats. According to legend, in ancient times it was the point of departure for large canoes which set sail in the 13th century on the 3000 mile (ca 5000 km) journey to New Zealand. Seven of the boats actually reached their destination. The intrepid

seafarers are honored to this day as the forefathers of New Zealand's Maori population.

From the Ara Metua, paths snaking along the **Turangi** stream allow for hikes into the island's interior region.

The coastal road travels further toward the north, past **Perfumes of Rarotonga**, where the intoxicating scents make perfect souvenirs. Shortly before Avarua, a street bears off to the left to the **Arai Te Tonga** complex. Before the arrival of the Europeans, this was the place where new chieftains were innaugurated. The places of worship are still regarded as sacred and cannot be entered.

A number of hiking trails of various degrees of difficulty lead into the interior. The *Cross Island Track*, for example, crosses through the middle of the island to the bizarre rock formations of **Te Rua Manga** (1321 feet/413 m), called "The Needle" by local inhabitants. Further inland is **Wigmore's Waterfall** and the **Papua Stream** to the southern coast, a hike of four to five hours. Brochures de-

175

scribe these hiking possibilities and list good guides. Exploring the valleys by car on the banks of the **Takuvaine** or **Avatiu Stream** is another attractive possibility.

AITUTAKI AND ATIU

Enchanting Aitutaki, an island with an area of barely 7.5 square miles (20 sq km), lies 140 miles (225 km) north of Rarotonga. The hilly main island with its nearly 400-foot-high (124 m) Maungapu hill is of volcanic origin. To the east, a string of uninhabited coral atolls *(motus)* stretch out like a pearl necklace, from a geological point of view an unusual combination of volcanic and coral formations.

The barrier reef surrounding the island bars larger ships from entering, thus pro-

Above and right: The beautiful sand beaches of Aitutaki – its marvelous lagoons and rich fishing grounds are attracting an increasing number of tourists.

tecting the shimmering emerald-green lagoon. The island is among the most beautiful places in the South Seas, which has earned it popularity among tourists. Prior to tourism, the only sources of income for its 2400 inhabitants were fishing, agriculture, especially planting copra and bananas, and financial aid from islanders living abroad.

Although Aitutaki has good overnight accommodations, most tourists visit it on organized day trips which they book ahead in their homelands because of limited space on aircraft servicing the island.

The first European to sight Aitutaki was Captain Bligh of the *Bounty* in 1789. The first missionaries arrived in 1821. American soldiers stationed on the island in World War Two built the airport and the Arutanga Wharf in the principal city of **Arutanga** on the west coast.

The coral islets sprinkled at the edge of the lagoon all boast much-sought fine white sand beaches and can be easily explored on a boat tour. On the inlet of **Aki-**

tua, southeast of the airstrip, there is luxury resort where the tropical paradise can be comfortably enjoyed.

The elevated coral atoll **Atiu** is just over 6 square miles (15 sq km) in area, 112 miles (180 km) from Rarotonga. Its main attractions are limestone caves, gentle bays, white sand beaches, red volcanic soil and bizarre coastal rock formations called *makatea*, which are formed from the coral limestone. About 1000 island inhabitants live in five villages on a 224-foot-high (70 m) volcanic plateau in the island's interior. They grow taro, pineapples and coffee. Individual travelers can enjoy Atiu and hike its numerous trails, explore caves, such as **Takitaki Cave**, with a guide, or simply laze in the sun on the beach.

Several beaches vie for attention: Taungaroro Beach, Orovaru Beach and Tunai Beach in the west, or Oneroa Beach and Takauroa Beach in the east. Bush beer, made of imported hops, malt, yeast and sugar is brewed on the island. The airstrip is in the north; **Taunganui Harbor** is in the northwest.

OTHER COOK ISLANDS

Mangaia (21 square miles/57 sq km, 112 miles/180 km southeast of Rarotonga) is surrounded by a 190-foot- high (60 m) wreath of *makatea*.

The interior is composed of swamps and fertile volcanic soil. Mangaia also has a number of interesting limestone caves to explore, e.g., **Teruarere Cave** in the north. The highest elevation on the island is 500 feet (169 m) above sea level. **Oneroa**, in the west, is the largest town. The famous ceremonial axes of Mangaia, with their tower-shaped shafts and fine carvings, are exhibited in museums all over the world.

Mitiaro (9 square miles/24 sq km; 143 miles/230 km northeast of Rarotonga) is an elevated coral island with *makateas*. It is swampy in parts. The settlements lie on the west coast. The airport is situated in the north.

Mauke is another elevated coral atoll (7 square miles/20 sq km), 150 miles/ 240 km northeast of Rarotonga. It has a number of caves, some filled with water. The 700 inhabitants live in the villages of **Areroa**, **Ngatiarua** and **Kimiangatau**. Most of the coastal areas are not recommended for swimming because of coral cliffs. The locals prefer the freshwater lake of **Vaitaongo Cave**, located 10 minutes from Ngatiarua and easy to find.

Palmerston Atoll and its 35 tiny islets stretch out 225 miles (360 km) west of Aitutaki. It was settled in the 1860s by the Englishman William Masters and his family. The **Northern Islands** are made up of six inhabited islands where life has gone on pretty much unchanged since the earliest days here: **Suwarrow**, **Nassau**, **Pukapuka**, **Rakahanga**, **Manihiki** and **Penryhn**. Regular flights serve Manihiki, Penryhn and Pukapuka. Accommodations are available on both Manihiki and Penryhn.

COOK ISLANDS

Country code: 682. No area code.

Travel In and Out

International connections: Fiji, Tahiti, Los Angeles and Auckland (New Zealand), with **Air New Zealand**, Tel: 26302, Fax: 23300.

Air Rarotonga flies nationally, Tel: 22888, Fax: 20979. Passes are available for accessing many islands. Air Rarotonga and local travel agents offer inexpensive packages. Airport tax on departure is NZ$ 20.

Currency

New Zealand dollar (NZ$). The Cook Island dollar is the same in value as the NZ$ and comes in coins and bills, but it is not easily reconverted abroad.

Business Hours

Banks: Mon-Fri 9 a.m.-3 p.m., at the airport on arrival and departure of international flights. **Shops:** Mon-Fri 8 a.m.-4 p.m., Sat morning. Smaller stores often have longer hours and open up awhile on Sun.

Electricity

240 V, 50 Hz – three-poled "English" plugs.

RAROTONGA

Accommodation

Accommodations must be substantiated when entering the country, or they will be arranged at the airport. Many hotels offer excursions, and rent cars, mopeds and bicycles. Just about all of them organize airport transfers.

LUXURY (beginning at NZ$ 150 per double): **Club Raro**, about a mile (2 km) east of Avarua, Tel: 22415, Fax: 24415, 39 rooms, restaurant, bar, pool, tennis. **Edgewater Resort**, northwest coast, Tel: 25435, Fax: 25475, 121 air-conditioned rooms, restaurant, bar, pool, tennis, water sports. **Lagoon Lodges**, Aroa, southwest coast, Tel: 22020, Fax: 22021, 18 units with kitchen, pool, tennis. **Little Polynesian**, south coast, Titikaveka, Tel: 24280, Fax: 21585, 9 units with kitchenette, pool. **Manuia Beach Hotel**, Arorangi, Tel: 22461, Fax: 22464, 20 bungalows, restaurant, bar, pool, water sports. **Moana Sands Hotel and Villas**, south coast, Titikaveka, Tel: 26189, Fax: 22189, 12 rooms, kitchenette, restaurant, bar, water sports. **Muri Beachcomber**, Muri Beach, southeast coast, Tel: 21022, Fax: 21323, 18 units with kitchen. **Oasis Village**, northwest coast, south of Black Rock, Tel: 22213, Fax: 28214, 4 air-conditioned bungalows, restaurant. **Palm Grove Lodges**, south coast, Tel: 20002, Fax: 21998, 13 units with kitchen, pool. **Raina Beach Aparts**, south coast, Titikaveka, Tel: 26189, Fax: 22189, 4 units with kitchen. **Rarotongan Sunset**, northwest coast, south of the Oasis Hotel, Tel: 28028, Fax: 28026, 20 units with kitchen, bar, pool. **Sokala Villas**, north of Muri, southeast coast, Tel: 29200, Fax: 21222, 7 bungalows with kitchenette, children 12 years and older welcome. **Pacific Resort**, Muri Beach, southeast coast, Tel: 20427, Fax: 21427, 53 bungalows, cooking opportunities, restaurants, bar, pool, water sports. **Rarotongan Resort Hotel**, southwest coast, Tel: 25800, Fax: 25799, 151 air-conditioned rooms some on the beach, restaurant, bar, pool, tennis, water sports. *MODERATE (from NZ$ 80 per double):* **Ati's Beach Bungalows**, west coast, south of Arorangi, Tel: 21546, Fax: 25546, 9 units with kitchen. **Central Motel**, Avarua, Tel: 25735, Fax: 25740, 14 rooms, pool. **Puaikura Reef Lodges**, southwest coast, Tel: 23537, Fax: 21537, 12 units with kitchen, pool. **Sunrise Beach Motel**, Ngatangiia, east coast, Tel: 20417, Fax: 22991, 8 units with kitchen, pool. **Wild Palms**, near the airport. Tel: 27610, Fax: 27611, 6 bungalows with kitchenette, pool. *BUDGET (up to NZ$ 80 per double):* **Arorangi Lodge**, Arorangi, west coast, Tel: 20796, 8 units with kitchen, on the waterfront. **Aremango Guesthouse**, south coast, Muri Beach, Tel: 24362, Fax: 24363, 10 rooms, communal kitchen, on the waterfront. **Are Renga**, west coast, Arorangi, Tel: 20050, Fax: 26174, 16 rooms with kitchen. **Ariana**, east of Avarua, Tel/Fax: 20521, 16 rooms with kitchen, pool, shop. **Aroko Bungalows**, south of Ngatangiia, Muri Beach, Tel: 29312, 4 units with kitchen, on the waterfront. **Backpackers International**, southwest coast, Tel/Fax: 21847, 7 rooms, communal bath and kitchen. **Kii Kii Motel**, east of Avarua, Tel: 21937, Fax: 22937, 24 units with kitchen, pool, on the waterfront. **Paradise Inn**, Avarua, near the Portofino Restaurant, Tel/Fax: 20544, 16 units with kitchen, on the waterfront. **Rutaki Lodge**, south coast, Tel/Fax: 21847, 7 rooms. **Tiare Village Motel**, west of Avarua, near the airport, Tel: 23460, Fax: 20969, 9 rooms. **Vara's Beach House**, southeast coast, Muri Beach, Tel: 23156, 5 rooms, on the waterfront.

Restaurants / Nightlife

INDIAN: **Priscilla's**, Avarua, Tel: 23530, international and Chinese as well. *INTERNATIONAL:* **Alberto's Steakhouse**, Avarua, Tel: 23596. **Blue Note Café**, Avarua, Tel: 23236, breakfast beginning at 7 a.m. **Kaena Restaurant and Bar**, near the Rarotongan Resort, southwest coast, Tel: 25433, open 6 p.m. **Liana's Restaurant**, south coast, on the beach, Tel: 26123, open 6 p.m., also Chinese. **Metua's Restaurant and Bar**, Avarua, Tel: 20850, breakfast as of 7:30 a.m. **PJ's Sports Café**, Arorangi, Tel: 20367, also Chinese. **Sails Restaurant and Bar**, Muri Beach, Tel: 27349. **The Flame Tree**, Muri Beach, Tel: 25123, exotic dishes, vegetarian as well, dinner begins at 6:30 p.m. **Trader Jacks**, Avarua, Tel: 26464. **Tumunu Bar and Restaurant**, Aorangi, Tel: 20501, vegetarian as well, as of 6 p.m. *ITALIAN:* **Portofino Restaurant**, Avarua, Tel: 26480, as of 6:30 p.m. **Spa-**

ghetti House, Arorangi near the Edgewater Resort, Tel: 25441, as of 5 p.m. *MEXICAN:* **Ronnies Bar and Restaurant**, Avarua, Tel: 20823, as of 11 a.m. Music and dancing is widespread on Fridays and Saturdays. Popular places in Avarua are: **Banana Court Bar**, **Metua's Café**, **Staircase**, **Hideaway Bar**, **Reefcomber Cabaret**, **Tere's Bar**, **TJ's** and **Trader Jack's**. The scene changes quickly. Ask locals what happens to be an in spot at the time of your sojourn.

Excursions / Transport / Rental Vehicles
Rarotonga is very suitable for touring about on your own. Guided excursions on Rarotonga and to other islands are offered by: **Hugh Henry & Associates**, Tel: 25320, Fax: 25320. **Island Hopper Vacations**, Tel: 22026, Fax: 22036. **Stars Travel**, Tel: 23669, Fax: 21569. For hikes into the interior of the island: **Pa's Mountain Walk**, Tel: 21079. **Reef Sub**, Tel: 22832, owns a semi-submersible, a boat that allows you to see underwater. Boat tours: **Captain Tama's Coral Cruizes**, Tel/Fax: 23810. The public **Cook's Island Bus** circumnavigates Rarotonga from Monday to Friday from 7 a.m. until 4:30 p.m., Sat until 1 p.m.. A bus stops in either direction about every half hour. Night buses also operate. If you want to rent a motorized vehicle, you will have to get a *Cook Island Driver's License*. It is available at the police station. You will need your own national license and NZ$ 10: **Avis**, Tel: 22833, Fax: 21702. **Budget**, Tel: 20895, Fax: 20888. **Polynesian Bike Hire**, Tel: 20895, Fax: 20880. **Rarotonga Rentals**, Tel: 22326, Fax: 22739.

Sports
FISHING: **Fisher's Fishing & Sightseeing Tours**, Tel: 23356. **Pacific Marine Charters**, Tel: 21237. **Seafari Charters Ltd.**, Tel: 20328.
GOLF: **Rarotonga Golf Club**, Tel: 27360.
RIDING: **Aroa Pony Trek**, Tel: 21415.
SAILING: **Aquasports**,Tel: 27350, Fax: 20932. **Captain Tama's Coral Cruizes**, Tel/Fax: 23810.
DIVING: **Cook Island Divers**, Tel: 22483, Fax: 22484. **Dive Rarotonga**, Tel: 21873, Fax: 29955. **Pacific Divers**, Tel: 22450. *TENNIS:* **Edgewater Resort**, Tel: 25435, Fax: 25475. **Rarotongan Resort Hotel**, Tel: 25800, Fax: 25799.

Cultural Events / Museum
Island Nights is held in several hotels. It involves dance performances and a Polynesian-European buffet. Cultural events held throughout the year include: **Cultural Festival Week**, during the 2nd or 3rd week in February. **Dancer of the Year**, 2nd or 3rd week in April. **Constitution Celebrations**, 10 days, beginning on the last Friday in August. **Tiare Week**, 3rd week in November. **Museum & Library of the Cook Islands**, Makea Tinirau Rd., Avarua, daily 9 a.m.-1 p.m., Tue 4-8 p.m., closed on Sun. **National Culture Center** with museum, Victoria Rd., Avarua, Mon-Fri 9 a.m.-3 p.m.; and library, Tue, Thu, Fri 9 a.m.-4 p.m., Mon, Wed 9 a.m.-8 p.m.. **Cultural Village**, Tel: 21314, guided tours Mon-Fri at 10 a.m.

Tourist Information
Cook Islands Tourist Authority, PO Box 14, on the main street, Avarua, Tel: 29435, Fax: 21435, open 8 a.m.-4 p.m..

AITUTAKI
Accommodation
LUXURY: **Aitutaki Lagoon Resort**, Akitua Island southeast of the airstrip, Tel: 31203, Fax: 31202, 25 air-conditioned bungalows with bath, restaurant, bar, pool, no cooking, pretty beach. **Aitutaki Lodges**, southeast coast, Tautu Jetty, isolated, Tel: 31334, Fax: 31333, 6 bungalows with kitchen, dining room, bar. The beach is nothing special.
MODERATE: **Maina Sunset**, south of Arutanga, Tel: 31511, Fax: 31611, 12 units, restaurant, shop, pool, tours. **Rapae Hotel**, north of Amuri, near the airstrip, Tel: 31320, Fax: 31321, 18 rooms, restaurant, bar, disco on Fridays, beach barbecue on Sundays. **Rino's Beach Apartments**, Ureia, Tel: 23369, Fax: 21569, 4 units with kitchen.
BUDGET: **Josie's Lodge**, Ureia, Tel: 21569, 6 rooms, communal installations. **Paradise Cove**, Anaunga, near the airstrip, Tel: 31219, Fax: 31456, 5 rooms, 6 Polynesian huts, communal kitchen, nice beach. **Tiare Maori Guesthouse**, Ureia, Tel: 31119, 7 rooms, cozy, good food. **Tom's Beach Cottage**, between Ureia and Amuri, Tel: 31051, Fax: 31409, rooms, communal installations, 2 bungalows with kitchen.

OTHER ISLANDS
Accommodation
All accommodations offer cooking opportunities and other self-provisioning possibilities (book in advance!). Meals are sometimes included in the price.
ATIU: *MODERATE:* **Atiu Motel**, in the south, Tel: 33777, Fax: 33775, 5 units with shower, kitchenette, tennis. **MANGAIA:** *MODERATE:* **Babe's Place**, Tel: 34092, Fax: 34078, 6 rooms, in part with shower and toilet, bar, weekend dances.
BUDGET: Some families rent out rooms or houses, among them: **Teinangaro**, Tel: 34168. **Atariki**, Tel: 34206. **Teaio**, Tel: 34164. **Papatua**, Tel: 34164. **MANIHIKI:** *BUDGET:* **Danny's Lagoon Lodge**, Tel: 23669 (Stars Travel), Fax: 21569, 2 rooms, communal installations. **MAUKE:** *BUDGET:* **Cove Lodge**, Tel: 35664, Fax: 35094, 3 units. **Tiare Holiday Cottages**, Tel: 35083, Fax: 35683, 5 units, communal installations. **MITIARO:** *BUDGET:* **Mitiaro Guesthouse**, Tel: 361 07, Fax: 36683, 2 units. **PENRYHN:** *MODERATE:* **Tarakore**, Tel: 42683, Fax: 42015, 3 units.

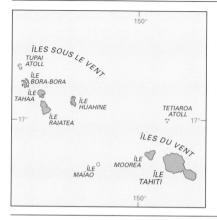

FRENCH POLYNESIA

TAHITI
MOOREA
HUAHINE
RAIATEA AND TAHAA
BORA BORA
TUAMOTU ISLANDS
MARQUESAS ISLANDS

More than any other island in the South Pacific, it's probably Tahiti that best conjures the image of a South Seas paradise. Since 1768, when the French count Louis-Antoine de Bougainville landed here, until this day, endless gushing travel reports, enticing films and millions of tourist brochures have kept this appealing picture alive. The reality must be looked at more objectively, of course, but one thing is certain: Tahiti and its islands do make vacation dreams come true. Crystal-clear waters ranging through all shades of blue, luxuriant vegetation in deep green valleys, rain forests and cascading waterfalls, coconut palms swaying in the breeze on a backdrop of permanently blue sky, pearly white, solitary and pristine sand beaches, all make for unadulterated South Seas romance – a veritable tract of Eden on earth. As is said locally, *maeva e manava*: welcome!

Bigger than France

French Polynesia measures over 1.5 million square miles (4 million sq km)

when including its territorial waters, which, if pasted onto Europe, would mean an area from southern Sweden to Sicily and from eastern Spain to the Black Sea.

This gigantic overseas territory belonging to France is divided up into five island groups with many special natural features. The **Society Islands**, thus named by Captain James Cook, are the most famous and most-visited. They include Tahiti, Moorea, Huahine, Raiatea, Bora Bora and Maupiti. Densely-forested mountains, the remains of ancient volcanoes, soar almost vertically into the sky in many places. Orohena, on Tahiti, is the highest mountain in the nation at 7171 feet (2241 m).

The **Tuamotu Islands**, on the other hand, consist of 76 coral islands and atolls spread out over a huge area and rising barely 10 feet (3 m) above sea level. They are covered with coconut palms. Rangiroa and Manihi are of most interest to the tourist. Nature in the interior of the lagoons is at its most beautiful, with coral gardens, colorful anemones, pearl oysters, starfish and schools of fish in all colors of the rainbow, in short, a perfect reason for divers and snorkelers to take to the waters as soon as possible.

The **Marquesas Islands** in the north are known for pristine nature. These vol-

Preceding pages: Mt. Pahia on Bora Bora. Left: Making flower garlands either for personal use or to welcome guests.

183

canic islands, with densely packed tropical vegetation, bear mighty mountains covered in low growth crisscrossed by deep and remote valleys. The coasts are harsh, because the cold currents prevented the growth of a protective coral barrier.

The ten rocky volcanic islets making up the **Gambier Islands** are embraced by a large reef belt. Plant life and isolated plantations are only found in the coastal plains.

The five tall **Austral Islands** (and one atoll) are about 400 miles (650 km) south of Tahiti. The colder climate is better for the cultivation of potatoes, carrots, tomatoes, lettuce and other vegetables, which are exported to the Society Islands.

The geological age of these islands, which were born from the eruptions of

Above: The stark coastline of the Marquesas Islands. Right: There can be heavy rain showers on Tahiti, especially between December and March.

underwater volcanoes over four "hot spots" (see introduction), increases from southeast to northwest. None of the islands is currently showing signs of volcanic activity, but new underwater volcanoes are appearing in the southeast.

Southeast Trade Winds from the Northeast

French Polynesia's large expanse has endowed it with various climatic zones. The Austral Islands are in a subtropical climate belt with a precipitation of about 80-120 inches (2000-3000 mm) per year. Other archipelagos considered to be in the tropics have wide ranges of precipitation. In Faaa on Tahiti, for example, annual rainfall has been measured at 67 inches (1700 mm) per year, on the leeward side of the island at over 120 inches (3000 mm) per year, and in the interior of the island at nearly 400 inches (10,000 mm) per year. Occasional hefty rain showers do occur, frequently at night from December to March.

Daytime highs during this period are between 86 and 90° F (30-32° C), nighttime lows are around 73° F (23° C). During the drier season, from June to September, the temperature is generally a little cooler. The mercury seldom gets above 86° F (30° C) and at night can drop to 68° F (20° C).

Some laws are generally applicable for the yearly weather pattern: the closer an island is to the equator, the less the fluctuations in its meteorological figures, and the flatter an island, the smaller the difference between daytime and nighttime temperatures. French Polynesia also lies in the sphere of influence of the southeast trade winds. It is frequently visited by a deviating side current of mainly northeasterly winds. The water temperature of the ocean averages 82.9° F (28.3° C). Fortunately, ground water sources near the shores in many places ensure cooler water for swimming.

History

Research into the early history of the islands has demonstrated conclusively that French Polynesia was settled from Samoa and the Tonga Islands during the Austronesian migration movements. This migration reached the Marquesas Islands about 2200 years ago, and then the Society Islands.

Raiatea was the *hawaiki* for a long time, the "original homeland," and served as the religious center. The strictly hierarchical society was ruled by an absolutist system. Gods and demigods, the ancestors of the ruling families according to local lore, had their say in everyday life and regulated both taboos and liberties. Puritanical codes as were common in Christian Europe were by and large unknown.

Many a daring seafarer taking off on a voyage of discovery into the virtually unknown expanse of the Pacific Ocean in the 18th century seldom had much to lose in his homeland. Living conditions on the ships were usually extremely bad, so by the time they made landfall somewhere, the sailors were promptly seduced by the lifestyle of the natives and the sheer natural beauty of the islands. They received a royal welcome, too, the climate was pleasant, fresh food was plentiful, and beautiful women offered themselves openly.

In 1767, the British captain Samuel Wallis was the first European to discover Tahiti. But it was the praise heaped upon it by Count Louis-Antoine de Bougainville, who spent 10 days on the island in the wake of a trip around the world, that made Tahiti famous in Europe as "La nouvelle Cythère," as he called it after the island where the Greek goddess of love, Aphrodite, was born.

Bougainville's *Voyage autour du monde* became a best seller. A year after it appeared, an English translation was prepared by Georg Foster from Danzig, who had accompanied his father Reinhold on Cook's second journey. The strong, young Tahitian Aotourou, whom

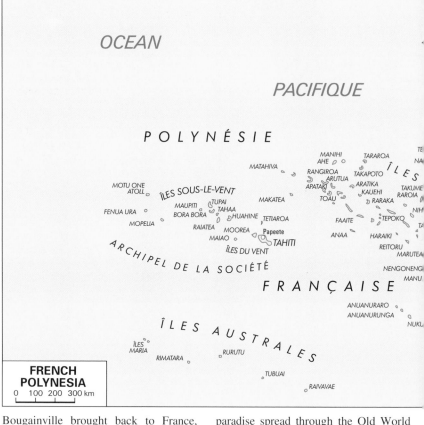

OCEAN

PACIFIQUE

POLYNÉSIE

TE
MANIHI   TARAROA   NA
MATAHIVA   AHE   RANGIROA   TAKAPOTO   ÎLES
ARUTUA
MOTU ONE   APATAKI   ARATIKA   TAKUME
ATOLL   ÎLES SOUS-LE-VENT   KAUEHI   RAROIA
TUPAI   MAKATEA   TOAU   RARAKA
MAUPITI   TAHAA   NIH
FENUA URA   BORA BORA   HUAHINE   TETIAROA   FAAITE   TEPOKO
MOPELIA   TA
RAIATEA   MOOREA   Papeete   ANAA   HARAIKI
MAIAO   TAHITI   REITORU
ÎLES DU VENT   MARUTEA
ARCHIPEL DE LA SOCIÉTÉ   NENGONENG
MANU
FRANÇAISE

ANUANURARO
ANUANURUNGA
ÎLES AUSTRALES   NUKL
ÎLES   MARIA   RURUTU
RIMATARA
TUBUAI
RAIVAVAE

FRENCH POLYNESIA
0   100 200 300 km

Bougainville brought back to France, seemed to be living proof of the existence of the "noble savage" who led a carefree life in the midst of abundant natural surroundings.

James Cook combed the South Seas during four trips undertaken between the years 1764 and 1780. The scientists and artists he had on board produced the first exact picture of one of the groups of islands they came across: the Society Islands (they are known as the *Archipel de la Société* in French) were named after the *Royal British Society of Sciences,* which had made its contribution toward the financing of his expedition.

The myth of the "happy islands" had its sequel; the reports of this newly-found

paradise spread through the Old World like wildfire and drew more and more adventurers into the distant ocean.

Mutiny on the Bounty

When Captain William Bligh was picking volunteers in 1788 – i.e., 20 years after the discovery of Tahiti – for the crew of his ship *HMS Bounty*, he had a large stock to pick from. His task was to transport a load of breadfruit saplings from Tahiti to the British West Indies. After a wonderful shore leave of five months on Tahiti, the crew was most reluctant to sail half way around the world to the Caribbean. The famous mutiny on the *Bounty* occurred in Tongan waters.

TAA
• MOTU ONE
/A
○ UA HUKA
hae
POU
uona HIVA OA

◌ FATU HIVA

QUISES

○ PUKAPUKA

U
KAHINA

A M ○ TAKAPOTO
U *O T U* ○ PUKARUA
AKIAKI ○ REAO
   ○ VAHITAHI
   ◌ NUKUTAVAKE
   ○ PINAKI
NUI

TUREIA
   ○

         ○○○○ MARUTEA
GI MURUROA ○ ○
 ○○ FANGATAUFA ○ MARIA
   ○
   ÎLES GAMBIER
   MORANE ○ MAGAREVA
         ○ ◌ TEMOE

fluence. The Tahitians no longer dressed in their traditional garb, but ran around in ragged clothing, they spoke a kind of pidgin language interspersed with rude English words. Furthermore, they had gotten hold of muskets and were making use of them, too – all in all, a deterioration of the former dignity and elegance.

Island society was not all that underwent severe change under the European influence. Too, who had been merely one of many local princes on Tahiti, subjugated the other chiefs with the help of weapons introduced by the Europeans, and had himself crowned King Pomare I.

A New God Arrives

On March 5, 1797, the good ship *Duff*, under Captain Wilson, laid anchor in Matavai Bay in Tahiti after a long and perilous journey. Of the missionaries from the *London Missionary Society* aboard, 14 pious craftsmen and four pastors went ashore.

Less than a year later, 11 of them departed again in a more humble frame of mind. Nevertheless, the missionary work they began paved the way to ultimate success: in 1819, King Pomare II agreed to be baptized of his own free will. With the help of the missionaries, he built up his kingdom according to European models. His one-year-old son succeeded him after his death in 1821. He died at age seven and was succeeded by his 14-year-old sister Aimata, who became Queen Pomare IV.

The French Hand

After laying hands on the Marquesas Islands for his nation, Rear Admiral du Petit Thouars sailed on to Tahiti in 1842 and declared it a French protectorate. Neither Queen Pomare IV nor the handful of English missionaries on the island were in any position to resist this territorial encroachment. The cries of help di-

The ship did make a detour to Tahiti to drop off some of the crew before the other mutineers headed off to the island of Pitcairn.

But Captain Bligh returned as well in 1792 with two ships. He found none of the mutineers. Two had been murdered, and the remaining 14 had been carted off to England the year before by Captain Edwards of the *HMS Pandora*.

Bligh collected breadfruit saplings again, and fulfilled the original task of bringing them to the Caribbean, where the trees produced a steady and abundant supply of food for the slaves on British plantations. Bligh was disappointed by his last sojourn on Tahiti. The "good old days" had succumbed to European in-

rected at England went unheeded. No one was willing to provoke a war with France for the sake of a few islands on the other side of the planet. Furthermore, the newly acquired colonies of Australia and New Zealand were far more significant politically and economically.

Thanks to their overwhelming weapons superiority and to the fact that Great Britain was neutral at the time, the French defeated the Tahitians in a war lasting from 1842 to 1844.

Queen Pomare IV died in 1877. Her son, reared under French influence, never had quite the necessary authority and power. In 1880, he finally signed the islands over to France in exchange for a substantial life-time pension for himself, his wife and his two brothers. The French never left.

France did little for its new colony until the year 1945. During World War Two, Polynesia did not hesitate to take the side of General de Gaulle, and France expressed its gratitude in the postwar years by showing more interest in her Pacific possessions.

Nevertheless, French Polynesia did remain a secret tip for artists, adventurers and the more well-to-do tourist crowd. In 1954, the Tahitian people voted to remain with France, whereupon the French government moved its atomic testing program from the Sahara Desert to the Pacific region.

In spite of large investments in the country, unrest broke out among the locals in 1958 and 1959. The opposition leader Oopa was exiled for eight years, and the opposition party RDPT dissolved in 1963.

Above: Shimmering black pearls are culti-vated in the lagoons of the Tuamotu Islands and represent one of the main export items of French Polynesia.

Independence? No Thanks!

French Polynesia was declared a French overseas territory with local au-

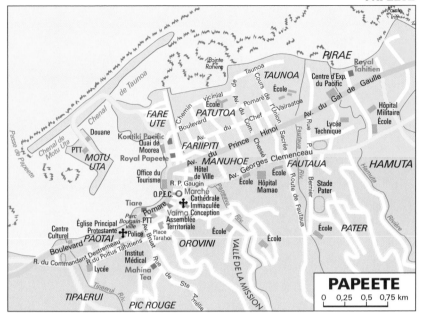

tonomy in 1984. It has indigenous political parties, a parliament, ministers and its own local president. All supra-regional tasks, however, are controlled by France. The French High Commissioner, whose function is mainly representative under normal circumstances, is officially the head of the territory. French Polynesia also has two deputies and one senator to represent its interests in the French National Assembly. All inhabitants have a French passport.

Referendums have shown till now that the majority of residents would like to remain French. Thanks to anti-nuclear testing protests, the referendum of March 1996 did give the independence parties quite a boost, but they still failed to capture even one-third of the vote.

Black Pearls and Tourism

About 200,000 tourists visit the islands of the southern Pacific each year. Over a third come from the USA, followed by the Japanese and the Germans in the number two and three spots respectively. Tourism has meanwhile become the third largest source of revenue for French Polynesia.

Ranking second in the local economy is trade with the unique black seeded pearls. The oysters producing them (*Pinctada mageritifera*) are found only in Polynesia, and have been cultivated mainly in the quiet lagoons of the Tuamotu archipelago. Until now, 80 percent of the export went to Japan, but Europe's jewelry market seems to be gradually getting a taste for these unusual artistic creations of nature.

Agricultural products, on the other hand, are not particularly abundant, with the exception of some coconut oil and vanilla. In recent years, a limited cosmetics industry has established itself with perfumed coconut oil (*monoi*), soaps, creams, etc. Exotic flowers are also increasingly being exported overseas.

The French state remains economic factor number one, however. If it would not receive massive support from the

189

mother country, French Polynesia would by no means be so wealthy. Over 50 percent of workers on Tahiti get their paychecks directly or indirectly from France's state coffers.

In January 1996, France once and for all ended its last atomic testing program after a final test series on the Tuamotu islands of Fangataufa and Mururoa (about 690 miles/1100 km southeast of Tahiti), carried out in the face of massive worldwide protest including a boycott of French products.

Once again, politicians have agreed on a ten-year development plan guaranteeing French Polynesia large sums. Everyone knows that the funds will be drastically cut after that. In the meantime, the local government hopes to hastily push other economic sectors, such as fishing and tourism, as well as mobilize other

Above: Papeete lies in the embrace of Tahiti's mountains. Right: The town really comes alive as soon as the sun has set.

subsidies – from the European Union, for instance – to do things like aid with road-building projects on Bora Bora.

Ethnic Mix

By the end of 1997, the ethnically-mixed population of French Polynesia had reached a good 220,000. Caucasians and Asians may not be important numerically, but they are economically. William Stewart, a Scotsman, brought over Chinese laborers to Tahiti from Hong Kong in the early 1860s to work on his cotton plantations. When their contracts ran out, they relied on their adaptability, mercantilism, diligence and skill to gradually become major landowners. As for the Europeans, they form about 11 percent of the population and generally are only on temporary work schedules in the region. The percentage of so-called "demis," people of mixed European and Maohi ancestry, is officially 14, but it is assumed that far more Polynesians have a non-Polynesian somewhere in their ancestry.

TAHITI

Papeete – a Busy City

The wide-eyed visitor expecting a dreamy, idyllic South Seas town will be as disappointed as Paul Gauguin was when he laid eyes on Papeete on his arrival over 100 years ago. **Papeete** (which means "water basket" and probably refers to the gourds used to find water) was always a vivacious business and trade town, a place of transshiping for wares from all over the world and a supply station for a huge area in the midst of the ocean. And yet, in spite of all the activity and the endless lines of cars that inappropriately squeeze their way through the narrow streets, modern Papeete has lost none of its ambient charm.

In 1827, Queen Pomare IV had a residence built for herself in Papeete. During the decade following, as whaling flourished in the South Pacific and anywhere from 50 to 80 whaling ships dropped anchor in the bay yearly, shops, bars, pool halls and a typical harbor red-light district (still located at the upper end of the shore promenade) proliferated to meat commercial demand.

Boulevard Pomare, a wide street lined with shops, restaurants and cafés – a mixture of Mediterranean and Polynesian exoticism – has a fine view over the harbor area. Free maps of the town and information brochures are available at the tourist information center **Tahiti Tourisme.** The big meeting place in town is the **Centre Vaima**, an expansive shopping center with all modern commodities. It consists of a three-story mall with shops and travel agents. A newsstand in the building carries international magazines and papers.

Ferries and catamarans to Moorea depart from a pier in the middle of town. Huge cruise ships tie up and disgorge their passengers at the **Quai d'Honneur** nearby. The colorful fishing boats of the natives, the *bonitiers*, unload their catches and carry them to the covered market and other fish stores to sell. Charter boats

and yachts berth next door. The outriggers of the canoe clubs are lined along the shore as one leaves town.

The light and airy **covered market** is a mere block away from the waterfront. It's a quiet place considering the hectic urban activity surrounding it. It is a very special place to visit. Exotic flowers and fruit, freshly-caught fish, clams and shellfish, meat, aromatic cakes and bread and many other delicacies are sold on the ground floor. All the brilliant and alluring smells of the tropics seem to have gathered here. On the upper floor is an unbeatable panoply of handicrafts from all the island groups. A shopping tour here can be tiring, and the **cafetaria** is a welcome spot for a break, even for locals. It's also a good opportunity to come in casual contact with Polynesian culture.

Above: The covered market of Papeete is a great place to go shopping for fresh fish.
Right: Cultural remains at the Musée de Tahiti et des Îles.

Nearby, to the south of the market, is the Catholic **Cathédrale Immaculée Conception**, completed in 1875, with Way of the Cross paintings definitely inspired by Polynesia. The **Hôtel de Ville** (Town Hall), which stands to the north of the market, is as pretty inside as out. It was inaugurated in 1990 for the 100th anniversary of Papeete's acquisition of city rights. The architecture is borrowed from that of the former palace of Queen Pomare IV, a much smaller building of course, whose construction was interrupted in the 1960s.

The **Centre Philatélique** in the main post office building, located between Boulevard Pomare and Avenue du Général de Gaulle, has all the coveted stamps and telephone cards a collector or any ordinary mortal might want.

The **Assemblée Territoriale** (parliament building) and the seat of the French High Commissioner are located on the plaza opposite, **Place Tarahoi**. In **Parc Bougainville** are two cannons from World War One, one from the German

ship *Seeadler*, the other from the French patrol boat *Zélée*. You will also find a statue honoring the great French seafarer Bougainville, the first Frenchman to circumnavigate the earth.

Also on Boulevard Pomare, but a little further on the way out of town, is the **Pearl Museum** (where black pearls are sold), the **Protestant Church** and finally the **Centre Culturel**, housing Papeete's public library.

Exploring Tahiti

Tahiti is the largest (about 402 square miles/1042 sq km) and economically most significant of the Society Islands. Almost 70 percent of the population of French Polynesia lives here.

The island consists of two joined extinct volcanoes and is surrounded by a coral reef. The surface is very uneven and covered with fairly dense tropical vegetation. The highest elevation is Mount Orohena right in the center at 7171 feet (2241 m).

A 71-mile (114 km) coastal road circumnavigates the larger island section Tahiti Nui. Two 12-mile (20 km) roads leave from Taravao and run along both coasts of the smaller peninsula Tahiti Iti (Tairapu), which is not visited nearly as much as the rest of Tahiti. All worthwhile sites can be easily reached by rental car, available either at the airport or at your hotel.

Any of the experienced local tour operators can arrange for a guided hike through the tropical jungle, boat tours along the coast lasting one to several days, jeep safaris to the interior, or horseback rides into the grandiose mountain world.

All distances in Tahiti are measured from the center of Papeete in kilometer points (Pk). Thus a place marked *Pk 6.4 – côté ouest* means it is on the west coast at 6.4 km (3.9 miles) from the capital. Beginning in Papeete and going counterclockwise around the island, you pass by **Faaa** and the **airport** of the same name (Pk 5.5 or 3.4 miles *ouest*), which is cur-

rently being used by ten national and international airlines. The Hôtel Tahiti situated right by the sea was the island's largest and finest in the 1960s, but was torn down in 1997. A new luxury outrigger hotel is scheduled to go up on the same spot.

Among the top addresses on this island paradise is the **Beachcomber Parkroyal Hotel** (Pk 7.2 or 4.4 miles), boasting "overwater" bungalows on stilts. Every Friday evening, delicious sea-food buffets are served in the park-like grounds to accompany a lively and colorful Polynesian show.

The most coveted residential area is the wealthy community of **Punaauia**, whose villas are built along the mountainside and have a spectacular view. Right near the modern town hall, the island's largest shopping center was built.

Right: Ancient Polynesian dances and ceremonies are performed at the Heiva i Tahiti-Festival in July.

The **Lagoonarium** (Pk 11 or 6.9 miles) is a special sight adjacent to the *Captain Bligh* restaurant. The giant maw of a shark built of brick opens up at the end of a wooden pier and leads to a fascinating underwater world. Colorful tropical fish and lagoon sharks swim around behind glass, and at noon the sharks are fed. The earth and stone used to fill part of the landing strip of the airport out on the reef was taken from the **Valley of Punaruu** (Pk 14.8 or 9.1 miles). A variety of little businesses have settled here. A short distance further is a road going off to the right to the **Musée de Tahiti et des Îles** (Pk 15.1 or 9.3 miles), about 1500 feet (500 m) from the main road at **Pointe des Pêcheurs**. The museum has a top-notch exhibition of natural and cultural history of French Polynesia, which must be seen for better understanding of the local social and natural environment.

In the village of **Paea** (Pk 21.9 or 13.6 miles) are two fine houses in colonial style, the white **town hall** and the neighboring **post office**. About 200 yards fur-

ther is the Catholic **village church** on the left-hand side, built out of coral rock. One of the tropical botanical miracles occurs here from December to about mid-February when the flaming red flowers of the leafless flame tree dispenses their colorful magic.

To reach the **Marae Arahurahu,** one of Tahiti's last visible remnants of Polynesian culture, leave the main road at Pk 22.5 (13.9 miles). This mysterious cultic site was very carefully restored during the 1960s by a team under the direction of archeologists from the Bishop Museum in Honolulu. Ancient Polynesian dances and ceremonies are performed before this historic backdrop during the *Heiva i Tahiti,* which takes place every year in July. The family put in charge of caring for this complex, which is under official protection order, has planted fruit trees and vegetables on the grounds. Breadfruit trees, avocados, grapefruit, mangos, limes, papayas, bananas, pineapples and coffee trees have turned the area into a botanical garden.

Wild ginger flowers, tiare Tahiti, frangipani and helicons spread their bewitching aroma.

At Pk 28.5 (17.7 miles) is an ice cold fresh-water lake with a depth of 480 feet (150 m) located in the stalactite cave of **Maraa**. The myriad shell species of the South Pacific area can be admired in the privately-run **Musée des Coquillages** (Shell Museum) in the center of **Papara**. Captain Cook described the cultic site (*marae*) of **Mahaiatea** (Pk 39.2 or 24.3 miles) as a pyramid with eleven steps on a base of 259 by 85 feet (81 by 26.5 m). It was at one time most probably the largest on the island, but only a sad pile of stones remains.

The road continues now through the widest part of Tahiti's coastal plain. William Stewart, the Scotsman mentioned earlier, set up a large cotton and sugar cane plantation in **Atimaono** (Pk 41 or 25.4 miles) during the American Civil War, but it went bankrupt after a few years. One Olivier Bréaud now runs French Polynesia's only golf course on

195

the former plantation's lightly hilly grounds.

The French painter Paul Gauguin (1848-1903) lived in the small, idyllic village of **Mataiea** (Pk 46 or 28.5 miles) from 1891 to 1893 with his Polynesian wife Tehaamana, hoping to find a wonderful world beyond the "civilized" one. He painted an amazing 66 tableaux within a year and a half.

Since the early 1980s, **Lake Vaihira** (1500 feet/470 m above sea level), which snuggles in the arms of steep slopes, has been exploited as a source of electrical power. The dirt road leading there (Pk 47.6 or 29.5 miles) can only be driven during good, dry weather. Back on the island road, however, another side road forks off to the **Gauguin Museum** and to the **Jardin Botanique** (Pk 51.2 or 31.8 miles).

Above: The Musée Gauguin documents the life and work of Paul Gauguin during the time he spent in Polynesia. Right: Cooling off at the Vaimahuta waterfall.

The latter, a wonderful garden, was designed and planted by the American professor of physics Harrison W. Smith in 1919. He had retired to Tahiti to devote himself to his favorite hobby, which was gardening. Many of the trees, shrubs and flowers that grow in the gardens of the island were originally brought here by him from the four corners of the world.

The two Galapagos turtles in the garden have been on Tahiti since 1930. The larger one in particular, the male, likes to have his neck scratched. There's a little restaurant directly on the water called *Snack Snack*, where the food is very good and which does a delicious earth oven dish, *ma'a Tahiti*, on Sundays (reservations are necessary).

As for the **Musée Gauguin**, it opened in 1965 and shows the life and art of this French impressionist, who, in 1901, moved from Tahiti to the Marquesas Island of Hiva Oa. There, plagued by illness and in conflict with the Church and the French administration, he died in 1903. The museum has a number of copies of his paintings, some photos, various items and a series of original pieces, including three paintings, three carved wooden spoons, two ceramic vessels and a color sketch for the illustration of a fan.

Just before reaching the isthmus of Taravao, the road, now lined on the shore side with tall casuarina trees, follows the **Baie du Port Phaéton**, where yachts often drop anchor. The little town of **Taravao** (Pk 60 or 37 miles) is Tahiti's second largest community after Papeete. The **fort** at the exit of town (Pk 53 or 32.9 miles *est*) is a remnant from the Franco-Tahitian war in the mid-19th century and still reveals some of its original walls with their embrasures. Four Germans and one Italian were imprisoned here during World War Two. The little **harbor** (Pk 52 or 32.3 miles *est*) was built as recently as 1994, but because of its unsafe location, it is hardly used.

The tour of the island proceeds now through the community of **Faaone** and on to **Hitiaa**. Many of the little houses on both sides of the road are weekend residences. The gardens here are different from those on the west coast in that they have more fruit and vegetables.

In spring 1786, Count Louis-Antoine de Bougainville anchored his two ships *La Boudeuse* and *L'Étoile* here (Pk 37.6 or 23.3 miles *est*). He mistook two offshore islets for the shanks of a broad bay. Being poorly protected from the powerful swell in this open berth, he ended up losing six anchors in ten days.

Mahaena (Pk 32.5 or 20.1 miles) was the site of the first major battle between French and Tahitian armies in 1844. The Tahitian resistance fighters had to retreat into the rugged interior of the island, for in spite of their numerical superiority, the French were able to prevail, thanks to more effective weapons.

At Pk 22.1 (13.7 miles), a signpost indicates the **Cascades de Fa'arumai** to the left. Three impressive waterfalls dis-

play their beauty there, the highest of which, **Vaimahuta**, is easily reached after an easy five-minute walk from the parking lot. This little detour also provides a good idea of the typical tropical vegetation and the smaller settlements of Tahiti.

Another spellbinding natural spectacle is the **Trou souffleur d'Arahoho** (Pk 22 or 13.6 miles). Big waves push sea water through a cave and little channels pierced in the cliff rock, and it shoots out on the surface like a fountain. Take careful note of the wet area around the blowhole while standing around and waiting for the next act!

In the village of **Papenoo** (Pk 17.1 or 10.6), the road crosses the eponymous river, which is the longest on the island and carries the most water. It rises in the crater of the extinct volcano that originally gave birth to Tahiti Nui. The coast at Papenoo is a favorite with body and board surfers for its wave conditions.

To get to the famous **Pointe Vénus** and the **Baie de Matavai**, you must take

a right off the main road in the village of **Mahina** (at Pk 10 or 6 miles). Captain James Cook gave this little peninsula its name, because it was here that he set up a small observatory in 1769 in order to watch the passage of Venus across the sun. On the way down to the beach are two monuments, one is fenced in and commemorates Cook's first sojourn on the island, and the other is the **Missionaries' Monument** and recalls the landing of the first missionaries from the *London Missionary Society* on March 5, 1797.

Tahiti's only lighthouse stands on the northernmost tip of the island. It was built in the 19th century by the father of Robert Louis Stevenson (the author of *Treasure Island*) and is still in operation. The black volcanic sand beaches on this spit of land are very popular with the local people.

Above: Pristine nature and beautiful solitary beaches can still be found on the Taiarapu peninsula (near Tautira).

On the way back to the main road, you should stop at the lookout point on the **Tahara'a** rise, which offers a magical view of the coast, the surrounding mountains and the island of Moorea. The **Royal Matavai Bay Resort** (formerly the Hyatt), nestled against the slope in this extraordinary location, opened in 1968 as one of Tahiti's first large hotels. The plan to turn the inconspicuous wooden house of **James Norman Hall** (Pk 5.4 or 3.3 miles *est* on the left-hand side) into a museum, has not yet materialized. Hall collaborated with Charles Nordhoff on the famous trilogy describing the trials and tribulations of *HMS Bounty* and also wrote many other interesting tales set in the South Seas. The last ruler of the Pomare dynasty is buried in the little village of **Arue**, just a short distance from Papeete.

The rather remarkable **Tomb of King Pomare V** (Pk 4.7 or 2.9 miles), the last king of the Pomare Dynasty, stands just a few miles before Papeete. In the vicinity lies the sanctified complex of the

Marae Taputaputea. King Pomare II had the complex torn down after he converted to Christianity, and had a huge house of worship built in its stead; a building 694 feet long, 51 feet wide and 18 feet high (217 x 16 x 5.5 m), with a capacity of 6000 people.

The **Chinese Cemetery** is up on the mountainside to the left on the way to the center. Its white grave stones can be easily made out in the distance. In the eastern suburb of **Pirae** begins the winding, unsurfaced Fare Rau Hape way to **Le Belvédère**, the point of departure for many trekking tours. At 1920 feet (600 m), it is also a favorite with day-trippers, especially for its unique panorama at sundown; Papeete with the volcanic island of Moorea in the background.

The Taiarapu Pensinsula

The peninsula of Taiarapu, also referred to as *Tahiti Iti*, or "Small Tahiti," extends to the southeast of the island, and has by and large remained free of tourist crowds and accordingly pretty.

A road leads along the southern shore from Taravao to **Tautira** (11 miles/18 km). Taiarapu's largest community lies in the valley of the Vaitepiha River and has a long and busy history. Captain Domingo Boenechea, an envoy of the Spanish viceroy in Peru, landed here in 1772 with two Catholic missionaries in order to annex Tahiti for the Spanish Crown. The two priests apparently never lost their fear of the "savages" and decided to leave a year later having achieved nothing.

James Cook also dropped anchor at Taufira during his second South Seas journey in 1773. An anchor lost because of the unfriendly winds and currents in the bay now adorns the entrance of the *Musée de Taïti et des îles*. In 1888, Robert Louis Stevenson also spent two months in this wonderful bay on his sailboat *Casco*.

Excursions to **Te Pari** and the eastern coast of the peninsula can be made from the point where the surfaced road ends. The path winds its way through the luxuriant vegetation of tropical forests, by-passing bizarre caverns, grandiose waterfalls and miles of pristine beaches resting at the feet of wild cliffs. These natural gems, however, are not easily accessible and require you to be in good physical condition. Tours with experienced guides generally begin in Tautira.

Another blacktop road begins at the hospital in Taravao and by-passes extensive pasturelands to climb up to the **Tareavao Plateau** (1920 ft/600 m). If the weather is good, you will have a spectacular view of the islands from here to compensate for the rather rough ride up.

Another route known for its lovely countryside begins in Taravao, and leads along the southern coast to **Teahupoo** via **Vairao**.

MOOREA

There is no doubt that the heart-shaped island 9 miles (14 km) northeast of Tahiti is one of the archipelago's prettiest. A ten-minute flight or a half-hour boat ride separates it from the main island. This popular "vacation island" has become a kind of suburb of Papeete and a secret idyll for artists who have grown weary of Tahiti.

Moorea, with a surface area of 51 square miles (132 sq km), has a character all its own, without the whirling activity of Tahiti and no irritating heavy traffic along the island's coastal roads. Bicycling is still a great joy here. Although a third of all the country's hotel beds are to be found on Moorea, with the ubiquitous Club Méditerranée operating the largest hotel complex, day to day life has remained rather simple. Agriculture is the second source of income for the island's 10,000 inhabitants, but comes way after tourism.

Geologically, Moorea is almost twice as old as Tahiti. The main landscape features are volcanic summits and two bays that cut deep gouges into the coastline, the Baie de Cook and the Baie d'Opunohu. Mount Toheia at 3862 feet (1207 m) is the highest peak.

The entire island is surrounded by peaceful bays lined with beaches of pure white coral sand and protected from the ocean swell by reefs. The waters of the lagoons shimmers in all shades of blue and green.

As with the other Society Islands, Moorea was first settled around 1500 years ago. Until the 18th century, it was called *Aimeho*. The current name, Moorea, means "yellow gecko" and refers to a vision a high priest had.

The first Europeans to visit the island were the Englishman Samuel Wallis, in

1767, Count de Bougainville, in 1768 and James Cook in 1769. Cook in fact had another small observatory set up on an offshore island to watch Venus. In 1777, he stopped in the Baie d'Opunohu, where some natives stole a goat. In retaliation, Cook ordered their houses be burned down.

In 1792, Pomare I used weapons taken from the *HMS Bounty* to invade the island. He then selected Papetoai as his royal residence. In 1805, Pomare II went to Moorea in exile accompanied by a few missionaries. In 1817, the first catechism was printed here in the Tahitian language using a printing press imported from England. A year later, members of the *London Missionary Society* planted the first sugar cane, cotton and coffee, and in the following year started operating the first sugar refinery.

The following tour of the island, which can be done by rental car, moped or bicycle, begins at the **Temae Airport** and goes counter-clockwise around the island on the ca. 37-mile (60 km) coastal

Above: The Baie de Cook on Moorea – a fjord-like bay that is a nice place for a relaxed conversation.

road. Every turn in the road seems to offer a new and more breathtaking vision, be that of coves with crystal clear waters, groves of coconut palms or splendid gardens. The kilometer stones on Moorea (Pk) are carved in the shape of the island.

Pareos of many colors and all sorts of handicrafts are peddled along the street of **Maharepa**, one of the island's most important towns. Opposite the **Hotel Bali Hai** (Pk 4 or 2.5 miles), which was opened in 1961, stands the **Maison Blanche** (White House) built around the turn of the century in colonial style. Tahitian souvenirs are sold nowadays in this erstwhile residence of a rich vanilla planter. For a good view of the **Baie de Cook** and the mountains that tower over the area, try the restaurant at the **Cook's Bay Resort Hotel**.

The following legend made the rounds of the 2876-foot (899 m) **Rotui** mountain, whose pineapple plantations can be spotted from a great distance already: Hiro, a divine creature from the island of Raiatea, wanted to steal the holy mountain one night. He had already tied a heavy rope around it (the gashes it left are still visible in the mountain's profile). The demigod Pai, however, saw what was happening from Tahiti and promptly threw his spear, which buried itself in the summit of Mount Mouaputa (this hole is visible, of course). The whine of the flying spear through the air woke up the sleeping birds, whose loud twittering chased away the robber. And so Rotui remained where it can still be admired today.

Hardly anyone sailing around the world will miss a shore leave in this marvelous bay. Also, one of Polynesia's great culinary specialties must be tried here, namely *poisson cru*, raw fish marinated in lemon juice and served in coconut milk.

In a chapel in the small but lively town of **Pao Pao**, the artist P. Heyman por-

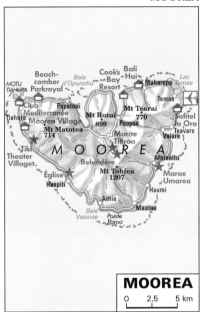

MOOREA

0   2,5   5 km

trayed the Holy Family in Tahitian style. Just before crossing the town limits, a road forks off inland (at Pk 9 or 5.6 miles). It is unsurfaced, and winds its way through pineapple fields, grapefruit and papaya plantations, and dense and generous vegetation, up to **Le Belvédère**. A trip to Moorea is always worthwhile, be it just for the incomparable view of the two bays from Mount Rotui.

A series of *maraes* are situated on either side of the dirt road. These special spots devoted to the gods were once at the heart of the local people's religious life. Information on the significance of these places is posted for visitors.

A short walk through the *mape* forest (Tahitian chestnuts) is recommendable from the parking lot at the **Marae Titiroa**. If you then continue driving, past the **Agricultural School**, you will rejoin the coastal road at the shrimp farm on the southern end of the **Baie d' Opunohu** (Pk 18 or 11 miles). There is a small **fruit juice factory** on the wild road joining the two bays. It offers guided tours, includ-

201

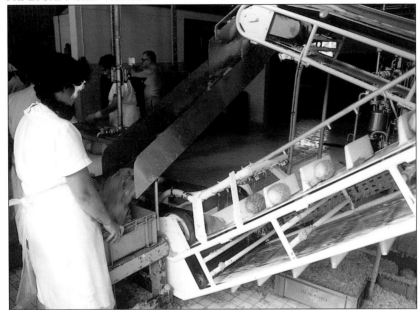

ing some sampling of the juices and liqueurs.

In **Papetoai** (Pk 22 or 13.6 miles) at the northern end of the bay stands the oldest remaning church in French Polynesia. The missionaries built this octagonal edifice on the foundation walls of an old *marae* to celebrate their victory over the heathens. A small obelisk standing in front of the church is all that recalls this former cultic place of the Polynesians. The mission also set up its first school here with the highbrow name of **Academy of the South Seas**.

Following the most beautiful beaches of the island, you come after a while to the highest concentration of hotels. The **Hotel Beachcomber Parkroyal** (Pk 28 or 17 miles), with its traditional bunga-

Above: Preparing and processing pineapple for canning on Moorea. Right: In Maeva, Huahine, archeologists have excavated one of the largest ancient Polynesian religious sites.

lows parked on stilts over the water, is the newest and most luxurious. The complex also has a small delphinarium. Opposite the **Club Med** is a quaint little shopping center with a bank, a restaurant, book stores and souvenir shops called **Le Petit Village** (the Little Village).

Just a little way to the south of **Tiahura**, a signpost points to the **Tiki Village**. This replica of a Polynesian village houses numerous artist families, who keep the traditions of their ancestors alive. You can learn the rudiments of flower binding, the dyeing of *pareos* and the grating of coconuts here; or enjoy an excellent Polynesian meal; or cast out to sea in an outrigger. Visitors are picked up by bus from wherever they are staying on the island.

The numbers on the kilometer stones start diminishing again, i.e., you have passed the half-way mark of your trip around the island.

The following southwestern, southern and southeastern coast has pretty much been spared the heavy hand of tourism.

202

The chapel in **Haapiti**, built by Easter Islanders out of coral rock, stands before a grand mountainous backdrop, and offers a wonderful photo motif.

The next village is dreamy **Maatea** (Pk 14 or 8.7 miles), which is followed by **Afareaitu** (Pk 10 or 6 miles). The latter actually serves as Moorea's administrative center. It boasts a church, built in 1912, and a hospital. Papetoai and Afareaitu were already the most densely populated parts of the island two centuries ago. The missionaries set up their second post, a school and a printing house in Afareaitu. The **Marae Umarea**, which is down by the water and unfortunately no longer in the best of shape, appears to be the oldest cultic spot on Moorea (about AD 900).

The ferries sailing in from Papeete unload their passengers and cargo in the bay of **Vaiare** (Pk 5 or 3.5 miles). For a nice view of the lagoon, the strait of Vaiare all the way to Tahiti, climb up to the **lookout point** located above the Sofitel Ia Ora hotel (Pk 1 or 0.6 miles).

HUAHINE

Painters and writers have repeatedly and unanimously bathed this island in a special light. It is, if you will, a kind of Provence of the South Seas. **Huahine**, 108 miles (175 km) northwest of Tahiti, is certainly part of the Society Islands, but belongs more precisely to the Leeward Islands. The natives in particular love their island for its unspoiled character and untamed beauty.

It consists of two volcanic ranges, the larger one, **Huahine Nui**, is in the north, the smaller one, **Huahine Iti**, in the south. The two are joined by an kind of natural bridge and embraced by a protective coral reef. This little gem of an island, dropped in the middle of a shimmering sea in all shades of blue and green, is surrounded by a host of lagoons and bays. Circumnavigating it should certainly not be missed.

The highest peak is **Mount Turi** at 2140 feet (669 m). The interior of the island is steep and covered in thick plant

growth. A road snakes for 20 miles (32 km) along the two halves of the island, through little villages with brightly colored houses.

Archeologists discovered one of the largest – though not the oldest – cultic places of the Society Islands in **Maeva**, but they only succeeded in excavating a part of it until now. Much of the excavation work was directed by Dr. Y. H. Sinoto of the Bishop Museum in Honolulu. He discovered the oldest evidence of the settling of the Society Islands here (AD 700).

An open market is held every morning in the picturesque village of **Fare** in the northwestern corner of the island, and every evening the fishermen sail out to sea. These two events are worth witnessing for a bit of local color. The place turns into a ghost town in the middle of the day.

Above: The island of Tahaa provides its visitors with delightful sunsets.

RAIATEA AND TAHAA

The two sister islands of Raiatea and Tahaa, separated by a narrow strait (2 miles/3 km) but surrounded by a common barrier reef, lie over 18 miles (30 km) to the west of Huahine. **Raiatea** is the second largest of the Society Islands, with a surface of about 77 square miles (200 sq km), and the town of **Uturoa** (with a population of about 3500) serves as the administrative center of the Leeward Islands, the so-called *Îles sous le Vent*. The landscape is very similar to the other Society Islands, so the visitor can expect the usual elaborate and thick vegetation in the valleys with numerous plantations and waterfalls. Raiatea's highest mountain, **Mount Toomaru**, rises to 3302 feet (1032 m), the highest peaks of the much smaller Tahaa never cross the 1900-foot mark (600 m).

Raiatea also has a significant historical background. It was known as the holy homeland *Hawaiki* to the ancestors of today's Polynesians, and served as the political and religious center of the archipelago.

The 60-mile (100 km) coastal road that circumnavigates the island leads to a slew of historic sites. The **Marae Taputapuatea** near Opoa (Pk 32 or 20 miles) is one of the main attractions for visitors with an eye for archeology; a complex with a stately ground surface of 137 by 25 feet (43 by 8 m). Even if all that's left is a pair of stone platforms on the beach, the place exudes a feeling of mysterious magic. Between the **Baie Faaroa** and the **Baie Faatemu** is a connecting road that leads through the interior of the island.

Although Raiatea is still relatively pristine, Tahaa is by comparison virtually untouched. It has been nicknamed *L'Île Vanille* because of its plethora of vanilla plantations. The 41-mile-long (67 km) coastal road connects the **Baie Apu** in the south with the main town of **Patio** in the north. The local economy is kept alive by agriculture, fishing and the recently started cultivation of pearls.

BORA BORA

No self-respecting traveler to the South Seas fails to put **Bora Bora** on the list of islands to visit. It is a mere 150 miles (240 km) from Tahiti, and therefore within comfortable distance by plane or ship. Arriving by air on the landing strip built on a coral reef off the shore of the main island already gives a fascinating view of the scintillating lagoon in every type of blue imaginable. The boat ride to Vaitape, which is included in the ticket, offers the kind of sight that makes most first-time visitors suspect they have reached Eden itself: water, palms, sand, blue, green, white – that's all. Towering over this scenery is the 2300-foot (718 m) volcanic peak **Otemanu**, sometimes crowned with a gentle wreath of clouds.

Bora Bora consists of a main island, whose 19-mile (32 km) coastal road can easily be cycled in a day, two smaller vol-

BORA BORA

0 1 2 3 4 km

canic isles (**Toopua** and **Toopuaiti**), and myriad flat coral islets that form a semicircular wreath around half of the main island. Aside from the southern tip, the coast of the main island is mostly cliffs. Near **Pointe Matira** are the nicest beaches and many tourist lodgings.

Vaitape itself is still a diminutive and sleepy village with a few shops, banks and cafés, as well as a very alluring **centre artisanale** (handicrafts center), located across from the pier.

The island was independent until the French grabbed it in 1888. American GIs, who set up a supply station during the Second World War, made waves in the peaceful life of the islanders (population today ca. 4500), and introduced tourism of sorts. None of the natives can live off fishing and agriculture anymore.

Naturally, the spectacular natural setting has been used as the backdrop for many a movie, from the 1931 silent production *Tabu* by German director Fritz Murnau, to the more recent *Hurricane* (1977) by Dino de Laurentiis. The lodg-

ings built for the film team of the latter became the **Sofitel Marara Hotel**.

The **Bloody Mary**, standing in the **Baie Povaie**, is a gourmet's delight which proudly looks back on a roster of illustrious guests. Handsome sculptures, colorful *pareos*, T-shirts, shells and black pearls are on sale at the **Jardin Gauguin**. Near the **Baie de Faanui**, the remains of *maraes* (**Maotetini**, **Taianapa**, **Fare Opu**), are witnesses of ancient Polynesian culture. A very special adventure is a trip across the lagoon in an outrigger canoe including dropping in on some very playful rays, shark feeding, snorkeling in a coral garden and a delightful barbecue on one of the *motus* (coral islets).

The little island of **Maupiti**, a mere 25 miles (40 km) from Bora Bora, has beautiful beaches and hardly any tourism to speak of. Lodgings are simple, and in addition, visitors are always made to feel

Above: Airborne approach to Bora Bora.
Right: The bungalows of the Manihi Pearl Beach Resort are on stilts.

welcome. The airport is near the main town of **Vaiea** on the *motu* **Tuanai**.

THE TUAMOTU ISLANDS

Any remaining South Seas expectations will be fulfilled by the Tuamotu Islands, which are spread over hundreds of square miles in the eastern Pacific; with snow white beaches of coral lined with swaying palm trees, lagoons rich in color with crystal-clear water and abundant tropical marine life. While the life of the natives may seem tranquil, it isn't necessarily easy: the meager vegetation of the islands puts serious limits on income opportunities. Copra production and fishing are basically the only games in town, and for the past few years, special farms have started cultivating seeded pearls.

Since tourism is in its inchoate stage on the islands, lodgings are few and far between. Only Rangiroa and Manihi have hotels, on other islands accommodations consist of either little bed & breakfasts or some other form of private rooming. In

Rangiroa, 199 miles (320 km) from Tahiti, the world's second-largest atoll, the huge turquoise lagoon (41 miles/67 km long and 16 miles/26 km wide) radiates nature in its most complete beauty. The two towns of **Avatoru** and **Tiputa** guard the entrances to the lagoon, which are deep enough for large ships. The little hotel complex of **Kia Ora Sauvage** is a special treat. A solid hour away from civilization by boat, it allows its guests to spend a modern Robinson Crusoe vacation on a small *motu*.

Manihi, with its unique underwater world, is about 320 miles (about 520 km) northwest of Tahiti. Copra and seeded pearls guarantee the local inhabitants' income. The town of **Turipaoa** was built at the entrance to the over 12-mile-long and 6-mile-wide lagoon (20 by 10 km).

The recently renovated **Manihi Pearl Beach Resort** provides a very special service: guests who are staying in the luxurious overwater bungalows are served meals by Polynesian beauties in dugout canoes.

To sum up: A visit to one of the Tuamotu Islands is the promise of stress-free vacationing, a terrific idea for those in search of peace and quiet; and for water sports enthusiasts there is diving, snorkeling, swimming, fishing, taking boat rides, walking and picnics on the beach. The annoying *nono* fly, whose sting can itch for days on end, can be avoided by using a good insect repellent.

MARQUESAS ISLANDS

The Marquesas archipelago, a sprinkling of islands and atolls spread over an area of 789 square miles (1270 sq km), were settled over 2200 years ago by seafarers from Samoa and the Tonga Islands. The northern islands of **Ua Pou**, **Ua Huka** and **Nuku Hiva**, which is the administrative center of the Marquesas, are about three hours by airplane from Tahiti. With the exception of Clark Atoll, all the islands are of volcanic origin. Almost all islands consist of a central mountain with steep slopes that drop in

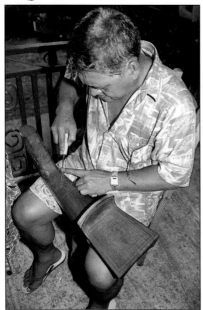

some parts directly to the sea. The climate is warm and humid; a tropical rain forest covers the eastern sides. The original name, *Las Islas Marquesas de Don Garcia Hurtado de Mendoza de Canete*, was given by Álvaro de Mendaña in 1595 to honor the then viceroy of Peru. The indigenous peoples call the islands simply **Te Henua Enata**, meaning the "land of the people."

The culture of the past is still evidenced by the large number of historic places, such as cultic grounds (*marae*), dance and residential platforms (*tohua* and *paepae*), fortified complexes (*aka-ua*), stone *tikis* and petroglyphs. The excellent wood carvings (tikis, bowls, spears, etc.) are known and coveted even beyond the borders of French Polynesia.

The best way to discover this unspoiled world is by the sea route. Catamarans ply these waters regularly, or you

Above: The inhabitants of the Marquesas Islands are known for their high-quality wood carving.

can opt for a 16-day cruise on the freighter *Aranui*, with four-wheel-drive or horseback tours of the islands generally included in the price.

The French painter Paul Gauguin and the Belgian-born *chansonnier* Jacques Brel were strongly attracted to the Marquesas for their cultural power and charisma, and brought these rather remote islands a good deal of publicity. Their graves can be found in the cemetery of the dreamy little town of **Atuona** on **Hiva Oa**.

Hiva Oa (77 square miles/199 sq km, pop. 1700) is the most important island of the southern group. The most beautiful landscapes are found at the **Baie de Taaoa** and in the **Valley of Puamau**.

Nuku Hiva, (127 square miles/330 sq km) is the main island of the northern group and boasts the largest population (2500). **Taiohae** is the economic hub, the **Baie de Hatiheu** and the beach of **Anaho** are worth visiting.

Ua Huka (23 square miles/60 sq km) is 20 nautical miles (36 km) east of Nuku Hiva. Men and women segregate themselves in their shops to sell unusual wood carvings.

Ua Pou (44 square miles/115 sq km) has one of the highest mountain of the Marquesas, **Mount Oave** (4005 ft/1252 m). Thousands of sea birds brood on an offshore *motu*.

Tahuata, the smallest of the inhabited islands (19 square miles/50 sq km), offers horseback tours into Hanatahu Valley and to some famous petroglyphs.

Fatu Hiva (31 square miles/80 sq km, pop. 500) is the southernmost and wettest of the Marquesas Islands. Well before embarking on his *Kon-Tiki* expedition, Thor Heyerdahl spent a year (1937-38) living amongst the indigenous people here, together with his wife Liv. A hiking trail about 11 miles long (18 km) connects the island's only two towns, **Hanavave**, on the picturesque Bay of Virgins, and **Omoa**.

FRENCH POLYNESIA

No area code, the country prefix is: 689.

Airlines

INTERNATIONAL: **Air France**, Tel: 436333, Fax: 410522, Los Angeles, Paris, Tokyo. **Air Nouvelle Calédonie**, Tel: 436333, via Wallis & Futuna or Fiji, New Caledonia. **Hawaiian Airlines**, Tel: 421500, Fax: 451451, from/to Honolulu. **Air New Zealand**, Tel: 430170, Fax: 424544, from/to Auckland, Fiji Islands, Los Angeles, Rarotonga. **Quantas**, Tel: 430665, Fax: 410519, from/to Los Angeles and Sydney via Auckland. *NATIONAL:* **Air Moorea**, Tel: 864141, Fax: 864299, offers hourly flights to Moorea, no reservations necessary, twice daily to Tetiaroa, Marlon Brando's atoll, Tel: 426302, Fax: 850051. The local airline is **Air Tahiti**, Tel: 864011, Fax: 864069, flies to 35 islands of French Polynesia, various attractive package tours (airplane pass and hotel). **Air Tahiti Nui** will begin operating at the end of 1998 and will fly Papeete-Los Angeles. The international airport of Faaa is 3.5 miles (5 km) from the center of Papeete. Taxi fare to the hotels is fixed.

Local Ferry Schedules

Two fast catamarans and two car ferries connect Tahiti with Moorea, reservations are not necessary: **Aremiti**, Tel: 428888, Fax: 420615; **Tamahine**, Tel: 450030, Fax: 421049. The fast boat **Ono Ono**, Tel: 4535 35, Fax: 438345, connects three times a week Papeete – Huahine – Raiatea – Tahaa – Bora Bora. The **Raromatai** ferry, Tel: 431988, Fax: 431999, (carries cars), also docks at Huahine, Raiatea, Tahaa and Bora Bora. There are the freighters that also take on passengers (see p. 239). The freighter and passenger ship **Aranui** sails to the Marquesas: Tel: 426240, Fax: 434889 (15-16 days). You can also fly one of the legs.

Cruises

Weekly cruises to the Society Islands are run seasonally on the five-mast **Club Med II**, Tel: 429699, Fax: 421683. **Archipels Croisières**, Tel: 563639, Fax: 563587, offers sailing tours on 58-foot (18 m) catamarans in the Marquesas, Tuamotu and the Society Islands. Numerous yacht chartering firms are based on Raiatea, some on Tahiti and Moorea. Recommendable are: **G.I.E. Mer et Loisiers**, Tel: 439799, Fax 433368. **Moorings Yacht Charter**, Tel: 663593, Fax 662094. **Stardust Marine**, Tel; 662318, Fax 662319. **Polynésie Yachting Charter**, Tel: 433752, Fax 432428. **Tahiti Yacht Charter**, Tel: 426746, Fax 439931.

Land Travel / Car Rental

The public bus **Le Truck** stops on hand signals. The driver or conductor takes the fare when you exit. Some lines are poorly serviced or only late in the afternoon (inquire!). **Taxis**: Daily basic fee of 800 CFP and 120 CFP/km, night fee 1200 CFP and 240 CFP/km. **Avis**, Tel: 429649, Fax: 410847. **Europcar Inter Rent**, Tel: 452424, Fax: 419341. **Hertz**, Tel: 420471, Fax: 424862. **Pacificar**, Tel: 419393, Fax: 421911.

Excursions

(On Tahiti and to other islands)

Paradise Tours, Tel: 454832, Fax: 419573. **South Pacific Tours**, Tel: 413970, Fax: 413472. **Tahiti Nui Travel**, Tel: 426803, Fax: 427435. **Vahine Tahiti Travel**, Tel: 9424438, Fax: 436006. To Tahiti's interior: **Adventure Eagle Tours**, Tel: 413763. **Safari Loisirs** ("boat office" near the main post office). **Tahiti Safari Expedition**, Tel: 421415. **Tahiti Trekking 4x4 Adventures**, Tel: 436566. Hikes of several days to Tahiti Iti: **Zena Anglien**, Tel: 572267.

Local Flights / Charters

AIRPLANES: in addition to the local companies: **Aero-Club UTA**, Tel: 838109. **Air Oceania**, Tel: 821047, Fax: 855211. *HELICOPTERS:* **Heli Pacific**, Tel: 856800, Fax: 856808. **Heli-Inter Polynésie**, Tel: 819900, Fax: 855556.

Festivals / Museums / Parks

Heiva-Festival in July with dance, music and sports competitions, parades and lots more. *TAHITI:* **Lagoonarium**, west coast, Punaauia, restaurant, Tel: 436290, 9 a.m.-6 p.m. and for dinner. **Musée de la Perle**, blvd. Pomare, by the sea, Tel: 424644, open during business hours. **Musée de Tahiti et des Îles**, west coast, Punaauia, Tel: 583476, 9:30 a.m.-5:30 p.m. except Mon. **Musée des Coquillages**, Papara, Tel: 574522, Tue-Fri 8 a.m.-4:30 p.m., weekends from 9 a.m. **Musée Gauguin**, south coast, southwest of Papeari, Taravao isthmus, Tel: 571058, 9 a.m.-5 p.m. **Jardin Botanique**, near the Gauguin Museum, 9 a.m.-5 p.m.

Business Hours

BANKS: Mon-Fri 8 a.m.-3:30 p.m. in Papeete, branch offices outside the town often have a lunch break but are open longer. WestPac at Faaa airport on arrival and departure of international flights. *SHOPS:* Mon-Fri 8 a.m.-noon and 2-5 p.m. Sat till noon; some of the larger supermarkets and most little stores are open until 7 p.m. Sat afternoon and even Sun morning. *PAPEETE MARKET:* Mon-Sat 5 a.m.-6 p.m., Sun 5-10 a.m.

Currency / Electricity

*CURRENCY:*French Pacific francs (CFP). Fixed rate with the French franc: 1 FF = 18,18 CFP. US dollars are accepted almost all over. *ELECTRICITY*: Generally 220 V – 60 Hz, rarely 110 V.

Tourist Information

Tahiti Tourisme, Tel: 505700, Fax: 436619, B.P. 65, Papeete. By the sea at the Fare Manihini, open Mon-Fri 7:30 a.m.-5 p.m., Sat 8 a.m.-noon.

TAHITI
Accommodation

LUXURY (over US$ 200): **Beachcomber Parkroyal**, Tel: 865110, Fax: 865110, 4,5 miles (7 km) southwest of Papeete, by the sea, 212 air-conditioned rooms/bungalows, restaurant, pool, tennis, water sports, diving. **Royal Matavai Bay Resort**, Tel: 421234, Fax: 482544, 5 miles (8 km) northeast of Papeete, 190 air-conditioned rooms, restaurant, pool, tennis. **Sofitel Maeva Beach**, Tel: 428042, Fax: 43 8470, 5 miles (8 km) southwest of Papeete, by the sea, 224 air-conditioned rooms, restaurant, pool, tennis, water sports. The **Lafayette** (near the Royal Matavai Bay Resort) and **Le Méridien** (at Pk 15 in Punaauia) opened in 1998.

MODERATE (over US$ 100): **Le Mandarin**, Tel: 421633, Fax: 421632, 51, rue Colette, Papeete, 37 air-conditioned rooms, restaurant. **Prince Hinoi**, Tel: 423277, Fax: 423366, corner avenue du Prince Hinoi/blvd. Pomare, Papeete, 72 air-conditioned rooms, restaurant, pool. **Relais de la Maroto**, Tel: 579029, Fax: 579030, in the center of the island, upper Papenoo valley, 24 rooms/bungalows, restaurant, access by 4-wheel drive or helicopter. **Royal Papeete**, Tel: 420129, Fax: 437909, blvd. Pomare, Papeete, stylish and elegant, 71 air-conditioned rooms, restaurant, nightclub. **Royal Tahitien**, Tel: 428113, Fax: 410535, 2,5 miles (4 km) east of Papeete, by the sea, 40 air-cond. rooms, restaurant, black sand beach.

MODERATE TO BUDGET (till US$ 100): **Fare Nana'o**, Tel: 571814, Fax: 577610, Faaone, south coast near Taravao, 5 bungalows on the lagoon, managed by an artist couple, imaginative and unusual, reservations. **Hiti Moana Villa**, Tel: 579393, Fax: 579444, Papara, south coast, 3 bungalows, pool, motor boat. **Kontiki Pacific**, Tel: 437282, Fax: 421166, northern inner city of Papeete, blvd. Pomare near Moorea ferry, 44 air-conditioned rooms, restaurant, nightclub. **La Belle Vue**, Tel: 584704, Punaauia, 10 miles (16 km) southwest of Papeete, one studio. *BUDGET (under US$ 50):* **Chez Myrna**, Tel: 426411, Chemin Vicinal de Tipaerui, Papeete. **Chez Tetua Lola**, Tel: 819175 (nights as well!), Faaa, near the airport, two rooms **Chez Vaa**, Tel: 429432, Punaauia, 5 miles (8 km) from Papeete. **Fare Opuhi Roti**, Tel: 532026, Paea, 13 miles (21 km) from Papeete. **Heitiare Inn**, Tel: 833352, Faaa, 2,5 miles (4 km) from Papeete, rooms/dorm. **Mahina Tea**, Tel: 420097, Vallée de Ste. Amélie, 16 rooms/studios. **Pension Armelle**, Tel: 584243, Fax: 584281, Punaauia, 10 miles (16 km) from Papeete, 8 rooms **Pension Te Miti**, Tel: 584861, Paea, 12 miles (19 km) from Papeete, rooms/dorm. **Pension Teamo Hostel** Tel: 420035, Fax: 435695, 8, rue du Pont Neuf, Quartier Mission, east of inner city, Papeete, atmospheric old house, rooms,

dormitory, tours. **Tahiti Budget Lodge**, Tel: 426682, rue du Frère Alain, Quartier Mission, Papeete, quiet, friendly, 11 rooms/dorm.

Restaurants / Nightlife

IN PAPEETE: CHINESE: **Le Cheval d'Or**, Quartier Faariipiti, Tel: 429889. **Le Dragon d'Or**, rue Colette, Tel: 429612. **Le Vaima Lagon Bleu**, Patutoa, Tel: 413941. *FRENCH:* **La Corbeille d'Eau**, blvd. Pomare, Tel: 437714, among Tahiti's best. **Le Doyen**, Vaima center, Tel: 420219. **L'Orchidée**, avenue du Prince Hinoi, Tel: 423747. **L'O à la bouche**, Tel: 452976. **Moana Iti**, blvd. Pomare, Tel: 426524. *ITALIAN:* **Don Camillo**, 14, rue des Écoles, Tel: 428096. **Pizzeria Lou Pescadou**, rue Anne-Marie Javouhey, behind Cathedral, Tel: 437426, inexpensive. *JAPANESE:* **Sakura**, Tel: 428042, Sofitel Meava Beach. **Shosai**, Tel: 461234, Hyatt Regency. *VIETNAMESE:* **La Saigonnaise**, avenue du Prince Hinoi, Tel: 420535, closed Sun.

OUTSIDE PAPEETE

CHINESE: **Chez Jeanine**, at the Taravao Isthmus, south coast, Taravao. *FRENCH:* **Auberge du Pacifique**, Tel: 439830, Punaauia, 7 miles (11 km) southwest of Papeete, excellent. **Belvédère**, Tel: 427344, 6 miles (9 km) from Papeete, 1900 ft up (600 m), free shuttle from the hotels. **Captain Bligh**, Tel: 436290, Punaauia, 7 miles (11 km) southwest of Papeete, no fee for the Lagoonarium. **Coco's**, Tel: 582108), Punuaauia, 8 miles (13 km) southwest of Papeete, among one of Tahiti's best. **École Hotelière**, Tel: 452371, Pirae, 2 miles (3 km) east of Papeete, hotel school, Tue noon to Fri evening. **Gauguin**, Tel: 571380, 3/4 miles (1 km) west of Gauguin Museum, southwest of Papeari, with a small garden. **Snack Snack**, Botanical Garden near Gauguin Museum, good Tahitian food Sun noon. *ITALIAN:* **Coté Jardin**, Tel: 432619, Punaauia, 5,5 miles (9 km) southwest of Papeete in the Moana Nui shopping center, until 8 p.m. *NIGHTLIFE:* **Club 106**, near blvd. Pomare, Vaiarni district. **Club Macumba**, avenue du Prince Hinoi, Temae. **Club Paradise**, blvd. Pomare, Arupa. **Le Piano Bar**, rue des Ecoles, next to Hôtel Prince Hinoi, Tel: 428824, transvestite shows. **Le Roll's Club**, in the Vaima Center, Tel: 434142, teens place, disco, karaoke.

Accommodation on other Islands
TETIAROA

Hotel Tetiaroa, Tel: 826302, Fax: 850051, simple bungalows on Marlon Brando's private atoll. (Not always open). 26 miles (42 km) north of Tahiti, bird and marine life sanctuary.

MOOREA

LUXURY (over US$ 200): **Cook's Bay Resort Hotel**, Tel: 561050, Fax: 562918, on the east side of the bay, 100 rooms, bungalows, restaurant pool, good dive shop. **Moorea Beachcomber Park-**

royal, Tel: 551919, Fax: 551955, north coast, west of Papetoai, Pk 24, beach, 147 mostly air-conditioned rooms, bungalows, restaurant, bar, pool, tennis, water sports. **Sofitel Ia Ora**, Tel: 561290, Fax: 561291, east coast between Vaiare and the airport, bungalows, beach restaurant, tennis, water sports, on one of the island's most beautiful beaches. *MODERATE (over US$ 80):* **Bali Hai Moorea**, Tel: 561359, Fax: 561922, Maharepa, Pk 5 east of Cook's Bay, 63 rooms, bungalows, restaurant, pool. **Hibiscus Hotel**, Tel: 561220, Fax: 562069, northwest coast, on the white sand beach near Tiahura, 29 pretty bungalows, kitchenettes, restaurant, pool. **Les Tipaniers**, Tel: 561267, Fax: 562925, northwest coast near Tiahura, on the beach, 22 rooms and 11 bungalows some with kitchen, restaurant. **Moorea Beach Club**, Tel: 561548, Fax: 410928, northwest coast near Tiahura, on the beach, 40 rooms most air-conditioned, bungalows with kitchenette, restaurant, pool, water sports, tennis. **Moorea Lagoon**, Tel: 561 468, Fax: 562625, north coast west of Pihaena, Pk 14 on a beautiful beach, 45 bungalows, restaurant, pool, tennis. **Moorea Village**, Tel: 561002, Fax: 562211, west coast south of Tiahura, Pk 27, on the beach, 50 bungalows, some with kitchen, restaurant, pool, water sports, canoes, bicycles. *BUDGET (under US$ 80):* **Motel Albert**, Tel/Fax: 561276, Cook's Bay, Paopao, Pk 8.5, 18 bungalows, kitchen, popular lodgings.

HUAHINE

LUXURY (over US$ 200): **Hana Iti**, Tel: 688505, Fax: 688504, west coast south of Bourayne Bay, 25 imaginative bungalows with whirlpool, restaurant, pool, one of the most beautiful and exotic hotels in French Polynesia. **Huahine Beach Club**, Tel: 688146, Fax: 410928, south coast near Parea, 17 bungalows, restaurant, beach, pool. **Sofitel Heiva**, Tel: 688686, Fax: 688525, east coast southeast of Maeva on a lagoon in a coconut palm forest, wonderful beach, archeological sites, 61 rooms/bungalows, restaurant, pool, cultural events. *MODERATE (over US$ 100):* **Bali Hai Huahine**, Tel: 688477, Fax: 688277, northwest coast north of Fare, 44 rooms/bungalows, good restaurant, bar, pool, nice location. **Relais Mahana**, Tel: 688154, Fax: 688508, south coast, beach, 22 bungalows, restaurant, pool, tennis. *BUDGET (under US$ 100):* **Chez Henriette**, Haamene Bay Tel: 688371, 6 bungalows with kitchenette. **Pension Poetaina**, Pk 1 Fare, Tel/Fax: 688949, rooms/dorm, community kitchen. *CHEAP (under US$ 50):* **Chez Lovina**, Tel: 688806, Fax: 688264, northwest coast bet. Fare and the airport, 13 bungalows/dorm, restaurant, bar.

RAIATEA AND TAHAA

LUXURY (over US$ 200): **Vahine Island Resort**, Tel: 656738, Fax: 656770, on the idyllic coral island of Tuuvahine northeast of Tahaa, 11 bungalows, restaurant, water sports. **Hawaiki Nui Hotel**, Tel: 662023, Fax: 662020, northeast coast of Raiatea, 1.5 miles (2 km) south of Uturoa, 32 bungalows, restaurant, bar, snorkeling.

BORA BORA

LUXURY (over US$ 300): **Bora Bora Lagoon Resort**, Tel: 604000, Fax: 604001, east on the island of Toopua, 80 bungalows, restaurant, pool, terrific atmosphere, jet-set appeal. **Moana Beach Parkroyal**, Tel: 604900, Fax: 604999, Matira Point, 51 bungalows on a white sand beach, restaurant. **Hotel Bora Bora**, Tel: 604460, Fax: 604466, southeast tip, on the most beautiful beach on the island, great snorkeling, 55 bungalows, top restaurant, it's one of the most exclusive hotels in the South Pacific, for millionaires, film stars and sundry VIPs. **Sofitel Marara**, Tel: 677046, Fax: 677403, Matira Point, 64 bungalows, restaurant, pool, relaxed atmosphere. *MODERATE (over US$ 150):* **Bora Bora Motel**, Tel: 677821, Fax: 677757, Matira Point next to the other Sofitel, studios, spacious apartments, on the beach. **Hotel Matira**, Tel: 677051, Fax: 677702, Matira Point, 28 bungalows some with kitchenette, on the beach. *BUDGET (under US$ 150):* **Chez Nono**, Tel: 677138, Fax: 677427, Matira Point, bungalows with bath, rooms, garden, tours; friendly house on the beach. **Chez Robert et Tina**, Tel: 677292, favorite beach house, Matira Point, rooms, cooking opportunity, tours.

RANGIROA AND MANIHI

LUXURY (over US$ 300): **Kia Ora Village**, Tel: 960384, Fax: 960220, Rangiroa, near Tiputa Pass east of the airport, 45 beachside bungalows, restaurant. **Kia Ora Sauvage**, Tel: 960384, Fax: 960220, Rangiroa, on Motu Avaerahi, south side of the lagoon, 1 hr by boat from Kia Ora Village, 5 bungalows, meals incl. *MODERATE (over US$ 150):* **Manihi Pearl Beach Resort**, Tel: 964273, Fax: 964273, Manihi, near the airport, 30 bungalows, pool, tennis, restaurant. **Rangiroa Beach Club**, Tel: 960334, Fax: 410928, Rangiroa, west of the airport, 12 bungalows, good restaurant, tennis, tours.

MARQUESAS ISLANDS

Hanakee, Tel: 927162, Fax: 927251, Atuona, 5 bungalows, TV, restaurant, beautiful view. **Keikahanui Inn**, Tel: 920382, Fax: 920974, Taiohae, 10 bungalows, beautiful view, restaurant. **Moana Nui**, Tel: 920330, Fax: 920002, Taiohae, 7 rooms with bath, restaurant, motorbike, scooter and bicycle rentals. **Moetai Village**, Tel: 920491, near the airport, 5 bungalows. **Nuku Hiva Village**, Tel: 920194, Fax: 920597, Taiohae, 15 bungalows with bath, restaurant, tours.

EASTER ISLAND

AROUND RAPA NUI

The monumental volcanic tufa sculptures (*moai*) make Easter Island one of the most mysterious places to visit in the entire South Seas region. About 1000 of these colossi with elongated heads and massive torsos are scattered about the small island; each weighs tons. Over the centuries, these enigmatic figures have sparked the imaginations of generations of travelers and researchers. Many people have presumed the sculptures to be the remains of the sunken continent of Atlantis, or of some unknown ancient culture. Today it is accepted that the Easter Islanders made these stone statues as a way of honoring their ancestors. Similar (but much smaller) figures can be found on the Marquesas and Tuamotu islands.

In addition to these singular ancient art works, the raw coastline and crater lakes typical of Easter Island are also attractive. The island's inhabitants are warm and open; visitors are welcome, despite the unusual conditions of life here in one of the most remote places on earth. The native people call their island, themselves and their language *Rapa Nui*. The official name of the island (which is under Chilean sovereignty) is *Isla de Pascua*.

Preceding pages: The Ahu Vai Uri on Easter Island outlined in the sunset. Left: A moai of the Ahu Tongariki – friend or foe?

Landscape

Easter Island, together with its small offshore island neighbor Sala y Gomez, represent the easternmost outpost of Polynesian culture. Located on the East Pacific-Antarctic ridge, far to the east of the Tuamotu archipelago, these two small islands officially belong to Chile – even though they are about 2170 miles (3500 km) distant from the west coast of South America.

The 64-square-mile (166 sq km) triangularly-shaped Easter Island lies within the subtropical climatic zone. The island is made up of volcanic rock, tufa, scoria and basalt. Old, partially eroded volcanic craters are characteristic features of the face of Rapa Nui; these may tower up in cone-like shapes, or may be worn and flattened into hills. Each of the three corners of the island is marked by a volcano. Two crater lakes serve as freshwater reservoirs; in fact, there are no watercourses here, since the bedrock is too porous and permeable.

The oldest stone of the 1214-foot (370 m) volcano Maunga Puakatiki on the peninsula of Poike has been dated at about 2.5 million years, whereas that of the 1037-foot (316 m) tall Rano Kau is about 1 million years old. A relative juvenile of only 25,000 years, Maunga Terevaka is

the youngest but also the tallest (1663 feet/507 m) of the three volcanoes. The last volcanic activity here seems to have taken place more than 2000 years ago. The coast is generally raw and rocky, with imposing cliffs reaching to a height almost 1000 feet (300 m); there are only a few exceptions to this rule, including the two beautiful beaches of Anakena and Ovahe in the northeast. Another interesting feature of the island is that it has neither a protective coral reef nor a safe natural harbor.

Climate

The maritime influence has an equalizing effect on Easter Island's climate. In the "cold months," from June to August, nighttime temperatures may fall to 50° F (10° C), while daytime temperatures often reach 64-72° F (18-22° C). In the

Above: The edge of Kano Kau's crater. Right: Easter Island – volcanoes, giant moais, grasslands and horses.

"warmer" season, from December to February, the mercury only drops to about 68° F (20° C) at night and usually rises to 81- 86° F (27-30° C) during the day. The humidity here is 83 percent. The dry season lasts from July to October, while the rainy season extends from March to June; the difference between them is in fact not very large.

Flora and Fauna

A comparatively small amount of plant and animal life has reached the island by natural means. Taro, yams, bananas, sugar cane and bottle gourds were probably brought here by Polynesian settlers. Pineapples, avocados, papayas, citrus fruits and vegetable plants, such as lettuce, tomatoes, corn and beans, were introduced later by Europeans.

The original vegetation also comprised tall trees. One of these is the *sophora toromiro*; today an extinct species on this island, it is now being replanted here. Presently, one mainly finds eucalyptus

and coconut palm trees on Easter Island, as well as guava shrubs and the Chinese elder tree, *miro tahiti,* which is used for wood carving.

Grasslands predominate on the inner part of the island. Only small portions of the original native varieties of plant life have been able to survive over the years. The first European visitors here spoke of the island's sparse vegetation – the Polynesian islanders had apparently largely destroyed the natural tree cover in order to obtain wood. The worst was yet to come: excessive cattle and sheep farming led to the final destruction of remaining flora starting from the 19th century.

Only a few insects and birds and two kinds of gecko reached Easter Island by natural means. The Polynesians brought rats and chickens, while the European expeditions later supplied the island with other domestic animals, as well as some animal species which now live outside of captivity here. The now quite prevalent gyrfalcon (*manu toke toke*) was also an artificial addition to the island's fauna.

European Explorers, Slave Traders and Missionaries

Scientists assume that Easter Island was already settled by Polynesians in about 500 BC; the settlers presumably came from the Marquesas or Tuamotu islands. Other waves of immigration may also have taken place. According to tradition – and almost all of the indigenous population today is convinced of this – it was the Polynesian king or chief Hotu Matua who first went ashore here with some hand-picked members of his tribe in order to found a new settlement. It is assumed that this event took place in the 12th or 13th century A.D., but no one knows the exact date.

The arrival of the first Europeans is also shrouded with uncertainty: did the English pirate Edward Davis, who found an island at 27° 20' southern latitude in 1687, in fact discover Easter Island? What is certain is that the Dutchman Jacob Roggeveen, who was in search of the island Davis described, arrived here

217

on April 6, 1722 (Easter Sunday), and named the place *Paasch Eyland* (Easter Island). He spoke of the island's "remarkably high carved pillars" which astonished him and his crew; he also reported seeing several thousand natives. In 1770, Don Felipe Gonzales annexed the island by order of the viceroy of Peru, bringing it into Spanish possession with the new name of *San Carlos*. Captain Cook came here in 1774, and although he only stayed four days, he was able to give quite an accurate picture of the island with the help of his scientists and draftsmen. In fact, at this point Easter Island made a rather desolate impression. Many tribal feuds had occurred, and rival parties had destroyed platforms and toppled statues.

In 1786, a French expedition under La Pérouse visited the island. The French gave the islanders pigs, goats and sheep, and planted fruit trees and field crops.

Contact with the Europeans brought considerable bad fortune to the island in the 19th century. North American seal hunters wreaked havoc on the island in 1805, raping and kidnapping women; and between 1859 and 1862, thousands of the islanders were abducted by unscrupulous Peruvian sailors and subjected to forced labor on South American haciendas and guano islands. The few survivors who were able to return home brought smallpox and tuberculosis to Rapa Nui, causing the death of the majority of the population. By 1876, there were only 53 men, 26 women and 31 children still living on the island.

Already in 1864, the French Captain Jean Dutrou Bornier recognized the island's potential for sheep-breeding; he "bought" most of the island and recruited workers for the project.

A Catholic missionary, Eugen Eyraud, also arrived on Easter Island in 1864; yet he left in disappointment 10 months later, allegedly due to constant disputes among the island's native inhabitants. After con-

vincing his superiors that a "proper" mission should be established there, he returned to Rapa Nui with a colleague in 1866. Eyraud died of smallpox just a few days after witnessing the baptism of more than 800 Easter Islanders. After a series of skirmishes with the plantation owner Bornier, the missionaries were driven from the island in 1871; Bornier for his part was killed by an islander in 1877.

Following Eyraud's death, Easter Island was without priests until 1937, when the Bavarian Capuchin priest Father Sebastian Englert (1888-1969) took over the pastoral duties here. Extensive scientific work concerning the culture and language of the Rapa Nui helped him to achieve an international reputation.

The Hard Road to Freedom

Easter Island was annexed by Chile in 1888. The Chileans leased the pasture areas of their new "protectorate" to an English wool company which conducted an intensive sheep-breeding operation on the island from 1897 to 1953. In 1954, the military-owned firm Corfo took over the expiring leases from the English; this development unfortunately brought no change in the catastrophic living situation of the indigenous population.

Until the mid-1960s, Easter Islanders had no basic democratic rights whatsoever. With few exceptions, they were not even allowed to leave their island, and in fact could only leave the village of Hanga Roa with special permission from the military. A small section of land around Hanga Roa was allowed them as a settlement area, while the rest of the island was used intensively for cattle breeding.

Only after desperate attempts by the islanders to flee their own home (usually in small, open boats) – and the consequent publication of these stories in the international press – did the world become aware of the unthinkable situation facing

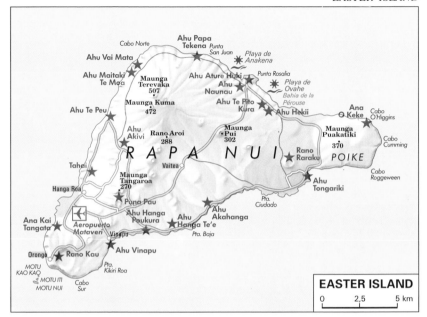

EASTER ISLAND

0   2,5   5 km

the islanders. In 1966, the Chilean government ultimately passed a law giving Easter Island a new status and ushering in a new period of openness to the world.

Since the restoration of democracy on the Chilean mainland, various political currents have arisen among the Easter Island's native population. What all of these have in common are the demands for more self-determination and for the promotion of trade and industry; yet no one seems to want Rapa Nui's complete political independence.

Population and Economic Activity

About 3000 people live on Rapa Nui today; about 800 of these are Chilean. The original residents of the island are Polynesian in origin (*Maohi*), but almost every family can point to at least one European member in the family tree.

Administratively speaking, Easter Island is a *departamento* that belongs to the Chilean province of Valparaiso. The locally elected mayor of the island is sub-ject to a governor appointed by the Chilean government. The island's only city is Hanga Roa ("big bay"), and the sole economic activity worth mentioning is tourism: roughly 12,000 visitors come here every year.

The airport of Mataveri was built here by the USA in 1964 as an emergency landing place for American space flights, and was improved in 1997; it is presently serviced by the Chilean airline LanChile. Residents of the island often receive financial support from former native residents who have immigrated to foreign countries – mostly to the USA or Chile. Until now, all plans to expand agricultural production for export have failed due to high transportation costs.

Moai, Ahu and Rongorongo

Towering stone sculptures (*moai*) on massive stone platforms (*ahu*) are the awe-inspiring emblem of the island. These figures, which were intended as ancestral images, were probably created

219

between A.D. 1100 and 1700. Today about 1000 of these statues exist, and experts argue about how they were transported from the quarry at the volcano Rano Raraku to the platforms. Most of the statues face inland from the coast. They originally wore cylindrical "hats" (*pukao*) of red volcanic slag (although these could also be understood as shocks of hair or as turbans), and several had "eyes" in the form of white coral.

Easter Island is the only Polynesian island on which wooden tablets with written symbols (*rongorongo*) have been found. These symbols most probably do not denote a written language as such; it is more likely that they served as memory and teaching aids for traditional songs. The individual symbols, some researchers think, stand for a word, a sentence or an entire sequence of events.

Above: Petroglyphs with birdmen in the archeological museum of Hanga Roa. Right: Hanga Roa, Rapa Nui's only town.

They start in the lower left corner of the tablet and continue toward the right. The symbols are upside-down in every second line, so that the tablet has to be turned 180 degrees at the end of every line while "reading." The *rongorongo* are to be found in various museums throughout the world.

AROUND RAPA NUI

The island can be easily explored either on foot or by jeep. Yet one also comes to less-frequented places on the island using guided tours which employ the additional means of buses or horses. The starting point for such expeditions is the tiny city of **Hanga Roa** (which has guest houses, hotels, restaurants, a post office, a bank and a hospital). It is important to note that there are no accommodations outside of Hanga Roa.

The Edmunds mayoral family (Juan and his son Petero) has succeeded in bringing about some positive developments in the town, including planting trees and paving the more important streets with bricks instead of asphalt. Hanga Roa's "main artery" is the Avenida Policarpo Toro, which is lined with small stores.

The **Catholic Church** lies somewhat outside of the town center; this church was consecrated in 1958 and contains some nice wood carvings created by local artists. The grave of Father Sebastian Englert is right next to the church. One can acquire primarily traditional wood and stone sculptures at the **Handicrafts Market**, which is located a bit further to the north. The objects here are often priced according to how well-off the clients look, and how friendly they are.

One finds the island's small **Archeological Museum** at the northern edge of Hanga Roa. This museum was founded by Father Englert. Besides sculptures, rock drawings and wood carvings, it contains the eye of a *moai* made of white

coral and red volcanic slag; this was found near Anakena in 1978. A museum visit can be combined with a side trip to the nearby ceremonial grounds of **Tahai**, which were excavated from 1968 to 1970. Three platforms can be seen here: the monumental **Ahu Vai Uri**, with five weather-worn *moai*, and the two smaller platforms **Ahu Tahai** and **Ahu Ko Te Riku**. A harbor was built between the platforms; canoes could be let into the water there via a ramp. The Ahu Tahai boasts evenly hewn, carefully jointed stones. The statue on the Ahu Ko Te Riku is over 16 feet (5 m) tall and is topped by a red "hat" (*pukao*); it features new eyes.

The surviving elliptical outlines of two huts made for sleeping (*hare paenga*) can also be seen here. These huts formerly consisted of a wooden framework covered with grass and reeds. The huts were entered by crawling in; the window-less construction resembled an upside-down canoe. Other remnants of the island's history include an earth oven, a henhouse and a boathouse.

Three miles (5 km) north of here, the remains of **Ahu Te Peu** loom up with outlines of more sleeping huts.

Leaving Hanga Roa on the coastal road in a southerly direction, you come to a space clearly reserved for parking after somewhat less than a mile (1 km). The large cave called **Ana Kai Tangata** is located right on the ocean at the foot of the jagged cliffs, which rise up to almost 1000 feet (300 m). In deference to tourists, the locals gladly call this the "cave of the cannibals." The remains of (heavily damaged) cave drawings are still identifiable on the walls here: sea swallows whirling in the air were executed in a life-like manner using red and white paint.

The road now heads inland, ascending through a small eucalyptus forest to the volcano **Rano Kau**. One of the places on the island where obsidian is found is on a hill to the left. Obsidian is a naturally occurring volcanic glass which can be used to make spearheads, knife blades, scrapers and other tools. The road ends in the village of **Orongo**, which was an import-

ant ceremonial site in Easter Island's pre-European times. Orongo now serves as a national park; the entrance fee is US$ 11. Among other attractions here are the fantastic views of the crater lake and of the offshore islands of **Motu Kaokao**, **Motu Iti** and **Motu Nui**.

Representatives of the island's families formerly met in Orongo to determine who would serve as chief for the next year. In a competition known as the "birdman cult," representatives of the various tribes each tried to bring the first tern egg of the nesting season safely back to Orongo. This involved climbing down the nearly 1000-foot (300 m) cliff and traveling about 2 miles (3 km) with a small float built of rushes in order to bring the egg (which was well-packed in a headband) to the aspiring chief. This cult was described in Kevin Costner's spectacular 1993 film, *Rapa Nui.*

Above: The 3000 inhabitants of Rapa Nui live off tourism. Right: The Ahu Tongariki, with its 15 statues, was restored in 1995.

About 50 restored stone houses can be seen in Orongo. Expressive reliefs of various human figures with bird's heads decorate the rocks; the god Makemake appears again and again in various poses, for instance as the free-standing sculpture of a head placed near the entrance of the houses.

People who enjoy hiking can make the 4-mile (6 km) upward trek from Hanga Roa to the crater lake.

To tour the island by car, you start from Hanga Roa and drive along the north side of the airport to the bay of **Vinapu** on the southwestern coast of the island. One of the first stops on the way is at the two stone platforms of the **Ahu Vinapu** (O Tahiri), which are surrounded by toppled statues. Even today, the nearly seamless gigantic stonework still attests to the unusual talent and skill of the ancient Rapa Nui's workers in stone. Another interesting point to be considered here is that, as Thor Heyerdahl noted, the precision and aesthetic values of Polynesian architecture show a recognizable similarity to the Incas' way of building.

The largely destroyed **Ahu Hanga Poukura** follows 2 miles (3 km) further to the east; it still has an impressive wall made of freestones. A little further, the eight stone figures of **Ahu Hanga Te'e** (Ahu Vaihu) lie face down on the ground. After another 2 miles (3 km) comes **Ahu Akahanga**, one of the island's largest stone platforms, with four toppled statues. The grave of the legendary chief Hotu Matu is nearby, according to tradition. Shortly afterwards, the **Te Ara Moai** (Street of the Moai) leads off to the left. This old road, which was used for the transportation of the gigantic sculptures, is lined with several fallen statues. Since the Te Ara Moai is only passable by all-terrain vehicle, it is more advisable to take the next turnoff to the left and to go to the volcano **Rano Raraku** and the "sculptor's workshop," where the *moai* were fashioned.

In fact, 95 percent of all *moai* were produced here at the slopes of Rano Raraku; its volcanic tufa stone offered an ideal material for Rapa Nui's sculptors. Even today nearly 400 finished or incomplete figures are strewn over the site. Heads with nearly identical, stiff facial features seem to rest in the grass or to grow strangely out of it. The largest of all the figures found to date lies in a niche in the rock, an unfinished *moai* with the impressive height of 69 feet (21 m). From here, the massive statues were transported throughout the island – they weighed up to 88 tons each. The view from the edge of Rano Raraku's crater is outstanding: it includes the crater sea which is partially overgrown with *totora* reeds, and extends out over the island.

About a mile (1 km) from the turnoff is the formation of 15 statues on **Ahu Tongariki**, restored by the Japanese in 1995. The surreal appearance of these weather-worn colossi is breathtaking. There is also a square in front of the statues where interesting petroglyphs can be seen.

The peninsula **Poike**, with its 1214-foot (370 m) volcano **Maunga Puakatiki**, is unfortunately not accessible by road. The volcano itself is easily recognizable by the "tuft" of trees growing in its flattened crater. The road runs along the north coast of the island by the base of the volcano. It is worth taking a side trip to the right here, in order to visit the **Ana O Keke** cave. This cave can be reached by foot after a cross-country trek of about 90 minutes.

The largest *moai* ever erected lies face down by **Ahu Te Pito Kura**, near the bay of **La Pérouse**. This 33-foot (10 m) giant is scheduled to be restored soon.

Directly on the raw rocks of the volcanic coast, there is a circle of black stones surrounding a large stone ball. This place is called **Te Pito O Te Henua**, for which "navel of the world" is a favorite translation. Yet *henua* also means "land" and "home."

White sand beaches are enchanting features of the two bays **Ovahe** and **Anakena**. Other alluring aspects of Anakena are its idyllic grove of coconut palm trees, as well as a picnic area which is especially popular with the locals on weekends. The partially-restored **Ahu Naunau** are also to be found on this beach. Five of the original seven *moai* on the ceremonial platform here are especially well-preserved, and four wear the trademark hats (*pukao*) of red tufa. These statues give a lifelike impression with their finely crafted facial features and the detailed design of their ears. Even details such as belly buttons and nipples can be recognized on these statues, and the lower back areas are·adorned with filigree relief ornamentation (see photo, page 22). The sculpted eye of white coral and red scoria on exhibition in the museum of Hanga Roa was found here. Reconstructed eyes are often put into the statues on festive occasions (e.g., for the Tapati festival week) and later removed. A footpath leads to the **Ahu Ature Huki**, which is the site where Thor Heyerdahl had the first of the figures restored and re-erected.

The road turns inland, passing a wooded area of eucalyptus trees, which belongs to the **Vaitea** federal forest station. Two miles (3 km) before Hanga Roa, one turns right toward Ahu Akivi (following the street sign). Shortly after, a footpath leads left to the crater of **Maunga Tangaroa** with the **Puna Pau** tufa quarry, where the red stone toppings (*pukao*) for the *moai* were cut. Several *pukao* can still be seen scattered in the grass.

Further to the north, the restored **Ahu Akivi** rises up in the island's interior. Its seven weather-beaten *moai* are visible from quite a distance; they face the sea. A trail leaves the road a little further to the north, proceeding to Anakena Bay via the flank of the **Maunga Terevaka** volcano and the north coast. This track is only for four-wheel-drives or hikers and horseback riders. Three hidden caves lie along this route; these are best explored with a guide or on a horseback-riding tour.

EASTER ISLAND
Country code for Chile: 56. For Easter Island: 32
Travel In and Out
The Chilean airline LanChile currently flies 5 times a week to Easter Island from Santiago de Chile (about a 5-hour flight) and from Papeete (about a 5-hour flight). Office: Avenida Policarpo Toro, Tel: 100279. Price for a round-trip ticket from Santiago is about US$ 900, and from Papeete about 700 US$. An airport tax of US$ 8 is levied on departure (for inland flights to Chile) or US$ 18 for international flights.

HANGA ROA
Accommodation
Accommodations always include a continental breakfast, a somewhat more substantial American breakfast is available for an extra fee. Half board is recommendable since the number of restaurants on the island is limited. Many accommodations arrange excursions and car rentals.

MODERATE: **Hotel Hotu Matua**, Tel: 100242, Fax: 100445, Avenida Pont, to the east of town near the airport, 57 spacious rooms with double or single beds, all rooms with a refrigerator, minibar, telephone, bathtub. The hotel has a pool and restaurant, bar, billiards, conference room, boutiques.

Hotel Iorana, Tel/Fax: 100312, Avenida Atamu Tekena, near the airport on cliffs overlooking the sea, 32 spacious rooms with breakfast, some with view of the sea, pool, restaurant, bar, tennis, occasional dance performances. About 25 minutes on foot to the city center. **Hotel O'tai**, Tel: 100250, Fax: 100482, Calle Te Pito Te Henua, near the post office in the center, 22 large and nicely furnished rooms, pool, good restaurant, pretty garden. Reservations are advisable. **Hotel Hanga Roa**, Tel/Fax: 100299, reservations are advisable through Panamericana, Santiago, Tel: 56-2-2349610, Fax: 2349608. Avenida Pont, western edge of town, view of the sea, but no beach, 90 rooms, restaurant, bar, pool. The one-time best hotel on Easter Island is currently being renovated, but has at printing (1998) about 30 new lodgings for US$ 220 per room, the old rooms at US$ 110 are pretty run down.

BUDGET: **Hotel Aloha Nui**, Tel: 100274, at the edge of town near the airport, 6 rooms, dining room. **Hotel Victoria**, Tel: 10027, Avenida Pont, centrally located with a nice view, 7 rooms, small restaurant. **Hotel Poike**, Tel: 100283, Petero Atamu, on the edge of town, 8 rooms, small restaurant. **Residencial Gomero**, Tuukoihu, near the church, Tel/Fax: 100313. This is a quiet, very nice house with 8 rooms, restaurant, bar. Traditional earth oven meals can be booked in advance (*kuranto*). The owner is an Austrian, Niko Kaltenegger. The house offers tours of the island in English, German and Spanish.

There are a number of other hotels, bed and breakfasts and private lodgings available in Hanga Roa. Most of them offer rooms with a bath, they are known for being very clean and managed by very helpful people. Among them are: **Chez Erika**, Tel: 100474, Calle Tuki Haka Hevari, 4 rooms. **Hotel Manutara**, Tel: 100297, Avenida Hotu Matua, near the airport, 20 rooms. **Hotel Orongo**, Tel: 100294, Avenida Policarpo Toro, centrally located near the market, 10 rooms.

There are also a number of private lodgings available, for example: **Tahiri House**, 4-6 people, US$ 65 per day, breakfast US$ 10 per person, other meals are also possible. Book via Pacific Direct, Tel/Fax: (689) 533237, E-mail: pitn@compuserve.com.

Restaurants

The most expensive and elegant restaurant on the island is **Kona Kona** (on a side street opposite the bank). It sometimes hosts dance performances for its patrons. Good and cozy too is the **Taverne du Pêcheur** on the little fishing port in Hanga Roa. Gilles, the owner, is French and an experienced professional cook, he also speaks Spanish, English and German. He can organize transportation from your hotel to the restaurant and back but only if you appear personally first, since he has no telephone in his establishment. Prices for an entrée range from US$ 12 to 30. The restaurant **Playa Pea** has a very nice view of the sea (near the fishing port), but its simple cooking only offers a small selection of dishes (US$ 10 to 25). **Aringa Ora** and **Mama Sabina** on the main street, Policarpo Toro, are two less expensive restaurants, as are the, **Kopa Kavana** and the **Pizzeria Giovani**, **Te Pito Te Henua**. The **Avareipua** restaurant is located in Caleta Hanga Roa O'tai. Meals in the restaurants of the hotels should be arranged in advance.

Excursions

It is recommended you take at least a full day or half day guided tour of the island. Excursions on horseback even for beginners are a nice way of exploring the island.

Another attractive possibility is taking a boat tour along Easter Island's steep cliffs. Two major agencies offer a panoply of tours: **Mahinatur**, Avenida Policarpo Toro, Tel: 100220, and **Kia Koe**, Tel: 100282, they offer tours in English as well as Spanish, Italian, German, and more. The **Rapa Nui agency**, which is led by a German fellow named Conny Martin, has good English-language tours as well: Tel/Fax: 100548.

Other English-language excursions are conducted by: **Archaeological Travel Service** (Tel: 100284, Edmundo Edwards Eastman).

Rental Vehicles

Cars (generally Suzuki jeeps) and in some cases cross-country motorbikes are provided by many of the hotels and shops. Inquire about the age of the vehicles and the current state of the roads. The prices for automobiles are in the US$ 60-80 range per day (officially 8 hours – longer periods can be negotiated for the same price as can be special rates for rentals lasting several days). **Insular Rent a Car**, Tel: 100480. In the shop of **Marco Rapu** in the middle of Avenida Policarpo Toro, you can rent bicycles, also in a few other little stores around town. Most of them are hardly suited to riding across the island.

Nightlife

The discothèques **Piriti** (near the airport) and **Toroko** (in the center of town) are open throughout the year (Thu-Sat), and for two more days a week during the main season. The fun begins right at the front door, where horses and cars are parked pell-mell. As a rule, however, you should go late in the evening.

Events / Museum

The **Tapati Rapa Nui Festival** with exhibitions, traditional competitions, folklore, handicrafts, cultural events and Miss Rapa Nui contest (it starts at the end of January or beginning of February and goes on for two weeks). The legendary landing of King Hotu Matuas on the beach of Anakena is represented with great care, and the absolutely unique banana sledding down the side of a volcano is also something spectacular (the riders slide at speeds of up to 38 mph/60 kmh). **Chilean Independence Day** (Sept 18th) with a parade. Inquire about the schedule for the dance performances at the Hotel Iorana. At the Catholic **Church** of Hanga Roa: daily at least one mass, three on Sunday. Archeological **Museum** at the northern border of town: Mon-Sat 9 a.m.-6 p.m. The handicrafts market to the north of the church has traditional wood and stone sculptures on sale.

Sports

Fishing: Using rods, harpoons or from boats: your landlords should be able to organize a tour. **Diving**: Michel Garcia, Tel: 100375, he is a specialist, and knows the waters around Rapa Nui best. **Tennis**: Inquire at the Hotel Iorana, or ask your landlord for other courts. **Riding**: The agencies in town should be able to advise you, your landlord as well.

Currency

Chilean pesos; US dollars are also accepted. Credit cards only at the major hotels and for a 5 to 8 percent fee. To change money, go to the Banco del Estado del Chile or to one of the private changers (who often offer a better rate of exchange). Banks take a US$ 7 charge per check for changing travelers checks.

Tourist Information

Tourist Office: About 150 feet (50 m) from the bank and Playa Pea, Tel: 100255.

HANDICRAFTS
AND SOUVENIRS

The works of South Pacific artists traditionally had and still have a certain social, religious, or physical function. Decorative elements are thought to endow certain everyday objects with special significance or power. This might explain the fact that "free art" in the South Pacific plays a subordinate role to this day, but good handicrafts are highly esteemed.

Natural resources are in limited supply on the islands. Plants and animal products are widely used, for example, leaves, plant fibers, bark, various woods, bones, skins, hairs, tortoise shell, sea shells, coral and even stone (on the volcanic islands). Clay

Preceding pages: "Nave Nave Mahana" (Day of Delight) by Paul Gauguin, 1896. Above: A piece of tapa being hand painted. Right: The ancient tradition of weaving with coconut palm leaves.

deposits are rare and hence pottery only developed in a few places, for example, in Sigatoka Valley on Fiji, one of the centers of traditional pottery.

Weaving with wool was never practiced, but women do plait artistic mats and other items such as handbags, hats, fans and baskets, often producing intricate patterns. The raw material used for the most part is the dried leaves of the screw pine (the *Pandanus* tree or *fara* on Tahiti). They occasionally use rushes as well, while coconut palm leaves, smoothed bark and various fibers are good for coarser structures.

The materials are often boiled before being used, softened by scraping and dyed using vegetable dyes. Decorations are made by plaiting in brown or black patterns, mats are given touches of color by the addition of feathers or colored wool threads. The soft, off-white hats used in the Cook and Tubuai Islands are made from the young shoots of the coconut palm. The most beautiful and most solid baskets are made by the inhabitants of the Tonga Islands. They are reinforced by an inner structure made from the middle ribs of palm leaves.

The bark bast so typical of the South Seas is called *tapa* (or *masi* on Fiji; *ngatu* on Tonga). It is produced by scraping out the inner bark of the paper mulberry tree, soaking it in water for a while and then beating it with wooden clubs until it thins out and becomes soft and malleable. Tapa is made by placing several pieces of this raw material atop one another and binding them using sticky plant juices and applying another beating with the clubs.

The resulting felt-like, whitish or at times brown or yellowish material can now be decorated with ornaments and geometrical patterns using reddish-brown and black natural dyes.

After traveling the South Seas and gaining a little experience, you will be able to tell what group of islands, or even what island in a group, a certain material comes from. The largest and finest tapas are produced on the Tonga Islands. Tapa works are also available in large quantities on the Fiji and Samoa islands.

The art of wood carving is a tradition on all the islands of the South Pacific. The quality of the craft ranges from breath-takingly beautiful to pure tourist trash. Preferred objects are ancestor figures, maces and spears, ceremonial paddles, headrests, kava chalices, animal sculptures and drums.

Wonderful vessels, sometimes well-done replicas of old kava or oil chalices, are available on the Fiji Islands. The wood carvers there bury their works in the mud of mangrove swamps in order to give them a black color.

Carvings with the finest ornamentation and the greatest attention to detail can be found in the Marquesas, and the best mother-of-pearl inlay work is done on the Solomons. Tropical hardwoods are most commonly used these days, carvings in sandalwood are only sold on a few of the

islands (on Tonga and in the Marquesas, for example). The Marquesas and Easter islands are also known for stone sculpting.

And what could thrill a woman's heart more than the abundance of beautiful jewelry made of shells, coral, or the bones of cattle or whales? The selection of mother-of-pearl is particularly large, items include engraved belt buckles, barrettes and the like. Beware in French Polynesia: much of the "pretty" stuff available is in fact *Made in Taiwan* or elsewhere.

Polynesians and Fijians do not use masks as a rule. Faces were either painted or tattooed. Masks of clay and plant fibers were used on Vanuatu. The carved masks available in handicraft shops are fantasy products made strictly for gullible tourists. The beautiful Polynesian dance costumes, splendidly decorated with plaitwork, shells and feathers, are difficult to come by. The traditional grass dresses of the native peoples are usually made of althea bark (*burao*).

TATTOOS

Long gone are the days when tattoos were only to be seen as anchors, pierced hearts or buxom sirens painted on the hairy chests and bulging biceps of sailors, ex-cons and other toughs.

A veritable tattoo culture has arisen in the meantime, especially among today's youth, as perhaps the newest form of protest against middle-class stodginess. Even famous athletes and actors show a little ornamented skin to their ecstatic public every now and then. What few realize is that the South Pacific is one of the centers of this age-old art of body painting.

The word *tattoo* is actually derived from the Polynesian word *tatau*, which translates more or less as "opening a wound."

Above and right: Tatau means quite literally to "open a wound." Tattoos are ornamentation and status symbol at the same time.

South Pacific tattoos consist by and large of abstract patterns and ornamentation. A special "design" made up of stylized objects could be used, in fact, to tell a story that meant a great deal to the person wearing the tattoo.

Traditionally, tattoos were not only mere ornamentation, but also a status symbol. It was a significant element in the initiation rites to becoming a warrior or as a sign of special merit for courage in battle. Expensive, exclusive tattoos increased a person's chance of finding a good partner; and certain "patterns of mourning" underlined the pain a person felt at the loss of a loved one.

Alone the decision to submit oneself to an extensive tattooing gave evidence of great courage, decisiveness and the ability to withstand a great deal of pain. In Samoa, a man without a tattoo was the subject of wagging tongues: "He is like taro," people would say, "without taste." Even today, in the heat of an argument, a person might tell another: "Go get a tattoo before talking to me."

The seafarers on the earliest exploratory expeditions brought home "souvenirs" in the form of tattoos.

The European Christian missionaries, with their usual respect for other cultures, strongly opposed the showing of naked and tattooed bodies in public; gradually the converted islanders began dressing in European garb, and traditional ornaments and patterns slowly disappeared or became hopelessly mixed with European elements.

In regions with a significant Melanesian population, on the Solomon Islands, for example, scar tattoos, which can be better seen on dark skin, are more common than color tattoos: the skin is cut open and the wound infected so that it only heals slowly and leaves behind a very obvious scar.

The Polynesians became absolute masters in the art of blue-black color tattooing, which shines forth dramatically, especially on lighter skin. On some islands, Tahiti for instance, machines are used for the job nowadays. On others, the dye is still pressed into the skin the old-fashioned way, using tattoo combs and mallets. These combs, which look like small rakes, used to be made of sea shells, tortoise shell or bone. The color was produced from the soot of the candelnut (*Aleurites Moluccana*). The tattoo masters worked together with assistants who stretched the section of skin being decorated and cleaned off the blood using cork bast tissues.

The most impressive tattoos are those from Samoa, which stretch from the hips to the knees. In men, large sections are covered with incredibly intricate patterns, giving the impression of wearing trousers. Women's ornamentation is finer and not as densely drawn.

An extensive, expensive tattoo could easily take weeks, months, indeed years to complete. The tattoo master, who was highly esteemed as a specialist, used to move with his entire family to his client,

who was supposed to keep them all supplied with life's necessities.

Even today, friends and relatives gather when someone is being tattooed. They sing songs, and tell stories and jokes to detract the "client" from the considerable pain caused by the comb.

In the old days, the biggest tattoos were worn by the inhabitants of the Marquesas. Every accessible body part was decorated, including such far away places as the top of the head, the hands, the inner nostrils and even the tongue.

For a while during the 19th century, checkerboard patterns were particularly popular. Karl von den Steinen, a German traveler who visited the Marquesas Islands in 1897, made drawings of the patterns and tattoos and published them in a book. The tattooers of French Polynesia and Samoa use it nowadays for their work.

Young Polynesians in particular are once again proudly showing off "decorated" skin – some of them even make a point of displaying their facial tattoos.

CHRONICLERS OF
THE SOUTH SEAS

The South Seas have always inspired writers, who have repeatedly attempted with varying degrees of success to capture the atmosphere and lifestyle of the islands. In doing so, they often contributed to the romantic South Sea dreams of world-weary Europeans.

Daniel Defoe (1660-1731) was almost 60 years old when he wrote his first novel in 1719, *The Life and Strange Adventures of Robinson Crusoe*. He was inspired by the actual adventure of the Scottish seafarer Alexander Selkirk, who was stranded on a solitary island off the coast of Chile from 1704 to 1709. The tale of a white man who civilizes an intelligent

Above and right: European artists and writers have entertained a long relationship with the South Seas – a depiction of Daniel Defoe's "Robinson Crusoe," and Paul Gauguin's last self-portrait.

and noble savage made Defoe famous overnight, and subsequently influenced missionaries, who unfortunately faced very real cannibals in the South Seas and ended their careers in an earth oven.

The explorer Count **Louis-Antoine de Bougainville** (1729-1811) gave an account of the first voyage around the world in his book *Voyage autour du monde* (1772). His gushing descriptions of Tahiti contributed greatly to the image of an idyllic South Seas paradise still very much in use in the field of tourism. He lived to see his book become a best seller even in other languages.

As a young man, **Georg Forster** (1754-1794) accompanied his father Johann on Captain Cook's second Pacific journey. His book *A Voyage round the World* (1777) is indeed a fascinating and critical travel account.

The American novelist **Herman Melville** (1819-1891) came to Tahiti as a sailor. *Typee*, written in 1846, and the follow-up *Omoo*, described the arrival of Western civilization in Polynesia. His most famous novel, *Moby Dick* (1851), perhaps the best portrayal of whaling in the Pacific Ocean, was made into a film starring Gregory Peck.

The Scotsman **Robert Louis Stevenson** (1850-1894) was already a well-known writer when he settled in West Samoa in 1890, hoping to ease his bronchial illness in the damp and warm climate of the tropics. His book *Treasure Island*, published in 1883, was a hit in its day and has lost little of its popularity since. His South Seas stories, among them "In the South Seas" and "The Bottle Imp," take place in Samoa, on the Marquesas and other islands. These masterworks of the art of storytelling are sensitive and compelling reflections of the islands of the South Seas and their inhabitants.

Jack London (1876-1916), the American adventurer and novelist, was attracted to Hawaii and Tahiti. His collection *South Sea Tales* was published in 1911.

The Englishman **W. Somerset Maugham** (1874-1965) chose the Pacific Ocean as a setting for many of his wonderful stories. His novel *The Moon and Sixpence*, which was published in 1919, is based on the life of the painter Paul Gauguin.

As for **Paul Gauguin** (1848-1903), who brilliantly captured the sensual beauty and peace of Tahitian women on canvas, as well as the light and colors of the Polynesian islands, he also discovered a talent for writing. His autobiographical writings, entitled *Noa Noa*, were published in 1900.

James Norton Hall (1887-1951) and **Charles Nordhoff** (1887-1947) both lived on Tahiti and wrote about a dozen books there. Though hardly known nowadays, they were the authors of the trilogy *Mutiny on the Bounty* (1932), *Men Against the Sea* (1934) and *Pitcairn's Island* (1934). It was the men of the *Bounty*, however, Fletcher Christian and Captain Bligh, who achieved world-wide fame thanks to several Hollywood films with star-studded casts. The South Seas atmosphere of times long gone is well depicted in Hall's gentle short story anthology *The Forgotten One and Other True Tales of the South Seas* (1952).

James Michener (1907-1997) joined the US navy during World War Two and was shipped to the South Seas. He later returned and traveled to many of the islands. Among his most famous books are *Hawaii*, *Return to Paradise* and *Rascals in Paradise*. He even won a Pulitzer Prize for *Tales of the South Pacific*, which was transformed into the hit Broadway musical *South Pacific*.

Paul Theroux, born in Massachusetts in 1941, traveled the South Pacific region for a year and achieved a delicate balance in his book *Happy Isles of Oceania* between very realistic travel writing and a poetic style.

One book that is somewhat controversial is *The Papalagi*, by **Erich Scheurmann**. It was first published in Germany in 1920 and has since that time found a large and loyal readership. These fictitious speeches of a Samoan tribal chief that in fact hold a critical mirror up to Western man, are a must for anyone traveling the South Seas.

Ever since the the University of the South Pacific first opened its doors in 1967 on Fiji, an independent body of South Seas literature has appeared on several islands. The most famous representative of this genre – and a very prolific writer indeed – is **Albert Wendt**, whose novels describe the contemporary social structures on Samoa (among them are *Sons for the Return Home*, *Pouliouli*, *Leaves of the Banyan Tree* and the collection of short stories *Flying Fox in a Freedom Tree*).

Epeli Hau'ofa, from Tonga, displays a humorous and satirical voice in his works. His *Tales of the Tikong* has become a classic of Pacific literature.

233

WHAT'S COOKING IN THE SOUTH PACIFIC

Virtually every island in the South Pacific has its own culinary specialty. There are, however, certain basic traits of the gastronomic arts that can be found throughout the entire South Pacific area, for example the slow cooking of food in an earth oven. Vegetables, fish, meat, sometimes even an entire pig, are wrapped in taro, breadfruit tree, or banana leaves, and placed on hot blocks of coral in a pit. An earth oven (called *lovo* on Fiji, *umu* on Tonga, Samoa and the Cook Islands, *umu ta'o* on Rapa Nui and *ahimaa* on Tahiti) can reach a temperature of 900° F (around 500° C); cooking time is about two hours.

Many hotels organize a South Seas banquet for their guests, naturally featuring earth oven dishes. Food typical of the region is usually offered including such local vegetables as taro, yams, manioc root, sweet potatoes, breadfruit and cooking bananas.

Fresh fish and other seafood are naturally the main aspect of South Pacific cuisine. Crabs, shrimp, lobsters, octopi, sea urchins, mussels, sea snails and a host of other fish leave the connoisseur of maritime food nothing more to be desired. The catch of the day is always the right thing to order. The coconut crab should be avoided as it is an endangered species. Most islands have to import meat. The exception here is New Caledonia, where venison is to be recommended as a local specialty.

The most important ingredient in South Pacific cuisine is coconut creme pressed from fresh coconut flakes. It is not only used for cooking; its slightly sweet flavor also serves to round off the taste of many dishes. One specialty on many islands that makes use of coconut creme is marinated fish: lemon juice is dripped on raw, filleted pieces of fish,

Above: A feast for the eyes as well! Right: Laplap, the national dish of Vanuatu – poi with fish or meat.

which are then left to marinate for about 10 minutes. Coconut creme and various chopped and diced vegetables are then added: onions, cucumbers, tomatoes and green peppers. This refreshing *hors d' oeuvre* is also eaten as an entrée, provided you have a robust digestive tract. The dish is called *kokoda* on Fiji, *oka* on Samoa, *'ota 'ika* on Tonga, *ika mata* on Cook, and simply *poisson cru* in French Polynesia – this dish is particularly popular on hot days.

Taro leaves cooked in coconut creme are served as a vegetable for many dishes. They taste particularly good together with corned beef or chicken meat (*palusami* on Samoa, *lu pulu* on Tonga, *fafa* on Tahiti).

Poi, *poe*, or *popoi* is a filling meal served up on many Polynesian islands. It consists of a creamy paste created from grated root vegetables or breadfruit to which coconut cream, spices – and sometimes bananas are added. The paste is wrapped in leaves and left to cook in an earth oven. *Laplap*, Vanuatu's national dish, is made up of a spicy paste with fish or meat (such as chicken).

Poi is also used as a basic building block for desserts by either adding sugar or fruits (*faikakai*, a Tonga specialty, is one example). A somewhat recent variation on the same theme is a solid pudding made with starch, to which fruits such as papayas or bananas are added. Coconut cream is used as a sauce in this instance. Tropical fruit is a good source of vitamins. Mangos, papayas, pineapples, grapefruit, guavas, passion fruit, carambolas, bananas, oranges, lemons and limes are available on most islands; though on the stark coral atolls they must often be imported.

The South Pacific islands don't really produce alcoholic beverages, though fruit, cocoa and coffee liqueurs are made on some of the larger islands. French Polynesia and New Caledonia have excellent wines from their own vineyards. Good local beers are sometimes available; the brewmasters are usually from abroad.

TRAVEL PREPARATIONS

South Seas Information

The national branches of the tourist offices are listed in the *Guideposts* at the end of each chapter.

Twelve South Pacific islands (Cook Islands, Fiji, French Polynesia, Kiribati, New Caledonia, Niue, Papua New Guinea, Solomon Islands, Western Samoa, Tonga, Tuvalu and Vanuatu) gathered together to form the **Tourism Council of the South Pacific (TCSP)** and have joint offices.

Main office on **Fiji**: Chief Executive, PO Box 13119, Level 3, FNPF Place, 343-359 Victoria Parade, Suva, Fiji Islands, Tel: 304 177, Fax: 301 995, e-mail: spt@infocentre.com.

The Tourism Council of the South Pacific, also has offices abroad:

Great Britain, 375 Upper Richmond Rd. West, London SW14 7NX, Tel: (44) 181 392 1838, Fax: (44) 181 392 1318.

USA, Lake Blvd., PO Box 7440, Tahoe City, CA 96145, Tel: (01-916) 583 0152, Fax: (916) 583 0154.

For information on **French Polynesia** contact **Tahiti Tourisme**:

Australia, 620 St. Kilda Road, Melbourne 3004, Tel: (3) 9521 3877, Fax: (3) 9521 3876.

USA, 300 Continental Blvd., Suite 180, El Segando, CA 90245, Tel: (01-310) 414 8484, Fax: (01-310) 414 8490. 444 Madison Avenue, 16th Floor, New York, NY 10022, Tel: (01-212) 838 7800 ext. 253, Fax: (01-212) 838 7855.

Internet: www.tahiti-tourisme.com; e-mail: tahiti-tourisme@mail.pf.

Information on **Easter Island** is available from Chilean embassies:

Australia, 10 Culgoa Circuit, O'Malley 2606ACT, Canberra, Tel: (61-2) 6286 2430, Fax: (61-2) 6286 1289, e-mail: echileau@dynamite.com.au.

New Zealand, 1-3 Willeston St., 7th Floor, Willis Corroon House, PO Box 3861, Wellington Tel: (64-4) 471 6270,

Fax: (64-4) 472 5324, e-mail: embchile @ihug.co.nz.

USA, 1732 Massachusetts Avenue, NW, Washington D.C. 20036 Tel: (1) 202 785-1746, Fax: (1) 202 887-5579

Clothing

Light, airy clothing, preferably made of natural fibers, is ideal for May to October, but don't forget a light pullover or a cardigan when visiting the islands. During this period, you will probably need some additional warm clothing on New Caledonia, the Austral Islands and Easter Island.

Horizon to horizon blue sky is only to be had in the brochures of your travel agent, in other words: bring some light rain-proof clothing, the kind that can be packed for day trips.

Sunglasses, sun hat, sun cream (with high blocking factor) and insect repellent should also be included in your pack. A sturdy pair of bathing slippers (of plastic if possible) should also come along, as they are hardly available on many of the islands. **Note**: These are needed to protect you from the very sharp coral which produces nasty cuts that take time to heal in tropical climates!

Snorkelers should not rely on the material available on location, it's often in bad condition if at all available. Diving goggles and snorkel are sufficient.

Packing a light, waterproof grip or some sturdy plastic bags is also advisable so that camera equipment and a second set of clothes stay dry during excursions in small boats. A pocket knife is always handy (put it in your luggage when traveling to avoid unpleasantness at the airports!), a flashlight will be of assistance finding your way round during the power cuts that are quite frequent, even in the better hotels.

You should make photocopies of all important documents (plane tickets, passport, driver's license, scuba license, etc.) and keep them in a separate place.

Visa and Entry Requirements

American Samoa: You need a return or ongoing ticket (except for US citizens), and a valid passport. A 30-day visa is granted on entry, it can be extended up to 90 days.

Cook Islands: You need a return or ongoing ticket, a valid passport, enough funds on hand and a written confirmation of reservations for lodgings (number of overnight stays is unimportant). A 31-day visa will be automatically handed out on entry, it can be renewed every month for up to 6 months.

Fiji: You need a return or ongoing ticket, a passport valid for at least 3 months and sufficient funds for your stay. Almost all nationalities receive a four-month visa on entrance, only a few must apply beforehand.

French Polynesia: You need a return or ongoing ticket and a valid passport. Visas are required, but not for French citizens. EU and Swiss citizens receive a three-month visa, which is extendible to 6 months.

New Caledonia: You need a return or ongoing ticket and a passport valid for at least three months Visas are required, but not for French citizens. EU and Swiss citizens receive a three-month visa, extendible to 6 months. Any questions should be directed to the French consulate or embassy nearest you, or contact the Haut Commissariat, Bureau des Etrangers, Rue Paul Doumer, BP C5 Nouméa, New Caledonia.

Easter Island: You need a return or ongoing ticket and a valid passport, visas are given on entry, extendible to six months.

Solomon Islands: You need a return or ongoing ticket, a passport valid for at least 3 months and sufficient funds for your stay (except citizens of the USA, New Zealand and Australia).

Samoa: You need a return or ongoing ticket, a valid passport and sufficient funds for your stay.

Tonga: You need a return or ongoing ticket, a valid passport and sufficient funds for your stay. All nationalities receive a visa valid for 30 days on entry. It may be extended to 6 months.

Vanuatu: Visas are available at: The Immigration Department, PMB 014, Port Vila, Vanuatu. Most nationals receive a 30-day visa on entering with a valid passport.

There is no rabies in the South Pacific, and quarantine regulations for bringing pets are extremely strict. If you happen to be on a yacht with pets aboard, you may run into difficulties. See the import regulations under "Customs," p. 241.

Money Matters

The currencies of the South Pacific states are either hard to reconvert into Western ones or impossible, so avoid changing too much money into the local currency.

Cash or traveler's checks in US$ are the recommendable means of payment; French francs in the French territories have a fixed exchange rate with Pacific francs. You can also pay with Australian or New Zealand dollars in the larger towns, and exchange most major European currencies.

Visa and Mastercard are the most commonly used credit cards, American Express is not accepted everywhere. It's often difficult to get cash with a credit card.

Health

None of the countries in this book require vaccinations unless you happen to be traveling from an "infected" country – for example, yellow fever vaccination if coming from certain African states or cholera if coming from Micronesia. Travelers heading to more remote parts should get tetanus and polio vaccinations or boosters and have antimalarial drugs handy (see "Medical Services," p. 244).

Purchasing insurance coverage at home is highly recommended, especially one providing transportation, as is bringing along a first-aid kit.

Any regular medication should be brought along in sufficient quantities for the entire trip. Your first aid kit should also include adhesive and regular bandages, antiseptics, pain killers, antibiotics, iodine, anti-diarrhetics, laxatives, something for colds and fevers, something against sunburn, infection and insect bites, and a thermometer.

Coral cuts can be painful and a nuisance. Some travelers recommend a simple, soothing camomile cream to help heal them. Also, if your repellant hasn't kept all bugs away, mentholated cold rubs might help with the itchiness.

Depending on where you will be going, bring flea powder, water purifier (see page 244) and even a mosquito net.

TRAVELING TO THE SOUTH SEAS

Getting There

Flight schedules and offers change constantly worldwide. The actual cost of flights is based on criteria that are often incomprehensible to the layperson, so that you may find it cheaper to travel the long way round rather than take the most direct route.

Various travel agents and airlines offer a wide range of fares. Comparing prices is advisable at any rate. What's important is to inquire about the conditions attached to the flight. For example, ask whether you can change your bookings during the trip and whether a special additional segment that you may want to add to your itinerary is being offered on the actual island at the same price as at home.

Air New Zealand has the most comprehensive flight network in the South Pacific. Besides a number of inexpensive package tours and special fares, the company also offers airline passes that allow you to make numerous stops during a tour.

When coming from Europe, the trip to the South Pacific from the USA and Canada is limited to those airlines that have stopovers along the American west coast, or to the few airlines that connect Los Angeles with the Pacific. Hawaiian Airlines is still the only US airline that flies to Tahiti from Honolulu (Hawaii).

Qantas and Air New Zealand and their partner airlines have the cheapest round-the-world flights from Europe at the present time. Fiji is the crossroads of the South Pacific and is serviced by Air New Zealand, Qantas, Canadian Airlines International, Air Nauru, Air Marshall Islands, Solomon Airlines, and more.

The Chilean airline LanChile connects Santiago de Chile to Easter Island and Papeete five times a week, Air France and the other French airline, AOM, fly Papeete-Paris with round-the-world tickets in connection with other airlines, such as Air Calin (Air Calédonie International).

Qantas flies Frankfurt-Brisbane-Sydney daily (three times a week via Singapore, four times a week via Bangkok and Singapore), and from Australia to Tahiti and the Fiji Islands. As an agent of Pacific Air, Qantas offers the inexpensive *Visit South Pacific Pass*, which has no time limit. It provides coupons for various itineraries. The first leg must be booked at home, additional coupons can be obtained on location from partner airlines.

Air New Zealand: *Australia:* Tel: 13-24-76; *Canada:* Tel: (800) 663-5494; *Great Britain:* Tel: (0181) 741-2299; *New Zealand:* Tel: (0800) 737-000; *USA:* Tel: (800) 926-7255.

LanChile: *Australia:* Sydney, Tel: (02) 9321 9333; Melbourne, Tel: (03) 9679-6860; *Canada:* Montreal, Tel: (1-514) 395-8812; Vancouver, Tel: (1-604) 683 7824; *Chile:* Tel: 600-600-4000. *Great Britain:* Tel: (0171) 730- 1180; *New Zealand:* Auckland Tel: (09) 912-7490; *USA:* Tel: (800) 735-5526.

Qantas: *Australia:* Tel: 13-12-11; *Canada:* Reservations and info, Tel: (800) 227-4500; *Great Britain:* Tel: (0345) 747-767; *New Zealand:* Tel: (0800) 808-767; *USA:* Reservations Tel: (800) 227-4500, info Tel: (800) 227-4500.

These are only three of many airlines that should be checked. Others with offices around the world are: Air France, Air Pacific, Air Fiji, Air Vanuatu, etc. You will find many pertinent Websites on the Internet.

Consultation

If you are interested in a package tour, consult a travel agent that specializes in the area. They are far better informed about the South Pacific than those who offer travel to the area as another part of their total range of services.

If you happen to be looking for a trip cut to measure, you will soon run into limitations. Even the most specialized offices are not able to keep up with what has been happening on the various islands: hotels are continuously being renovated, restaurants change cooks or owners, transportation companies suddenly have a new bus and a travel agent starts offering unusual and top-notch tours – yes, even the little world of the South Pacific is subject to the current laws of rapid change.

One company that offers individual advice and some unusual itineraries is *PITN Pacific Direct.* It has offices and agents in various island states. *Pacific Direct* can be accessed at following locations (among others): Easter Island, Tel: (0056-32) 100220, Fax: 100420 and on Tahiti Tel/Fax: (00689) 533237, or e-mail: pitn@compuserve.com.

TRAVELING IN THE SOUTH SEAS

Traveling among the Island States

All island states described in this book – with the exception of Easter Island –

have their own airline companies that also offer international connections (see *Guideposts* at the end of each chapter). They offer air passes for their own network or in connection with other regional airline companies, making round trips a great deal cheaper than the sum of all the individual flights: *Pacific Triangle Pass*, *Triangle Pass* or *Polypass*.

Tourist with a great deal of time travel the routes between Fiji, Tonga, Samoa, New Caledonia and the Solomon Islands by ship. However, you will need a lot of patience to organize passage. Information is available in the harbor of Suva (Fiji), in the *Fiji Times* or at **Carpenter's Shipping**, Suva, Tel: 312244, Fax: 301572; **Pacific Forum Line**, Suva, Tel: 315444, Fax: 302754; **Shipping Services Ltd.**, Suva, Tel: 313354, Fax: 301615.

Traveling within a Country

In just about every state there are national air passes available to visit many islands. This also allows for lots of savings.

The air passes are already worth buying if you just want to visit two or three islands besides the main one. Inquire at each of the airlines (the addresses are at the end of each chapter).

A somewhat quieter means of traveling around the larger islands is by ferry. Info in *American Samoa:* **Polynesia Shipping**, Pago Pago, Tel: 6331211. *Cook Islands:* **Outer Island Shipping**, Rarotonga, Tel: 27651. *Fiji:* **Patterson Brothers**, Suva, Tel: 315644, Fax: 301652.

The island world can be explored as a passenger on a freighter in Papeete in *French Polynesia* – e.g., to Moorea and Bora Bora or to the Marquesas and the Tuamotu Islands. Information is available at the tourist office or the **Compagnie Française Maritime de Tahiti**, Papeete, Tel: 426393, Fax: 420617. *New Caledonia:* **Ballande Maritime**, Nouméa, Tel: 283384, Fax: 287388. **Société**

Maritime des Îles Loyauté, Tel: 289318. *Solomon Islands:* **Marine Division**, Honiara, Tel: 21535. *Tonga:* **Shipping Corporation of Polynesia**, Queen Salote Wharf, Nuku'alofa, Tel: 21699, Fax: 22617. *Samoa:* **Samoa Shipping Corporation**, Apia, Tel: 20935, Fax: 22352. *Vanuatu:* **Ifira Shipping**, Port Vila, Tel: 24445, Fax: 25934.

If you have more money to spend, you might want to charter a yacht with a crew or take part in a cruise.

Most of the larger islands have an excellent network of buses, allowing you to get about without a rented car and to make contact with the local population. The flatter islands in particular are ideal for cycling. Many lodgings rent out bicycles, but they are often not very well suited for longer stretches. If you are planning a tour with your own bike – preferably a rugged mountain bike – you can usually have the bike shipped on international flights either for free or for a minor fee. Ferries also take bicycles. If you're intending a longer bike tour, make sure you have enough replacement parts and that you can repair a bicycle!

Some of the islands are also ideally suited for exploration on horseback. Easter Island and Tonga are particularly romantic for this means of transportation.

Driving

Rental cars or motorcycles are very often the only way to get to some of the more remote areas on some of the islands.

Right-hand driving on the following islands: Samoa, New Caledonia, Vanuatu, French Polynesia and Easter Island.

Left-hand driving on: the Cook Islands, Fiji, Tonga and the Solomon Islands.

Local regulations:

Cook Islands: A local driver's license is needed, it is available at the police station in Avarua on presenting your regular license and paying a NZ\$ 10 fee.

New Caledonia: The minimum age to rent a car is 25.

Samoa: International driver's licenses are permitted. If you happen not to have one, then you can get a local one at the police station with your national license and a W\$ 10 fee. The minimum age requirement is 21.

Tonga: You will need a local driving permit, which is available at the Central Police Station on presentation of your valid national license and payment of a T\$ 10 fee. The minimum age requirement is 21.

Vanuatu: The minimum age for renting cars is 23, for motorcycles it's 17. Your own driver's license must be older than one year.

PRACTICAL TIPS

Bargaining

Haggling over prices is not customary in the South Seas, the sole exception being in the shops run by Indians on the Fiji Islands.

You also always buy the commodities in markets and on the roadside in the unit they're offered in, for example: a pile of five mangos, a bundle of three pineapples or one string of fish. It's not common to take only a portion. What you don't need can be given away, for example, which very much corresponds to the community spirit of the islanders.

Crime

The crime rate on the islands of the South Pacific is very low in comparison to many other parts of the world. Visitors are, of course, under protection of the laws of hospitality on the islands.

Violent crimes are very rare, larceny, however, has been on the rise during recent years. This applies to the towns especially, which are no different from those in the rest of the world, and also for some of the solitary beaches that are visited by tourists now and then. There is no need to take any special precautions, but objects of value should not be left lying around without supervision and your rental car should be locked. There's no need to tempt anyone.

Fights often break out on weekends in discos and other dance establishments where the abuse of alcohol is high. Tourists seldom get mixed up in them, nevertheless, just to be sure, keep a sharp eye open for the general mood of the place and get out in time.

Women are safe in general, but to avoid any harassment, do not go alone to places where alcohol is flowing freely and men are gathered together in large crowds. Even though this hardly means danger, it can be construed as provocative behavior.

Customs (Exports)

The law in all countries basically prohibits the export of artifacts with special archeological, ethnological or historical value. If you wish to take older items out of the country go to the local authorities and inquire about the individual regulations. If you have any doubts, obtain official permission in order to avoid any unpleasantness when departing.

Otherwise there are hardly any strict rules about export. The same applies to plant and animal products, including shells. Many of the South Sea nations have not signed the Washington accords on species protection, so you should therefore inquire about the import regulations in the country you are heading to.

Australia, New Zealand, the USA and Canada have especially strict regulations, but Europe also prohibits the import of some protected shellfish and snail types. Importing them can lead to considerable problems and be quite expensive.

Even if a clam or snail is widespread in the country of origin, it doesn't mean that it's not protected. This applies to the black corals of Tonga, and to whale's teeth as well (by the way, the export of

tabua – sperm whale teeth, which are used for ritual ceremonies – is prohibited in Fiji).

Customs (Imports)

Generally, each country prohibits the import of drugs, as well as photographs, films or books with pornographic content. For munitions and weapons, you should apply for permission beforehand; in some countries bringing in weapons is prohibited.

Importing plants, animals, meat, sausages, fruit, vegetables, seeds and other foodstuffs is basically prohibited and the law prescribes strict quarantines. Many visitors find the regulations exaggerated but they are very justified. Each year new insects, viruses and bacteria are brought to the islands thanks to inattention, and they can cause havoc with the sensitive eco-systems there.

Shells and corals are very popular souvenirs, and hardly a visitor to the South Seas fails to pick some up. It is important to make sure that they are free of sand and earth – which are excellent media for micro-organisms – to avoid immigration problems when island hopping. That is why camping gear has to be registered and checked at the customs office in just about every South Pacific island. Make sure, too, that the inhabitants of your shell have left to avoid smelly surprises later on!

If you happen to be carrying "hot" wares in your luggage and you are only passing through, you should give the stuff to customs for safe-keeping until you leave again.

Duty-free wares:

American Samoa: Travelers to the USA are permitted one US gallon of alcohol, 400 cigarettes.

Cook Islands: 200 cigarettes, 50 cigars or 0.5 pound of tobacco, 2 l of spirits or wine or 4.5 l of beer, as well as taxable items up to a value of NZ$ 250.

Fiji: 500 cigarettes, 500 g of tobacco or cigars, 4 l of beer or wine or 2 l of spirits, other taxable items up to a value of F$ 400.

French Polynesia (travelers 17 years of age or older): 200 cigarettes, 100 cigarillos, 50 cigars or 250 g of tobacco, 2 l alcohol, 50 g perfume, 500 g of coffee, 40 g tea.

New Caledonia: 200 cigarettes, 50 cigars or 250 g of tobacco, 2 l of wine or 1 bottle of spirits, perfume for personal use.

Easter Island (travelers 18 and older): 400 cigarettes and 500 g of tobacco and 50 cigars plus 50 cigarillos, 2,5 l spirits, perfume for personal use.

Solomon Islands: 200 cigarettes, 50 cigars or 250 g of tobacco, 2 l spirits, other taxable items up to a value of SI$ 40.

Samoa: 200 cigarettes, 1 bottle of alcohol (max. 40 fl. ounces).

Tonga: 400 cigarettes, 2 l of spirits.

Vanuatu: (travelers 15 and older) 200 cigarettes, 50 cigars or 250 g of tobacco, 1.5 l of spirits and 2 l wine, 25 cl of eau de toilette, 10 cl of perfume, new items up to a value of Vatu 20 000.

Drinking Water

The quality of the water varies sharply on the islands, both from island to island and within the islands themselves. The rule here, if any, is that the mountainous volcanic islands usually have enough water for drinking, on the atolls and other coral islands water is in short supply and often a little salty.

The quality and drinkability of tap water depends on the disinfecting methods and on the reservoir and conduit systems, which are out of date and unhygienic in many places. Inquiring on location is seldom of any help, since the local stomachs have to a great extent adapted to the water quality.

Water quality also depends on the weather: both a long, dry period or a heavy period of rain can cause water quality to drop. For safety's sake, you should either disinfect your water or boil it for at least seven minutes.

Bottled local spring water is often available for purchase on many of the islands. Tap water is generally good enough for brushing teeth. The following information is only a general orientation: *American Samoa:* Tap water is drinkable. *Cook Islands:* Tap water is drinkable on Rarotonga at least. *Fiji:* In cities and hotel resorts the water is drinkable. *French Polynesia:* Tap water can only be drunk in Papeete. *New Caledonia:* With the exception of the small islands, water quality is quite good throughout the country. *Easter Island:* Tap water can be drunk without question. *Solomon Islands:* It's advisable to only drink boiled or disinfected water and to use it for brushing teeth. *Samoa:* Tap water is only drinkable in Apia. *Tonga:* Tap water can be drunk but it doesn't taste good at all. *Vanuatu:* in Port Vila and Luganville the tap water can be drunk, just be a little careful after a long dry spell.

Electricity

Electrical power on American Samoa is 110 V, and 220-240 V AC in all other island states. In addition, there are different plugs in the various countries, ones for flat, bipolar sockets in American Samoa, round bipolar Euro sockets in the French territories, tripolar "English" sockets on the islands with a British colonial past. Bring an adapter from home with you in case, and make sure your electrical equipment switches from 110 to 220 V.

Foreign Representation

American Samoa: There is no diplomatic representation in the country, none that might issue a visa for the USA.

Cook Islands: **High Commission of New Zealand**, 1st floor, Philatelic Bureau Building, Takuvaine Road, Avarua (PO Box 21), Rarotonga Tel: (682) 22 201, Fax: (682) 21 241.

Fiji: **Australian Embassy**, 7th and 8th Floors, Dominion House, Thomson

Street, Box 214, Suva, Tel: (679) 312844, Fax: (679) 300900. **British Embassy**, Victoria House, 47 Gladstone Road, Suva, Tel: (679) 311033, Fax: (679) 301406. **New Zealand Embassy**, Reserve Bank of Fiji Building, Pratt Street, Suva, Tel: (679) 311 422, Fax: (679) 300 842.

New Caledonia: **Australian Consulate-General**, 7/8th Floor, Immeuble Foch, 19 rue du Maréchal Foch, Noumea, Tel: (687) 272414, Fax: (687) 278001.

Easter Island: No representation.

Solomon Islands: **Australian High Commission**, Hibiscus Avenue and Mud Alley, Honiara, Tel: (677) 70160, Fax: (677) 23691. **British High Commission**, Telekon House, Mendaña Avenue, Honiara, Tel: (677) 21705, Fax: (677) 21549. **New Zealand High Commission**, City Centre Building, Mendaña Avenue, Honiara, Tel: (677) 21 502/503, Fax: (677) 22 377.

Samoa: **Australian High Commission**, Fea Gai Ma Leata Building, Beach Road, Tamaligi, Apia, Tel: (644) 23411, Fax: (644) 23159. **British High Commission**, Apia, Tel: (644) 472 6049, Fax: (644) 473 4982.

Tonga: **Australian High Commission,** Salote Road, Nuku' Alofa, Tel: (676) 23244, Fax: (676) 23243. **British High Commission**, PO Box 56, Nuku'alofa, Tel: (676) 21020, Fax: (676) 24109. **New Zealand High Commission**, corner Taufa'ahau and Salote Roads, Nuku'alofa, Tel: (676) 23122, Fax: (676) 23487.

Vanuatu: **Australian High Commission**, KPMG Hse, Rue Pasteur, Port Vila, Tel: (678) 22777 (24 hours), Fax: (678) 23948. **British High Commission**, KPMG Hse, Rue Pasteur, Port Vila, Tel: (678) 23100, Fax: (678) 27153.

Holidays

Special festivals and events are listed in the *Guideposts* at the end of each chapter. In the countries with Anglican influence, the non-Christian holidays are taken on the nearest Monday or Saturday, assuming they do not already fall on a Monday or Saturday. The following holidays are observed all over the place:

January 1 (New Year's Day); March/April (Good Friday and Easter); May 1 (Labor Day); May/June (Whitsun); May/June (Ascension Day); December 25 (Christmas Day), and additionally:

American Samoa: Third Monday in January (Martin Luther King Day); third Monday in February (President's Day); April 17 (Flag Day); last Monday in May (Memorial Day); July 4 (Independence Day); first Monday in September (Labor Day); second Monday in October (Columbus Day); November 11 (Veterans' Day).

Cook Islands: March/April (Easter Monday); April 25 (ANZAC Day); first Monday in June (Queen's Birthday); October 26 (Gospel Day); October 27 (Flag Raising Day); December 26 (Boxing Day).

Fiji: Friday in March (National Youth Day); March/April (Easter Monday); Monday at the end of May (Ratu Sir Lala Sukuna Day); Monday after June 14 (Queen's Birthday); Monday end of July (Constitution Day); Monday end of July or beginning of August (Prophet Mohammed's Birthday); October 10 or Monday before (Fiji Day); October/November (Diwali); December 26 (Boxing Day).

French Polynesia: March 5 (Arrivée de l'Évangile); March/April (Lundi de Pâques, Easter Monday); May/June (Lundi de Pentecôte, Whitsun Monday); July 14 (National Holiday); August 15 (Assumption); November 1 (Toussaint, All Saints' Day); November 11 (Armistice Day).

New Caledonia: July 14 (National Holiday); March/April (Easter Monday); May/June (Whit Monday); August 15 (Assumption Day); September 24 (Nouvelle Calédonie); November 1 (All Saints' Day); November 11 (Armistice Day).

Easter Island: March/April (Easter Saturday); May 21 (Batalla); May/June (Cuerpo Cristi); August 15 (Assumption Day); September 11 (Pinochet); September 18/19 (Independencia de Chile); October 12 (Discovery of America); November 1 (All Saints' Day); December 8 (Fiesta Religiosa).

Solomon Islands: May/June (Whit Monday); second Friday in June (Queen's Birthday); July 7 (Independence Day); last Monday in August (Liberation Day); December 26 (National Thanksgiving Day).

Samoa: January 2 (day after New Year's Day); March/April (Easter Monday); April 25 (ANZAC Day); first Monday in May (Mother's Day); June 1 to 3 (Independence); October/November (Palolo Day); November (Arbor Day); December 26 (Boxing Day).

Tonga: April 25 (ANZAC Day); May 4 (Crown Prince Tupoutu'a's Birthday); June 4 (Emancipation Day); July 4 (King Taufa'ahau Tupou IV's Birthday); December 4 (King George I's Birthday); December 26 (Boxing Day).

Vanuatu: March 5 (Custom Chief's Day); July 24 (Children's Day); July 30 (Independence Day); August 15 (Assumption); October 5 (Constitution Day); November 29 (National Unity Day); December 26 (Family Day).

Medical Services

The little South Pacific islands do not have the means for a very high medical standard. Equipment is lacking, as are medication and doctors. The larger towns have some private practices, you would be best advised to make use of their services should the need arise, since waiting times in the hospitals are often very long.

In the case of serious illness you should take the next plane to the USA, Australia or New Zealand. Only New Caledonia and French Polynesia have proper care. The following is a brief list of available medical services:

American Samoa: Mediocre standards. The hospital (Tel: 633-1222) is in Fa-ga'alu south of Fagatogo, drugstores.

Cook Islands: Mediocre standards on Rarotonga, the hospital is east of the airport (Tel: 20066). Service on the other islands is poor. Ambulance: Tel: 998.

Fiji: Mediocre to decent medical standards in towns, poor in the country. Lautoka Hospital (Tel: 660399), has a dental clinic. There's no malaria, but there is the painful dengue fever; sexually transmitted diseases and AIDS are also spreading, so take precautions.

French Polynesia: Medical standards are high (except on the smaller, remote islands), but treatment is relatively expensive. AIDS is spreading here as well. Papeete: Mamao Hospital, private clinics, for example Clinique Paofai, Blvd. Pomare, Tel: 430202. 24-hour emergency service: S.O.S. Médecins, Tel: 423456. Ambulance, Tel: 15. On the island of *Moorea:* the hospital (Tel: 561197) is located in Afareaitu, numerous doctors, a pharmacy, a dental clinic (Tel: 561051). *Bora Bora:* private clinic (Tel: 677062) and dental clinic (Tel: 677055). There is a pharmacy near the ferry embarkation.

New Caledonia: Medical standards in Nouméa are high, the hospital (Tel: 272121) is located on Av. Paul Doumer, for emergencies only; otherwise there are private clinics, for example, Clinique Magnin, Tel: 272784. There are also community hospitals in the small towns. Beware of AIDS! Ambulance, Tel: 15, or S.O.S. Médecins, Tel: 286600.

Easter Island: Medicinal standards are low. The hospital is in Hanga Roa.

Solomon Islands: Mediocre medicinal standards in the towns, in the country they are poor. Pharmacies are only in Honiara, the hospital is north of Chinatown (Tel: 23600) only in case of emergencies; otherwise use the private clinics, for example the Island Medical Center, Cluck St., Tel: 23277. Dental clinic, Ashley St., Tel: 22754. High risk of malaria, prophylaxis is highly recommended.

Samoa: Mediocre medical standards. The hospital is in Apia, Tel: 21212.

Tonga: Mediocre standards in Nuku'alofa (Vaiola hospital, Tel: 23200. German clinic, Wellington Rd, Tel: 22736); services are poor out in the country.

Vanuatu: Mediocre standards in Port Vila, on the island of *Efatu* (hospital is in the proximity of Erakor lagoon, Tel: 22100, private doctors) and Luganville, *Espiritu Santo* (hospital, Tel: 36345), service is poor out in the country. High risk of malaria, prophylaxis is strongly recommended for travel outside Port Vila.

Photo, Film and Video

The South Seas are very photogenic, especially the people. You should always ask permission beforehand. This also includes photographing children. Generally it's allowed, in many places people even like to be photographed. If permission is not given, please respect this. Sometimes people request money for filming or photographing them.

Skylight and polarizing filters do help with the sun. Film, batteries and equipment are often difficult to get hold of; the following list will help you determine how much film to bring along:

American Samoa: limited selection in Pago Pago. *Cook Islands:* Films are only available in Avarua. *Fiji:* Wide and inexpensive supply of film and cameras. *French Polynesia:* Good selection of photographic material, very expensive, however. *New Caledonia:* good selection of photographic material in Nouméa, but it's expensive. *Easter Island:* Limited selection of photographic material. *Solomon Islands:* Film can only be purchased in Honiara and Gizo, the selection is very limited. *Samoa:* Films are only available in Apia, limited selection, cameras are expensive. *Tonga:* Film can only be purchased in Nuku'alofa the selection is limited, cameras are expensive. *Vanuatu:*

Selection of film and cameras is available only in Port Vila.

Post and Telecommunications

As a rule of thumb, the more frequent the international flights, the faster letters and postcards will arrive at their destination. Mail should therefore only be sent from the main island, and then only from the main town or capital. This is still no guarantee of fast mail.

It takes a week at best for mail to reach New Zealand and Australia and the west coast of the USA, and a week to Europe from New Caledonia and Tahiti. Otherwise count on three to four weeks to Europe, and if not sent airmail, three to six months!

For telecommunications you should not have a problem in the larger towns and from the big hotels, though calling from them is quite expensive. Card-operated public phones have started appearing on the Cook Islands, Fiji, New Caledonia and Tahiti. E-mail is also on the rise. If in urgent need, you may want to try a large hotel or a tourist office.

Sports and Tours

If you happen not to be the kind of person that heads to the South Seas to lie about in a hammock and let your soul drift, you will also find something to do in the South Seas, especially where aquatic sports are concerned.

The *Guideposts* at the end of each chapter list all the businesses that organize programs for various kinds of sports and tours, from diving and fishing vacations, advanced scuba diving, surfing, kayaking, yacht excursions and even individual ecological hiking tours, bird-watching tours and excursions by bicycle and on horseback.

Tipping

Many travel guides state that tips should not be given in the South Seas, indeed they are not even welcome because they force the beneficiary to give something in return, or so the usual argument goes.

This assumption, however, is not wholly true. It is correct that no one expects a tip. But it is also correct that people do rejoice at a small token gift. But no waitperson will understand what's going on if you just leave a few coins on the table.

There is a special way of giving the tip: it should be handed over with a few words, such as "Thank you very much for the especially fine service." This clarifies the situation, since the gift of money is a gift for something that has already been given to you.

SOUTH SEAS ETIQUETTE

The people of the South Seas are especially polite people, and strangers, be they locals or tourists, are given great respect, which is often expressed as exaggerated reserve.

By and large, foreigners who break the rules are granted understanding, however, if you behave correctly from the word go, you will get a lot further faster. If you accidentally severely violate manners and customs, you should turn to a competent local in all trust and ask what is the best way to compensate for the error of your ways.

Some of the following basic rules, which for the most part apply to the entire South Seas, are actually self-explanatory, but they really should be written out in full for the sake of completeness.

Visit to a Village

Do not visit any village without first asking permission to do so. Before entering the village, ask to speak to the chief. He or his deputy will generally grant permission to visit after you have explained your reason for wanting to do so.

Even a simple reason suffices: "The houses are pretty, I would like to photo-graph them and show them to my friends back home." It is good to offer a small present, which can be given to the chief in the form of money (a few dollars or more) for a planned village project or as a contribution to the church.

Overnight Guests

If you are staying for one or several days with a family, a gift of about US$ 10 per day and/or household goods should be made to your hosts to cover your cost and the extra effort that was made by them owing to your presence. Things that the family has to buy – i.e., not cans of fish, but rather soap, sugar, flour, butter, bread, school books, etc. – are good gifts.

Guaranteeing hospitality is considered one of the unshakable laws on the islands, and visitors are often mystified by the fact that a family will slaughter its last pig for a guest or even go into debt to satisfy him or her. Of course, no one will tell the guest that. And many have thoughtlessly or, worse yet, shamelessly abused the hospitality of the island people in this manner.

Presents

It is customary to bring a present even for shorter visits (regardless of whether it's to a village or a family). Food and cigarettes or cigars are good possibilities, *waka* (kava root) should never be lacking on the Fiji Islands.

Invitations to Meals

Hierarchical seating arrangements are often the rule in households, and they follow certain very well established customs:

The guest begins eating alone or together with the highest ranking host(s), followed by the men, then women and children. What's important is to act in such a way that there should be enough to go around at all times! So don't eat up the three lobsters and leave only breadfruit and manioc for the others!

Conversation Level

Conversations are held at the same level, not meaning content-wise but physical. In other words, either everyone is sitting or everyone is standing. Sitting is not only a great deal more comfortable but it is also seen as more polite. If you are invited into a house (take your shoes off at the door), you should sit down before starting to talk.

Sitting Arrangements

Speaking of sitting! Most foreigners have great difficulty with this particular aspect of South Seas life. Usually everyone sits down in a circle. You should always ask what seat has been reserved for you, don't automatically take the one that offers the best opportunity for photography. You then sit cross-legged on a mat on the floor.

Sitting in this fashion is a question of practice. Some people can do so for an hour or two, others hold out for about 30 minutes, for others it becomes torture after a few minutes.

One thing is certain, the islanders in the South Seas can stay that way forever. You can stretch your legs out to the left or right, or angle them out back, but never stretch them forward into the circle. If you can no longer sit cross-legged, you should stand up with an apology and go away from the circle to stretch your legs

"It's Beautiful!"

Enthusing is not always the best way of expressing appreciation of something. If you happen to admire, say, an item with too much enthusiasm, you will run the risk of receiving the object in question as a present, and that means you will have to give something in exchange!

Always Share – Especially Food

Never eat without offering others some of it, and always invite to eat. On many islands foreigners have been greeted for centuries with a casual "come eat!" This tradition has lost none of its importance and meaning to this day.

Fast Food Style

It is impolite to eat while standing or, heaven forbid, walking – and anyway it all tastes a lot better when sitting.

Land Ownership

Plots of land seldom have fences around them. Do be careful, however, this is not meant as an invitation to wander about them freely!

Fruit and Vegetables

Fruit and vegetables that grow far from human inhabitation are not for the community of humans at large. If you would like some you should ask permission. This applies equally to bananas hanging on the tree or coconuts that have fallen on the ground.

Fees for Entry or Usage

It is common on Vanuatu, Samoa and the Solomon Islands (especially on Malaita) to pay the owner a so-called custom fee for using or visiting certain places (beaches, caves, freshwater pools, waterfalls, historic places, etc.). This can range from a small fee to some pretty hefty sums in the regions with larger tourist crowds.

Greetings

It is habitual to greet people you meet – except in the larger towns – even from a car or a motorbike. A hand signal is the usual way. Greetings are proffered when entering shops, approaching the stalls at a market, before taking a close look at the wares on the stalls and photographing. The language you use is not important, it's the gesture that counts.

Eye(brow) Language

A lot of communication takes place with the eyes, be that a twinkle of the eye, a blinking motion, a sideways glance... The most visible sign for foreigners is the brief raising of the eyebrows, and you should practice it in front of your hotel mirror the first night in the South Seas. You'll need it when passing someone in the street as a quick greeting, as an abbreviated form of affirmation, as a brief way of expressing agreement during a discussion, a concise "yes" during conversation. In short, you need it.

Any tourist learning to use the fast eyebrow raising will have overcome one of the great obstacles to understanding. And if you are interested in learning more about this South Seas language, just observe carefully the reserved mimicry and gestures of the islanders.

Offering

Politeness requires that you first refuse something offered. The giver then renews his offer and hence makes it clear that it is indeed his own desire that the gift be accepted.

Loud Sounds

It is impolite to speak loudly or to suddenly raise your voice during a conversation. It is evidence of having lost control over oneself and a sign of disrespect towards others.

Off Limit Heads

You should avoid touching the heads of people, be that as a friendly stroking of the neck or a gentle caressing of the head. Doing something over someone else's head is considered very bad manners or handing an object over his head. If you can't avoid doing so, then at least apologize effusively – several times at best – while doing so.

Shirt and Trousers

Even in the expensive hotel resorts, comfortable casual dress is widely accepted, so a jacket and tie are not required for men.

Women should always wear clothing that covers their upper arms and shoulders in public, and that reaches at least down to the knees. This even applies to areas of Melanesia where the locals sometimes run around almost naked. Trousers on women are not good form in churches, and are even considered offensive in other more conservative circles. Male visitors should not appear bare-chested in public even if the islanders themselves do it.

Bathing Clothes

Bathing clothes should only be worn at the beach or around the pool! Bathing suits raise fewer eyebrows than bikinis (the women of the islands usually wear a wraparound and a T-shirt, which is recommendable for more remote areas). Topless bathing is only permitted – or at least it's widespread – in Nouméa and on the well-trodden islands of French Polynesia. Some female tourists have run into considerable trouble bathing in the nude on a remote beach and thinking she was alone.

Respect

Generally the people on the islands show great respect for each other and show extreme politeness in their daily meetings.

Older people, people with titles and guests are granted special respect. It is imperative you return the favor, and always keep in mind that the position a person holds in the somewhat sad economic life of the islands says nothing about his position in the traditional system. A bus driver, hotel porter or taxi driver might easily be a high chief.

Taking Time

Being calm and serene are important basic aspects of community life and an expression of politeness and respect toward others. You should avoid being hectic and excited and generally take your time (which shouldn't be too diffi-cult while vacationing). For example, make a point of stopping before shaking someone's hand.

INTERNET ADDRESSES

Tourism Council of the South Pacific:
http://www.tcsp.com
American Samoa:
http://members.gnn.com/samoa/
welcome.html
Western Samoa Visitors Bureau:
E-mail: samoawsvb@pactok.peg.apc.org
Fiji:
http://www.infocentre.com
E-mail: spice@is.com.fj
Fiji Visitors Bureau:
http://www.fijivb.gov.fj
E-mail: matatolu@fijifvb.gov.fj
or infodesk@fijifvb.gov.fj
French Polynesia:
http://www.tahiti-tourisme.com
New Caledonia:
http://www.travelfile.com/get?newcal
Sabre: XX ORG/NEWCAL
Apollo: TD*TF/LINK/NEWCAL
Worldspan: XX TVL/NEWCAL
Amadeus: 1TVO.NEWCAL
Abacus: XX TVL/NEWCAL

AUTHOR

Michael Brillat, Project Editor of the *Nelles Guide South Seas*, has been travel-ing the South Pacific for almost 20 years. He wrote his doctorate as a Physical Geographer on a Fiji topic, and spent eight months there doing professional training. After working for several years as a scientific assistant at the Geographi-cal Institute of the Technical University in Berlin, he decided once and for all to devote himself to the South Seas. He has traveled the Germany-Tahiti-Rapa Nui triangle since 1990 together with his wife Kina Pakomio Paoa, an Easter Islander.

He guides study tours, among others, for several travel organizations, and was one of the founding partners of the South Seas travel consulting group *PITN Pa-cific Direct.*

PHOTOGRAPHERS

Archiv für Kunst und Geschichte,
  Berlin   19, 23, 26, 27, 28, 31, 95,
                  226/227, 232, 233
A.N.T. (Silvestris)   17
Bernhart, Udo   223
Borredon, Thierry   15, 49, 185, 191,
                  192, 193, 207, 228
Brillat, Michael   55, 170
Eberhardt, Matthias 182, 200, 208, 229
Erbst, Holger   10/11, 16, 111, 156
Fischer, Peter   110, 190, 196
Gross, Andreas M.   217, 220, 221
Helms, Bernd   146
Herion, Peter   cover
Janicke, Volkmar E.   14, 22, 32/33, 34,
          39, 42, 50, 53, 54, 94, 99, 100,
        102, 104, 105, 108, 127, 134, 139,
        147, 148, 151, 154, 158, 160, 175,
                  180/181, 198, 203
Kaehler, Wolfgang
  (Fotoarchiv Peter Fischer)   18, 161
Kohnen, Björn-Eric   107
Krall, Richard (Sivestris)   164/165
Lahr, Günther   8/9, 93, 109,
                  126, 155, 174, 202
Leue, Holger   12, 21, 29, 37, 41, 46,
        57, 59, 70, 74, 81, 86/87, 101, 112,
        120, 131, 133, 144, 149, 157, 166,
        171, 173, 197, 230, 234, 235
National Tourism Office, Vanuatu 48
Pelzing, Jürgen   184, 206
Pleynet, Gérard   62/63, 64, 68, 69, 73,
          75, 76, 77, 78, 79, 80, 83
Siebig, Udo (Mainbild)   176
Spierenburg, Paul   25, 44/45, 88,
        92, 96, 98, 106, 113, 118/119,
        123, 124, 130, 142/143,
        188, 195, 204, 231
Stadler, Hubert   168, 177, 212/213
Storck, Manfred   214, 216, 222.

Explore the World

AVAILABLE TITLES

Afghanistan 1 : 1 500 000
Australia 1 : 4 000 000
Bangkok - *Greater Bangkok,*
Bangkok City 1 : 75 000 / 1 : 15 000
Burma → *Myanmar*
Caribbean Islands 1 *Bermuda,*
Bahamas, Greater Antilles
1 : 2 500 000
Caribbean Islands 2 *Lesser Antilles*
1 : 2 500 000
Central America 1 : 1 750 000
Colombia - Ecuador 1 : 2 500 000
Crete - Kreta 1 : 200 000
China 1 - *Northeastern*
1 : 1 500 000
China 2 - *Northern* 1 : 1 500 000
China 3 - *Central* 1 : 1 500 000
China 4 - *Southern* 1 : 1 500 000
Dominican Republic - Haiti
1 : 600 000
Egypt 1 : 2 500 000 / 1 : 750 000
Hawaiian Islands
1 : 330 000 / 1 : 125 000
Hawaiian Islands – **Kaua'i**
1 : 150 000 / 1 : 35 000
Hawaiian Islands – **Honolulu**
- O'ahu 1 : 35 000 / 1 : 150 000
Hawaiian Islands – **Maui - Moloka'i**
- Lāna'i 1 : 150 000 / 1 : 35 000

Hawaiian Islands – **Hawai'i, The Big**
Island 1 : 330 000 / 1 : 125 000
Himalaya 1 : 1 500 000
Hong Kong 1 : 22 500
Indian Subcontinent 1 : 4 000 000
India 1 - *Northern* 1 : 1 500 000
India 2 - *Western* 1 : 1 500 000
India 3 - *Eastern* 1 : 1 500 000
India 4 - *Southern* 1 : 1 500 000
India 5 - *Northeastern - Bangladesh*
1 : 1 500 000
Indonesia 1 : 4 000 000
Indonesia 1 *Sumatra* 1 : 1 500 000
Indonesia 2 *Java + Nusa Tenggara*
1 : 1 500 000
Indonesia 3 *Bali* 1 : 180 000
Indonesia 4 *Kalimantan*
1 : 1 500 000
Indonesia 5 *Java + Bali* 1 : 650 000
Indonesia 6 *Sulawesi* 1 : 1 500 000
Indonesia 7 *Irian Jaya + Maluku*
1 : 1 500 000
Jakarta 1 : 22 500
Japan 1 : 1 500 000
Kenya 1 : 1 100 000
Korea 1 : 1 500 000
Malaysia 1 : 1 500 000
West Malaysia 1 : 650 000
Manila 1 : 17 500

Mexico 1 : 2 500 000
Myanmar (Burma) 1 : 1 500 000
Nepal 1 : 500 000 / 1 : 1 500 000
Trekking Map *Khumbu Himal /*
Solu Khumbu 1 : 75 000
New Zealand 1 : 1 250 000
Pakistan 1 : 1 500 000
Peru - Ecuador 1 : 2 500 000
Philippines 1 : 1 500 000
Singapore 1 : 22 500
Southeast Asia 1 : 4 000 000
South Pacific Islands 1 : 13 000 000
Sri Lanka 1 : 450 000
Tanzania - Rwanda, Burundi
1 : 1 500 000
Thailand 1 : 1 500 000
Taiwan 1 : 400 000
Uganda 1 : 700 000
Venezuela - Guyana, Suriname,
French Guiana 1 : 2 500 000
Vietnam, Laos, Cambodia
1 : 1 500 000

FORTHCOMING

Central Asia 1 : 1 750 000
Trekking Map *Kathmandu Valley /*
Helambu, Langtang 1 : 75 000

Nelles Maps in European top quality!
Relief mapping, kilometer charts and tourist attractions.
Always up-to-date!

Explore the World

AVAILABLE TITLES

Australia
Bali / Lombok
Berlin and Potsdam
Brazil
Brittany
Burma → *Myanmar*
California
  Las Vegas, Reno,
  Baja California
Cambodia / Laos
Canada
  Ontario, Québec,
  Atlantic Provinces
Canada
  Pacific Coast, the Rockies,
  Prairie Provinces, and
  the Territories
Caribbean
  The Greater Antilles,
  Bermuda, Bahamas
Caribbean
  The Lesser Antilles
China – Hong Kong
Corsica
Crete
Croatia – *Adriatic Coast*
Cyprus
Egypt
Florida
Greece – *The Mainland*
Hawai'i

Hungary
India
  Northern, Northeastern
  and Central India
India – *Southern India*
Indonesia
  Sumatra, Java, Bali,
  Lombok, Sulawesi
Ireland
Israel - *with Excursions*
  to Jordan
Kenya
London, England and
  Wales
Malaysia
Mexico
Morocco
Moscow / St Petersburg
Munich
  Excursions to Castles,
  Lakes & Mountains
Myanmar (Burma)
Nepal
New York – *City and State*
New Zealand
Paris
Philippines
Portugal
Prague / Czech Republic
Provence
Rome

Scotland
South Africa
South Pacific Islands
Spain – *Pyrenees, Atlantic*
  Coast, Central Spain
Spain
  Mediterranean Coast,
  Southern Spain,
  Balearic Islands
Sri Lanka
Syria – Lebanon
Tanzania
Thailand
Turkey
Tuscany
U.S.A.
  The East, Midwest and South
U.S.A.
  The West, Rockies and Texas
Vietnam

FORTHCOMING

Canary Islands
Costa Rica
Greek Islands
Maldives
Norway
Poland
Sweden

Nelles Guides – authorative, informed and informative.
Always up-to-date, extensivley illustrated, and with first-rate relief maps.
256 pages, approx. 150 color photos, approx. 25 maps